DOG

◆

THE COMPLETE GUIDE

◆

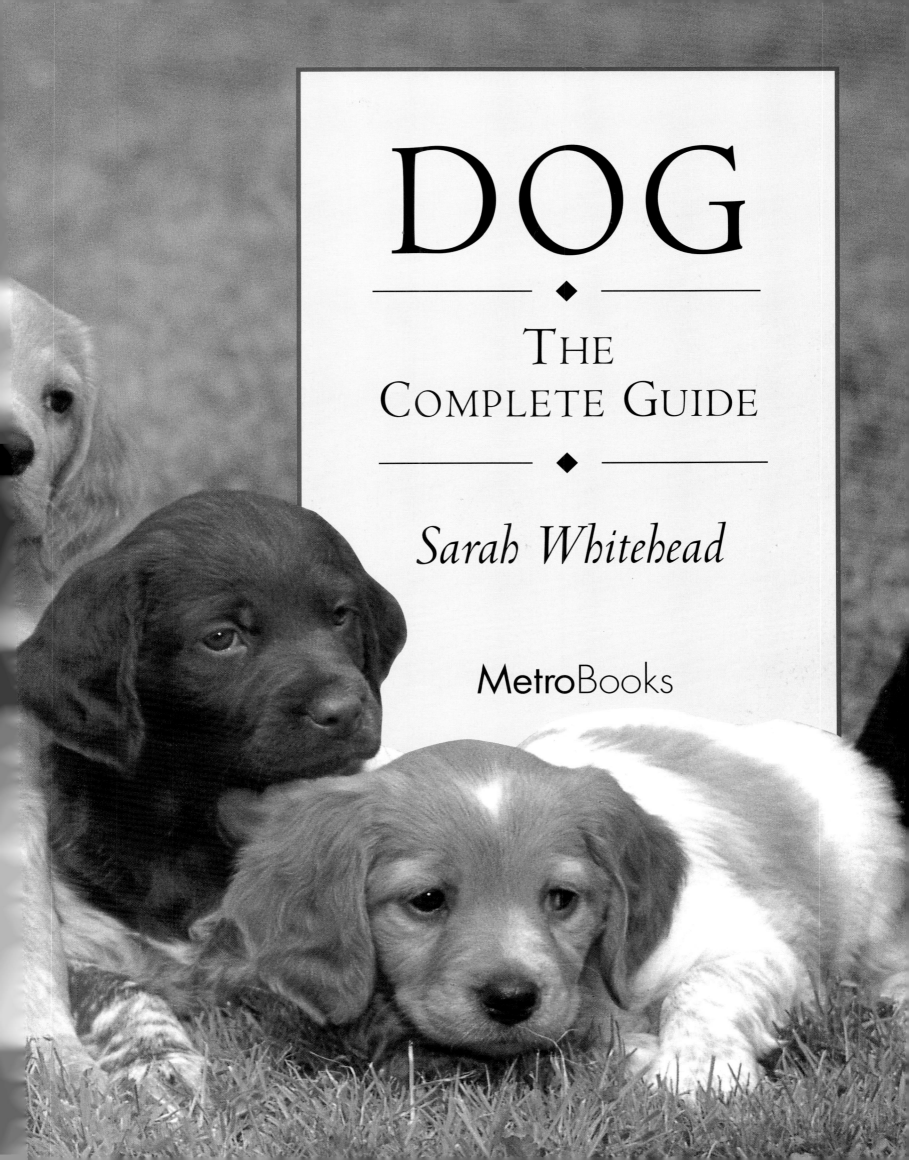

DOG

♦

THE COMPLETE GUIDE

Sarah Whitehead

MetroBooks

Dog – The Complete Guide
was conceived, edited and designed by
Team Media Limited
Masters House
107 Hammersmith Road
London W14 0QH

Authors

Sarah Whitehead	What is a Dog?
	Caring for Dogs
	Your Dog's Health
	(pp152–160)
Bradley Viner	Your Dog's Health
	(except pp152–160)
Beverley Cuddy	Dog Breeds
Karen Sullivan	pp 242–249

Consultants

Peter Neville	Jim Breheny
Bradley Viner	

Project Editor	Karen Sullivan
Editors	Simon Hall
	Rupert Matthews
	Fiona Plowman
	Gwen Rigby
	KC Trommer
Art Editor	Ruth Prentice
Designer	Darren Bennett
Design Assistants	Max Newton
	Zoe Quayle
Picture Research	Julia Ruxton
Illustrators	David Ashby
	Wildlife Art
	Michael Woods

Team Media

Editorial Director	Louise Tucker
Managing Editor	Elizabeth Tatham
Art Directors	Eddie Poulton
	Paul Wilkinson

Copyright © 1999 by Team Media, Ltd.,
London, UK

This edition published by **Metro**Books,
an imprint of Friedman/Fairfax Publishers
by arrangement with Team Media, Ltd.

2000 **Metro**Books

ISBN 1-58663-072-5

Book design by Team Media, Ltd.

Printed and bound in China

01 02 MC 9 8 7 6 5

LFA

Sarah Whitehead runs four pet behavior clinics and has an established chain of puppy socialization classes. She has co-authored several books on dog behavior, and is a regular contributor to pet magazines. She also appears on television and radio.

Bradley Viner runs a highly respected three-center animal practice. He contributes regularly to a number of pet magazines and has written several books about pet care. He presents a weekly pet program on radio and frequently appears on television.

Beverley Cuddy is an acknowledged authority on dog breeds, their habits, characterist cs and history, and an established expert in the field of pet writing. She is currently the editor of *Dogs Today*, a leading magazine for dog enthusiasts.

Peter Neville has been in practice for the referral and treatment of behavior problems in pets for over ten years. He is a frequent media broadcaster, public speaker and regular feature writer in leading pet publications such as *Dogs Today* and *Wild About Animals*.

Jim Breheny is the Curator of Animals for the Education Department at the Wildlife Conservation Society's Bronx Zoo. He manages the 3.5 acre, award-winning Children's Zoo and the zoo's collection of handleable animals used for teaching.

Contents

6 Introduction

8 Man's Best Friend

Part 1: What is a Dog?
14 Introduction • 16 Evolution & Domestication • 18 Structure of a Dog
20 Body Shapes • 22 Skin & Coat • 24 Body Systems
26 Sight • 28 Hearing • 30 Scent & Taste • 32 Movement
36 Hunting & Retrieving • 38 Scent & Defense • 40 Life Cycle of the Dog
44 Dog Behavior • 46 Socialization
50 Intelligence & Communication

Part 2: Caring for Dogs
56 Introduction • 58 Why a Dog? • 60 What's Involved?
62 Choosing a Dog • 66 Making the Right Choice
68 Supplying the Basics • 70 Early Days • 72 Understanding Your Dog
74 Your Dog's Needs • 76 Basic Practicalities • 78 Introducing Your New Pet
80 Settling In • 82 Handling Your Dog • 84 Training a Puppy
86 Continuing Training • 88 Training an Adult Dog • 90 Establishing Roles
92 Dog Discipline • 94 House Hygiene • 96 Living Areas
98 Dog-proofing Your Home
100 Traveling • 102 Problem Dogs
106 Your Dog's Well-being • 108 The Healthy Dog • 110 Nutrition & Diet
112 Grooming • 118 Essential Equipment • 120 Dogs & Play
122 Dogs & Exercise • 124 Toys & Games

Part 3: Your Dog's Health
126 Introduction • 128 Preventative Healthcare
130 Hereditary Diseases • 132 Neutering
134 Eye, Ear, Mouth & Tooth Disorders
136 Nervous & Circulatory Disorders • 138 Skin Disorders
140 Bone, Muscle & Joint Disorders
142 Digestive & Respiratory Ailments
144 Reproductive & Urinary Disorders • 146 Natural Medicine
148 Nursing & First Aid • 152 Having Puppies
154 Selecting a Mate
156 The Pregnancy • 158 The Birth • 160 The New Arrival

162 Dogs in Action

Part 4: Dog Breeds
168 Introduction • 170 Hounds • 180 Gundogs
194 Terriers • 206 Utility Dogs
216 Working Dogs • 230 Toy Dogs • 240 Show Dogs

242 Dogs in History
244 Famous Dogs & Dogs of the Famous
246 Dogs & the Imagination

250 Useful Addresses • 251 Further Reading
252 Index • 255 Credits

Introduction

The millions of proud dog owners around the world are testimony to the fact that a healthy, happy and well-behaved dog is a joy to own. No other pet lavishes on its owner the devotion that dogs do, nor fits so easily into the households of every country in the world. For most people, a dog is more than just a pet – it is a lifelong friend and a genuine responsibility.

Dog – The Complete Guide focuses on understanding today's domesticated and working dogs and provides both present and prospective dog owners with all of the information they need to care for and build a relationship with their pet. From choosing the right dog, taking care of him and finding the best training methods, through to an in-depth analysis of dog intelligence, behavior and special skills, this book is filled with sound, practical advice, based on up-to-date research from around the world.

DOGS AND THEIR CARE

The book opens with a discussion of the evolution and domestication of dogs, and goes on to provide detailed information about their anatomies, external features and senses. Skills and intelligence are examined, and a unique section is included on how dogs communicate with each other and people. The life-cycle of the dog, from birth to old age, is explained, with particular emphasis on the socialization stage and how this period of a dog's development affects its behavior during its life.

Part 2 consists of a practical guide to caring for dogs, with information, tips and expert advice on choosing a dog, tending to its needs, handling and training, establishing roles, ensuring that the home and yard are safe, traveling, grooming, diet and exercise. Part 3 deals with veterinary care, health conditions, breeding and the different problems that might arise throughout a dog's life.

THE BREEDS OF DOG

Part 4 of the book examines a wide variety of breeds, which have been grouped into six categories (see page 169). The breeds are recognized by the American Kennel Club (AKC), the Canadian Kennel Club (CKC), the British Kennel Club (KC) and the Federation Cynologique Internationale (FCI). Here, there is information about a breed's history, development, physical characteristics and temperament. Key features of each breed are listed in a handy breed assessment, which pinpoints exercise and grooming needs, size, how noisy the dog is likely to be, and possible health problems. It should be noted that these assessments are based on knowledge of the breed in general, and that characteristics vary enormously between individual dogs. Whether or not docking is customary is also noted. It is important to remember, however, that while some breeds are docked for the show ring in the US, many experts now consider the practice outdated and barbaric unless medically prescribed.

DOGS IN HISTORY

The final part of the book is an engaging and informative look at the importance of the dog in history, the arts and entertainment, and in the news. Finally, readers will find an authoritative resource section, with addresses of key organizations and suggestions for further reading.

Dog – The Complete Guide is an invaluable and inspiring reference – a thoroughly modern book that will help every dog owner, prospective or experienced, to understand their dog and give it the life that it deserves.

MAN'S BEST FRIEND

Since the dog was first domesticated, more than 12,000 years ago, it has provided warmth and affection to its owners, taking on the dual role of companion and worker with ease. Dogs are content to be our companions because they need to be guided by a pack leader, appreciate the availability

of food and comfort, and thrive in a relationship that is ever more defined. Dogs are sociable creatures and, because they share many of our social behaviors, are unique in their ability to respond positively to us. Loyal, unquestioning and comforting, the dog has earned the distinction of being "man's best friend".

The great pleasure of a dog is that you may make a fool of yourself with him and not only will he not scold you, but he will make a fool of himself too.

SAMUEL BUTLER, NOTE-BOOKS, *"HIGGLEDY-PIGGLEDY"*, 1912

The dog was created specially for children. He is a god of frolic.

HENRY WARD BEECHER, PROVERBS FROM A PLYMOUTH PULPIT, 1887

In order to really enjoy a dog, one doesn't merely try to train him to be semihuman. The point of it is to open oneself to the possibility of becoming partly a dog.

EDWARD HOAGLAND, "DOGS AND THE TUG OF LIFE", HARPER'S MAGAZINE, FEBRUARY 1975

A door is what a dog is always on the wrong side of.

OGDEN NASH, A DOG'S BEST FRIEND IS HIS ILLITERACY, *1953*

He is my other eyes that can see above the clouds; my other ears that hear above the winds. He is the part of me that can reach out into the sea. He has told me a thousand times over that I am his reason for being; by the way he rests against my leg; by the way he thumps his tail at my smallest smile; by the way he shows his hurt when I leave without taking him. (I think it makes him sick with worry when he is not along to care for me.) When I am wrong, he is delighted to forgive. When I am angry, he clowns to make me smile. When I am happy, he is joy unbounded. When I am a fool, he ignores it. When I succeed, he brags. Without him, I am only another man. With him, I am all-powerful. He is loyalty itself. He has taught me the meaning of devotion. With him, I know a secret comfort and a private peace. He has brought me understanding where before I was ignorant. His head on my knee can heal my human hurts. His presence by my side is protection against my fears of dark and unknown things. He has promised to wait for me . . . whenever . . . wherever - in case I need him. And I expect I will - as I always have. He is just my dog.

GENE HILL, "HE'S JUST MY DOG", TEARS & LAUGHTER, 1997

Animals are such agreeable friends. They ask no questions, they pass no criticisms.

GEORGE ELIOT, SCENES OF CLERICAL LIFE, 1858

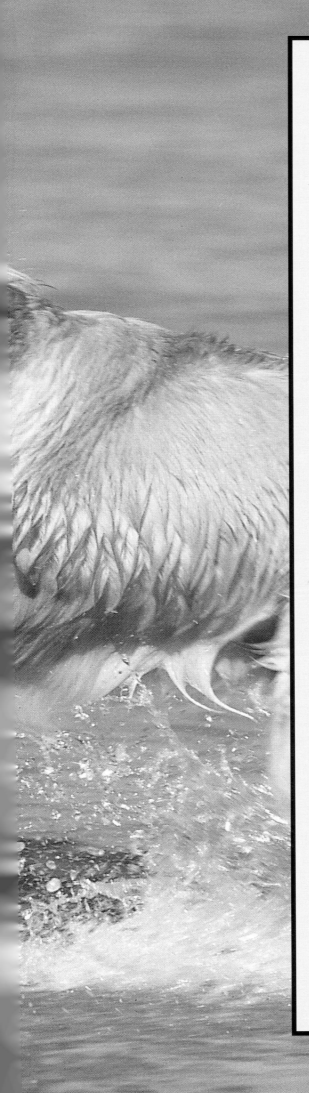

PART I

WHAT IS A DOG?

The domestic dog, *Canis familiaris*, is descended from a wolf-like creature that lived several million years ago. History suggests that the dog was one of the earliest of domesticated animals, having lived in close association with humans for more than 15,000 years. Today's pet dog is hardly recognizable as the wolf it once was. At least 400 different breeds are now recognized worldwide, engineered through selective breeding to look and behave in specific ways that people have found attractive or useful. The way in which we live with our dogs has also changed dramatically. It is no longer feasible for us to allow the dog to follow all the basic drives that come naturally to it. In return, the dog has to cope with the rigors of modern life – fast traffic, limited exercise and the values of a species that must seem incomprehensible at times. It is only by reinventing itself that the dog will continue to be valued, needed and loved. Looking at the evidence so far, it seems likely that *Canis familiaris* is here to stay.

Evolution &
Domestication

Genealogy ✦ Evolution ✦ Development of breeds

Below: The bond between human and dog stretches back many centuries, as shown in this marble carving from Ancient Greece.

The dog is a carnivore, a meat eater with four carnassial teeth designed to tear through flesh. Such carnivores are thought to have evolved between 54 and 38 million years ago, in reaction to changes in climate and habitat. The dog's earliest ancestor was probably a creodont (a small, meat-eating creature) known as *Miacis*, a ferret-like animal that lived in trees in the Paleocene epoch.

Between 38 and 26 million years ago *Miacis* was slowly replaced by a variety of canids (dog-like animals), including *Hesperocyon*. An inhabitant of what is now North America, *Hesperocyon* possessed a similar inner-ear formation to the modern canine family, confirming its evolutionary link. From this creature, the more dog-like *Cynodictis* developed, spreading to many parts of the world.

By the late Miocene period, around 12 million years ago, 42 different canids had evolved. Of these, the canid *Tomarctus* had long jaws, a large brain and a close resemblence to the modern dog in shape and tooth anatomy. This canid rerepresents the modern dog's foundation stock.

EVOLUTION OF THE DOG

Different theories of the evolution of the dog have been explored. The wolf, the fox and the jackal have each been claimed as direct ancestors of the dog. The domestic dog, the wolf and the jackal all belong to the family of dog-like animals, *Canidae* (canids). The close ancestry of these three species,

Above: Some modern dogs, like the Siberian Husky, have a wolf-like appearance. In general, dogs have inherited the wolf's extraordinary sight, hearing and sense of smell.

and the fact that they can breed together successfully, has led to historical speculation about whether the dog descended from a cross with the wolf or jackal. However, scientists now believe that the dog's most likely ancestor was a strain of the grey wolf, *Canis lupus pallipes*, which still exists in India and the Middle East today.

HUMANS AND DOGS

Humanity's association with the dog is an ancient one. Cave paintings show dogs hunting alongside humans, and bones from early encampments prove that dogs and humans have lived side by side for at least 10,000 years. However, the image of human and dog as friends and hunting companions may not have been so idyllic in the early stages of our relationship.

While research indicates that there can be little doubt that the wolf is the forefather of the modern dog, how the process of domestication took place is another question. The stretching of the wolf's elastic genes to create the sizes and shapes of dog we know today probably did not begin with taming a highly reactive, adult member of a predatory pack.

It is also unlikely that humans hand-reared cubs and brought them up as "domestic" animals, since even hand-reared animals will eventually develop into fully grown predators, and will always revert to the natural hunting lifestyle of their species.

Instead, it is possible that around the time that humanity's own lifestyle was changing from nomadic hunter to settler, there was a genetic shift in some wolves that arrested their development at a juvenile stage – at somewhere between four and six months of age.

DOMESTICATION BEGINS

The rubbish dumps around early human settlements would have been a good source of scavengable food, and those wolves that were less fearful of humans would have had more to eat. As humanity gradually changed from being predominantly hunters to partly farmers, these juvenile wolves might have provided an easily obtainable meat supply.

In turn, humans would have tolerated the scavenging activities of the less reactive wolves and been aware of those that produced the strongest offspring. Eventually, these juvenile wolves would have moved right into the village. Domestication had begun.

As humans developed a different way of life, farming crops, hunting from a home base and rearing captive livestock, they would have recognized certain useful qualities in some of these wolves. Some would have remained extremely adolescent and playful, without any vestige of dominant or predatory traits, and they would have been ideal for guarding livestock. Others would have been noted for their possessive instincts, and these would probably have been encouraged if there was a need for a retriever on the hunt.

Those that proved useful would have been kept and bred from; the rest would have been killed, eaten or driven away. This selection of certain aspects of wolf behavior by humans was to result, over many generations, in the emergence of the domestic dog.

THE DEVELOPMENT OF BREEDS

Once selective domestication of the wolf had begun, breeding would eventually have followed. The earliest objective of breeding would have been for the animal's usefulness in either hunting or defense. Ancient breeds of dog such as Mastiffs, Greyhounds, Pointers and Sheepdogs reflect this. At this stage, and for the millennia that followed, humanity was not concerned with the dog's appearance, and was only interested in the usefulness of the animal.

As humanity progressed towards modern times, the popularity of the dog slowly started to spread around the world, presumably via the trade routes. As working animals, dogs would have been universally valued, but the type that was good at herding in a settlement in one part of the world may have looked entirely different from the dog that had evolved to do the same job in another.

The nature of the task to which the dogs were suited, however, would have resulted in a sort of "type profile". Large, heavy dogs like Mastiffs would be good at hunting forest animals; lighter and more supple dogs like Collie- or Greyhound-types would be good at chasing, herding and flushing animals on the open plain.

The dog's appearance and its behavior naturally evolved side by side. It has only been in the 20th century that we have bred dogs purely for the way they look.

Below: The dog is thought to be directly descended from a subspecies of the grey wolf that inhabits Asia and the Middle East. Despite the grey wolf's name, its coat colour includes white, red-brown and black.

The Structure of a Dog

The skeleton ◆ Types of bite ◆ The skull ◆ Teeth

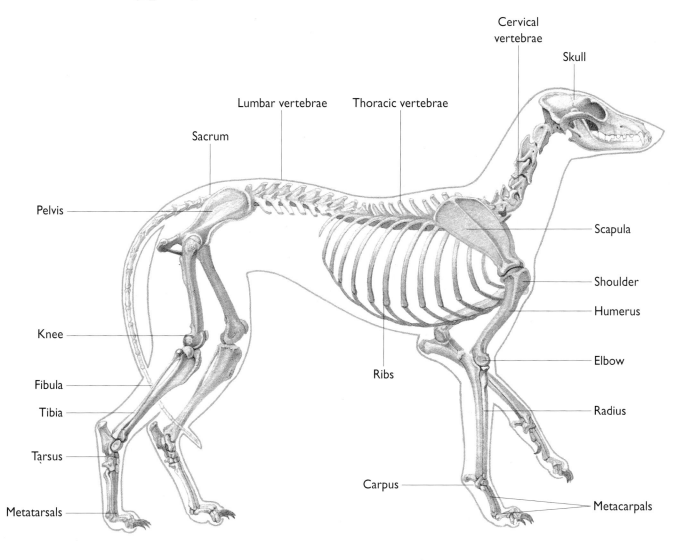

Cervical vertebrae

Skull

Lumbar vertebrae

Thoracic vertebrae

Sacrum

Pelvis

Scapula

Shoulder

Humerus

Knee

Elbow

Ribs

Fibula

Tibia

Radius

Tarsus

Carpus

Metatarsals

Metacarpals

With good care, exercise and nutrition, most dogs live long and happy lives. However, being able to identify a problem with your dog's health at an early stage is a key part of responsible dog ownership, and having a good basic understanding of the way in which your dog's body works can make this much easier.

THE DOG'S SKELETON

The dog's skeleton provides the structural framework for the animal's entire body. Along with a complex system of muscles and tendons, it enables the dog to stand, sit, run,

Above: Just like the skeleton of a human being, the main function of the dog's skeleton is to support and protect the internal organs of the animal's body.

jump and walk. The skeleton is moved by these muscles, which are anchored to the bones themselves.

Bones are hollow tubes made up of a latticed structure of hard, calcified material, filled with bone marrow. They are nourished via blood vessels that enter the bone though tiny holes. If a bone is broken, its surface produces new cells to fill the gap. During development, growth occurs at the end of the long limb bones. This

growth is controlled to a large extent by hormones, and stops once sexual maturity has been reached.

Unlike humans, dogs do not have a collar bone: the forelimbs are held together by muscles alone. This allows the dog great flexibility in movement.

All dogs have 30 true vertebrae, plus a varying number in the tail. Of the true vertebrae, 7 are cervical, making up the neck; 13 are thoracic, making up the spine (which lies over the chest and connects with the ribs); and 7 more are lumbar, forming the lower back. The vital spinal cord lies within a vertebral canal in the spine, for protection.

Skull shapes in different dog breeds vary enormously, yet contain the same bones in different formation. There are three basic skull shapes. Elongated, or narrow-headed breeds, such as Borzois and Afghan Hounds, are classified as dolichocephalic, while those with very short, broad heads, such as Bulldogs and Boxers, are brachycephalic. Dogs with heads of average length between the two extremes, are classified as mesocephalic.

Each skull, no matter what its exact dimensions, effectively forms a box shape. The upper part of this is called the cranium. The upper jaw is made up of the maxilla bone, while the mandible, or lower jawbone, is hinged to the skull.

The bony plates that make up the top of the skull fuse together in the middle of the forehead after birth, in a similar way to the skull of a human baby.

In some breeds with very domed heads, such as Chihuahuas, the fusion fails, leaving a gap known as the fontanelle. This can leave the animal vulnerable to brain injury.

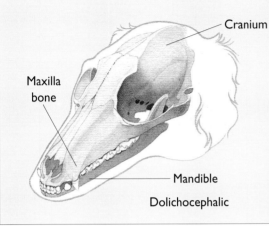
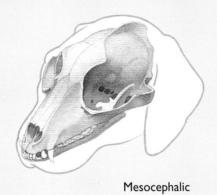
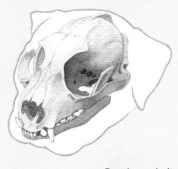

Maxilla bone — Cranium — Mandible

Dolichocephalic

Mesocephalic

Brachycephalic

THE DOG'S BITE

A dog's bite is determined by the length of his lower jaw. The four main types of bite that a dog may have are: scissor bite (with top teeth fitting over the bottom teeth); undershot (lower jaw extending beyond the upper); overshot (upper jaw extending beyond the lower); and level (teeth meeting). Any of these bites may be considered correct, depending on the breed or type of dog. For example, an undershot jaw would be considered a serious fault in a Golden Retriever, but is considered correct in a Bulldog. The shape of the jaw varies greatly between breeds, and official breed standards include requirements for the bite of each dog.

Level

Undershot

Overshot

Scissor bite

Below: The Bulldog's upper lip hangs low over the sides of its undershot jaw. The front of the jaw is prominent and turns upward.

TEETH

Adult dogs have a total of 42 teeth. Incisors are for cutting, the canines are for rending and tearing, and the molars are for crushing. Special teeth called carnassials are strong enough to chew through tough materials.

Below: Although dogs' teeth are strong, they may chip or fracture when bones are chewed. Regular dental care can prevent many problems from developing.

Body Shapes

Breed distinctions ✦ *Special designs* ✦ *Selective breeding*

Selective breeding in dogs has created more variety in one single domestic species than in any other on earth. Dogs range in size from the tiny Chihuahua to the massive Irish Wolfhound, with every possible size and shape in between.

Body shapes among dogs vary from the elongated form of the Dachshund to the upright elegance of the Saluki. This incredible variety in the shape, size and temperament of different dog breeds is partly due to the genetic elasticity of dogs. But it is also the result of man intervening in breeding in order to achieve the shape and behavior that best suits a dog to a particular function.

GOING UNDERGROUND

Generally, body shapes reflect the type of work that a dog has been bred to do. For example, dogs that can go down holes in the ground after fast-moving and sometimes formidable prey are likely to be relatively small, wiry and very supple. Most terriers

Right: The German Hunting Terrier was developed to hunt vermin and small game both above and below ground. Its small, supple body reflects this function.

Above: Dogs like the Scottish Deerhound, with their aerodynamic bodies and deep chests, are clearly designed for speed.

fall into this category. Although some large terriers do exist – such as the Airedale – on the whole, the build of terriers such as the Jack Russell, the Cairn and the Border clearly shows their ancestry as hunters of underground vermin and game.

A GOOD VIEW

Sight-hounds, on the other hand, are generally large dogs, able to view open ground and cover relatively short distances at high speeds. The

Greyhound is probably the best known of this type. This dog's thin skin and short coat leaves no part of his dramatic body shape concealed. Quite clearly, this is a dog built for speed, but not endurance. With long legs and a deep chest, the Greyhound can extend his gait to cover short distances effortlessly, hardly needing to pant at the end of the chase.

Sight-hounds are probably closest in body shape to the world's fastest land mammal, the cheetah, which can achieve speeds of up to 81mph (129k/ph). However, although it can easily outstrip the average wolf, which can run at up to 35mph (56k/ph), the Greyhound, at 44mph (70k/ph), is still considerably slower than the cheetah.

ENDURANCE RUNNERS

Other types of dog may be slower to cover the ground, but may be able to continue for far longer stretches at a time. Siberian Huskies, Malamutes and Eskimo Dogs have more stamina than the sprinters and can carry a reserve of fat to draw on during long journeys. Such dogs are still used as sled animals for long-distance transportation in some of the coldest and

Above: Dogs with strong, bulky, bodies, like this Bull Mastiff, have given man formidable protection as guard dogs. Mastiffs have also been used for fighting.

most inhospitable parts of the world. These types of dog tend to trot rather than sprint, which allows them to conserve energy and use their resources effectively.

STRENGTH, NOT SPEED

Dogs that have been selectively bred for guarding may have yet another different basic body shape. Many of these dogs are squarely built, for strength,

Below: Flat-nosed breeds, like the Pug, are susceptible to breathing problems because their short muzzles have been accentuated.

Height in dogs is measured from the ground to the shoulder, the highest part of the back. Despite great diversity in size, dogs have the same basic anatomy, with differences in the size of bones accounting for most of the visible difference.

The tallest breed in the world is the Irish Wolfhound, which usually stands at well over 31in (78cm) at the shoulder, and often more. At the other end of the scale, Chihuahuas may stand only 7–8in (17–18cm) tall, and may weigh a mere 6lb (2.7kg). Such huge diversity in size and weight is entirely due to selective breeding by man, where the largest or smallest specimens in each breed have been mated to produce extremes in

offspring. Giant breeds were often bred to intimidate intruders or to hunt formidable prey, such as wild boar. Some smaller breeds, such as Jack Russells, were bred to be small enough to follow vermin to ground. Other miniatures, such as the toy breeds, were favoured for their diminutive size, which made them easy to pick up and cuddle. Some of the smallest breeds were used to keep their owners warm, as they fitted neatly inside clothing. Dwarfism, where a dog never reaches its true size and retains the proportions and height of a puppy, occurs in some breeds, especially the German Shepherd. Sadly, this condition often results in early death.

not speed, and have an outline that reflects power and solidity rather than great agility. Their bones are normally straight and strong, while the neck and skull may be massive in comparison to the rest of the body. The Rottweiler and Mastiffs generally display these characteristics.

EXPERIMENTAL DESIGN

Man has been responsible for most of the diversity in body shapes present in dogs today. As our leisure time has increased in recent years, we have selected characteristics relating more to a dog's aesthetic appearance than to his particular function. Selective breeding for looks has resulted in hereditary diseases and physical anomalies, of the following kinds:

◆ The eye shapes and facial skin folds have become so exaggerated in breeds such as the Shar Pei and the Bloodhound that their eyesight can be seriously affected.
◆ Excessive lengthening of the spine in breeds such as the Dachshund can mean serious back problems, particularly in older animals.
◆ Sheer size and weight can also cause problems. Giant breeds, such as the St Bernard, can suffer heart conditions, which means that their life-expectancy is greatly reduced.
◆ Some breeds have been so "manufactured" that they can no longer give birth naturally. Many Bulldogs, for example, are now born by Cesarean section because their heads will not fit into the birth canal.

Skin & Coat

Skin ◆ Coat ◆ Hair growth

*A*dog's skin and coat often mirror overall health and fitness, and an unhealthy coat is frequently one of the first signs of illness.

The skin acts as physical protection against the elements and helps to control the dog's body temperature. It gathers information about the external environment, how hot or cold it is and whether it is comfortable or not. Skin is sensitive to pain and is the primary warning system about danger in the environment. Dogs' coats may vary greatly from breed to breed and from individual to individual. Indeed, some breeds have developed with no hair at all. The Mexican Hairless Dog and the Chinese Crested Dog are born without any coat, as a result of a genetic mutation that was encouraged through selective breeding.

STRUCTURE OF THE SKIN

A dog's skin is made up of two main layers – the epidermis and the dermis. The epidermis is the outer layer of cells, which continually replaces itself

Right: A dog's skin consists of a tough outer epidermis and a flexible inner dermis, over a layer of subcutaneous fat.

Above left: The Chinese Crested Dog's bald skin is a genetic mutation which would die out if not continued for selective breeding.

Above: Historically, the Komondor's corded coat provided protection from the elements and from wolves in his native Hungary.

as the top surface is shed or gets worn away. Under the epidermis lies the dermis, which is strong and flexible and provides the nerve and blood supply to the epidermis. Hair grows from papillae in the lower part of the the epidermis, through follicles. In dogs, a number of hairs appear from the same follicle. One hair is often thicker and longer than the others, and is known as the guard hair. Sebaceous glands in the dermis feed oil into the hair follicle to keep the skin lubricated and the coat glossy.

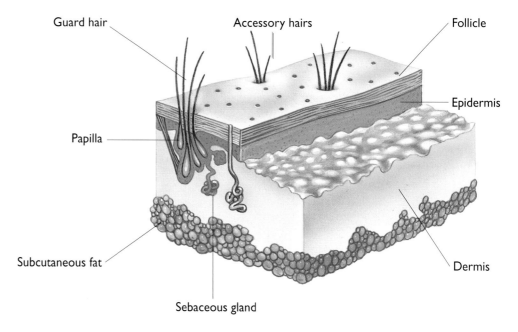

Guard hair · Accessory hairs · Follicle · Papilla · Epidermis · Subcutaneous fat · Sebaceous gland · Dermis

A small drink taken on the morning after a night of excess has traditionally been called "hair of the dog". This idea is based on an eighteenth-century cure for dog bites, on the principle that whatever caused the pain would also cure it. In *The Treatment of Canine Madness*, the author writes: "The hair of the dog that gave the wound is advised as an application to the part injured." It has never been recommended that drunken revellers swallow dog hairs in any form, but the occasional drink the morning after may well ease any withdrawal symptoms.

Sweat glands also open through the epidermis. In dogs these are primarily on the pads of the feet and in the ear canals. Dogs lose most of their excess heat through panting, rather than through sweating as we do.

Small muscle fibers contained inside the dermis – the deeper layer of the skin – can control movement of the guard hairs on the surface. By contracting or lengthening these muscles, dogs are able to achieve "piloerection", which is more commonly known as "raising the hackles".

This usually happens when the dog is in a state of arousal – aggressive, anxious, uncertain or excited.

HAIR-GROWTH CYCLES

A dog's hair grows and sheds in cycles. Any individual hair is either growing, is in a transitional phase or is in a resting phase. It is only shed when a new one is ready to replace it.

There are three main stages of hair growth: anagen is the stage of active hair growth; catagen, when the hair has stopped growing but is still attached to the papilla; and telogen, when the papilla contracts, loosening the hair before it begins growing a new one in its place. In a natural environment, the length of time between resting and regrowth is determined by the prevailing climatic conditions, the number of daylight hours and the dog's hormonal state. Dogs usually shed hair in the spring when they least need it, and again in the autumn, prior to growing a thick winter coat. Where central heating and artificial lighting interferes with this rhythm, shedding may be constant.

Four other parts of the body are classified as modified skin structures: the mammary glands, which have been specially modified to produce milk; the anal sacs, which are inversions of the skin where it joins the end of the digestive tract; the pads of the paws and the claws.

Dogs' coats have evolved in a variety of colors and patterns. The following are examples of the most common coat types:

MERLE
A marbled effect of blue-grey with flecks of black.

WHEATEN
Pale yellow or fawn.

TRICOLOR
Three colors in the coat in distinct areas. Black, white and tan is the most common tricolor.

ROAN
A mixture of colored and white hairs: blue roan, orange roan, lemon roan and liver roan are the most common.

SABLE
Black-tipped hairs overlaid on a background of gold, silver, grey, fawn or tan.

BRINDLE
An even mixture of black hairs, with gold, brown or grey, usually in tiger stripes.

GRIZZLE
A real mix of muted colors, including grey, red and black, in combinations.

CHOCOLATE
A rich brown color. Also known as the color "liver" in some breeds.

PAWS AND CLAWS

◆

Both the pads of the paws and the claws are regarded as modifications of the skin. This is because the material that makes up the nail is produced from an extension of the epidermis. The pads have a thick, protective epidermal layer, which makes them less sensitive to temperature and contact than other parts of the skin. The pads also contain sweat-producing glands, which help to prevent them from drying out. Sweat may be produced from the pads when the dog needs to cool down, and also when it is stressed.

Body Systems

Main body functions ✦ *Nervous system* ✦ *Glands & hormones*

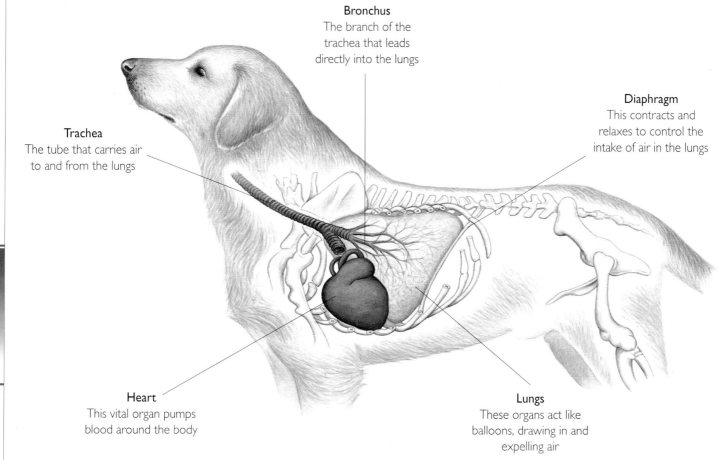

Bronchus
The branch of the
trachea that leads
directly into the lungs

Diaphragm
This contracts and
relaxes to control the
intake of air in the lungs

Trachea
The tube that carries air
to and from the lungs

Heart
This vital organ pumps
blood around the body

Lungs
These organs act like
balloons, drawing in and
expelling air

Most of the dog's major organs and body systems correspond to that of a human being and have the same functions.

RESPIRATION
The lungs take up most of the space in the thoracic cavity that is not taken up by the heart. The muscles used to control respiration – the diaphragm and some of the trunk muscles – expand and contract dramatically during periods of exertion.

DIGESTION
The dog's strong jaws and teeth are the first part of the digestive system.

Above: The respiratory system allows oxygen to be taken in and carbon dioxide to be removed. During normal respiration the dog breathes around 10 to 30 times per minute.

Food is chewed and then moved to the back of the dog's mouth, into the esophagus or gullet. Unlike ours, the dog's esophagus has thick but elastic walls, which allow large items to be swallowed. The stomach contains glands which produce acid and enzymes to aid digestion. It also acts as a holding unit until the food is ready to leave through the pyloric sphincter to enter the duodenum, the first part of the small intestine. Here,

peristalsis – contractions of internal muscles in the intestine wall – moves the food down the gut. Once the food is mixed with enzymes from the liver and pancreas, nutrients are absorbed into the bloodstream. Fluid is removed from the food via the large intestine, which also contains a large number of bacteria to help to break down the waste. This is then excreted.

EXCRETION
The excretory system removes toxic products and metabolic wastes from the body, as well as regulating fluid contents. The kidneys filter waste products from the blood. These are

then carried through the ureters to the bladder, where they are stored until disposal. The urethra carries urine out of the body through the dog's penis or the bitch's vulva.

REPRODUCTION

The reproductive system allows the animal to breed. In the male, this involves sperm production in the testes. In the female, eggs are produced by the ovaries and then move through the fallopian tubes to the uterus. The uterus in a bitch is a very distinct shape, having two "horns" that meet at the cervix. During pregnancy, the fetuses are positioned similar to peas in a pod in rows along each horn (see pages 156–7).

BREATHING

The cardiovascular system ensures the circulation of essential products, especially oxygen, in the blood and lymphatic system. A dog's circulation rate and distribution of blood depends on his level of activity. The brain constantly receives about 20 per cent of the blood pumped by the heart around the system. During periods of activity, increased amounts of blood are pumped to the heart muscles and the limb muscles, to provide higher levels of oxygen. Nerves and hormones regulate the blood supply to various parts of the body.

NERVES AND BRAIN

The nervous system controls many other body mechanisms, responding to the animal's needs and to the demands of the environment. The dog's central nervous system consists of the brain and the spinal cord. The spinal cord extends to the base of the tail. Information about the environment, such as heat and cold, as well as about the dog's state, such as its position, is gathered from nerve receptors in the skin, muscles and joints, and is constantly fed back to the spinal cord and the brain.

There is much we have yet to learn about how the dog's brain functions. We do know that dogs have learning centers that deal with sensory information, particularly the senses of smell and vision. Like us, dogs also have "emotional centers" which generate chemical responses that are then manifested as behavioral activity. However, whether dogs "feel" in a similar way to us remains a mystery.

HORMONES

The endocrine system aids internal control through the function of a number of glands and tissues that produce hormones. The pituitary gland controls the entire hormonal system. Hormones influence stress responses, sexual activity and blood sugar levels, all of which directly influence observable behavior.

Below: A basic knowledge of your dog's digestive and excretory systems will help you to understand how its body works.

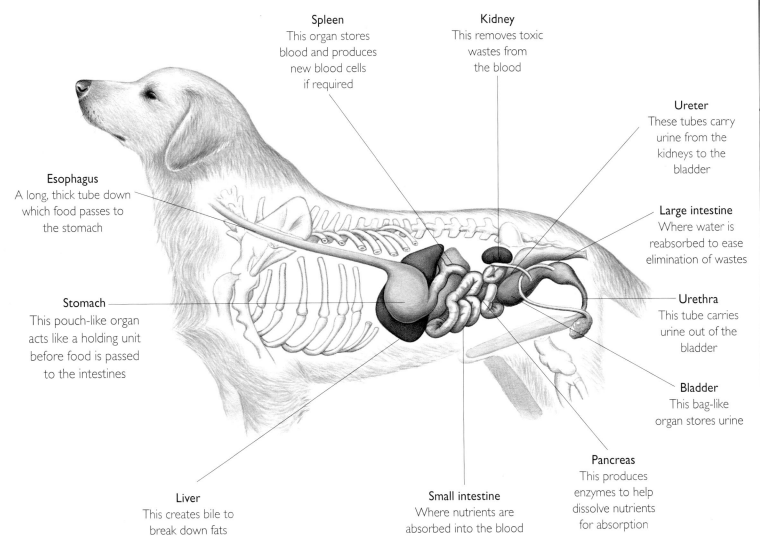

Spleen
This organ stores blood and produces new blood cells if required

Kidney
This removes toxic wastes from the blood

Ureter
These tubes carry urine from the kidneys to the bladder

Large intestine
Where water is reabsorbed to ease elimination of wastes

Urethra
This tube carries urine out of the bladder

Bladder
This bag-like organ stores urine

Pancreas
This produces enzymes to help dissolve nutrients for absorption

Small intestine
Where nutrients are absorbed into the blood

Liver
This creates bile to break down fats

Stomach
This pouch-like organ acts like a holding unit before food is passed to the intestines

Esophagus
A long, thick tube down which food passes to the stomach

Sight

The role of the eye ✦ Vision ✦ Eye shapes

A dog's eyes are more sensitive to light and movement than a human's eyes, but they are less effective in discerning the outline of objects. The eye itself is relatively flat when compared with a human eye, and although the dog is able to alter the focal length by changing the shape of the lens, they cannot do this as effectively as humans. Some breeds, such as Collies, may have incredible awareness of even the tiniest movement, being able to percieve such minute changes as the dilation or constriction of the pupils in human eyes.

HOW THE EYE WORKS

The eye is a fluid-filled globe that is housed in an orbit in the skull. It is held in position by strong muscles that allow it to move up, down and from side to side. The outer layer of the eye is a tough membrane called the sclera. This membrane is transparent over the front of the eye and is called the cornea.

The lens is attached to the cilary body, a muscle that can contract to alter the shape of the lens, enabling the dog to focus at different distances. It also holds and moves the lens.

The retina lines the back of the eye. Nerves here are sensitive to light and transmit messages through the optic nerve to the brain, where they are decoded into an image. The back of the eye also contains a separate area that reflects light, called the tapetum. This produces the characteristic

Right: The dog's eye is much like a human eye, but its flatter shape means that it cannot adjust focal length as effectively. The retina has more light-sensitive rods so the eye is better able to perceive light and movement .

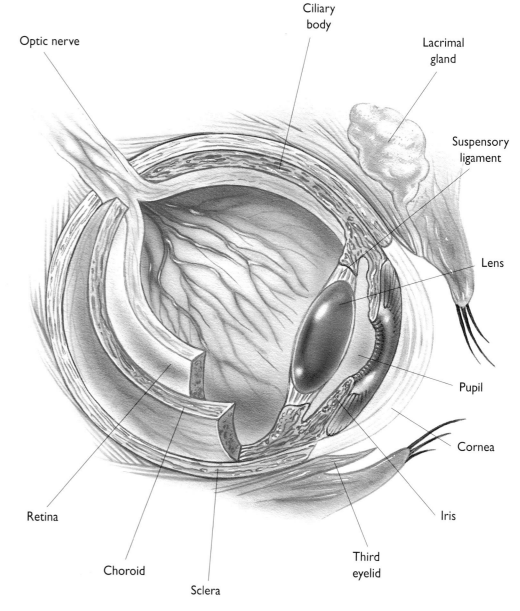

Optic nerve · Ciliary body · Lacrimal gland · Suspensory ligament · Lens · Pupil · Cornea · Iris · Third eyelid · Sclera · Choroid · Retina

reflection in a dog's eyes when caught in a direct beam of light. Dogs have a third eyelid, which lies hidden in the corner of each eye. This is usually only visible in a dog which is in poor condition, as it moves across to protect the eye. The lacrimal gland produces tears, which keep the cornea moist and clean. Any excess tears are carried away in ducts which are situated in the inner corner of the eye and lead to the nose. If these ducts become blocked, tears may run down the face, causing staining of the coat and skin.

Dogs cannot see color in the same way that we do, because of the way the eye is constructed. They cannot differentiate colors ranging from greenish yellow through orange to red, but they can distinguish between colors at each end of the spectrum.

FIELD OF VISION

♦

The dog usually has a wider field of vision than the human, due to the shape of the head and the set of the eyes. Flat-nosed breeds, such as the Pug or the Boxer, are likely to have a 200-degree field of vision, whereas sight-hounds, such as the Saluki or Greyhound, have a 270-degree field of vision, but poor stereoscopic vision. The human has a 100-degree field.

Below: Brachycephalic breeds, such as the Bulldog, have eyes in the front of their heads, which give them a better overlap in the field of vision than their longer-nosed counterparts. This overlap allows a better appreciation of depth and distance. The sleek bone structure of the Borzoi (Dolichocephalic) gives it a wider range of lateral vision but relatively poor overlap.

Brachycephalic type

Dolichocephalic type

EYE SHAPES

♦

The shape of a dog's eyes, and their placement in the head, modifies the field of vision, which varies between breeds.

Chow Chow

German Shepherd

Whippet

Bull Terrier

Hearing

The role of the ears ✦
Ear shapes ✦ A sixth
sense?

The hearing of a healthy dog is highly developed, as any owner who has ever tried to open a can of food quietly will know. Dogs can detect a sound in six-hundredths of a second and, by using the muscles in the outer ear to funnel sound into the inner ear, many can hear noises four times further away than we can.

HOW THE EAR WORKS

While the ear flap varies from breed to breed, the structure and function of the middle and inner ears is the same in all dogs.

The ear flap consists of cartilage, muscle and skin and is fairly mobile in most dogs. It assists in capturing sound and then funneling it down through the ear canal to the tympanic membrane, or eardrum, which vibrates as sound waves strike it.

Beyond the eardrum is the middle ear. It consists of a chamber, with the auditory ossicles – three small bones known as the hammer, anvil and stirrup because of their shape and function. These bones are the smallest in the body; they transmit the vibrations of the eardrum to the inner ear, amplifying them at the same time.

Inside the inner ear, the spiral-shaped cochlea converts these vibrations into signals that are then sent to the brain. Also in the inner ear are the organs that provide the dog with a sense of balance. These organs also give the dog information about the alignment of its head at any time.

Right: The ear consists of four parts: the ear flap, the external ear canal, the middle ear and the inner ear.

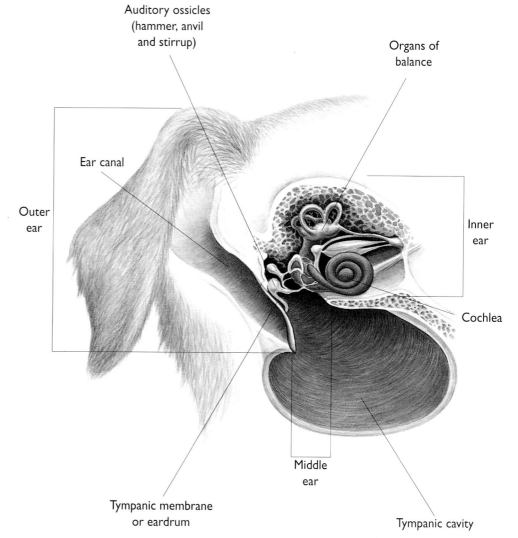

Auditory ossicles
(hammer, anvil
and stirrup)

Organs of
balance

Ear canal

Outer
ear

Inner
ear

Cochlea

Middle
ear

Tympanic membrane
or eardrum

Tympanic cavity

EAR SHAPES

More than any other part of the dog's body, the shape of the ears has been modified through the practice of selective breeding. The dog's natural ear shape is illustrated in its ancestor, the wolf. Upright and highly mobile so as to scan the whole environment, the wolf's ears are assisted by 17 different muscles, which help it to move its ears independently.

Our dogs' ear shapes now show as much variety as the breeds themselves. Some, such as the German Shepherd, still sport upright ears, much like the wolf's, and this gives them an impression of alertness. Other breeds, such as the Bloodhound or the Cocker Spaniel, who perhaps do not rely so heavily on their hearing, may have heavy, pendulous, or folded, ears. In contrast to these types, dogs such as the French Bulldog and the Boston Terrier have large, bat-like ears, which stand erect.

Selective breeding has inevitably led to ear problems. The dog's ear canal does not normally grow hair, but changes in ear skin has caused hair growth and some breeds need to have the hair plucked from their ears.

Above: As the name suggests, the Papillon has 'butterfly ears', resembling the wings of a butterfly.

DO DOGS HAVE A SIXTH SENSE?

◆

Some owners claim that their dog has a sixth sense and can even tell what they are thinking. Dogs that get excited long before their owner takes them for a walk or gives them their dinner may appear to be telepathic, but they are actually reading their owner's body language as the owner thinks about getting up to go out or to prepare food. Dogs are very good at picking up on the tiniest non-verbal cues. Some have even been known to spot the dilation of the pupils of their owner's eyes.

Less easy to explain are stories of dogs predicting their owners' homecoming after an absence, or even howling at the exact moment that their owner has died in hospital some distance away. Other mysteries include dogs that have traveled hundreds of miles to reach their owners, despite having never traveled such routes before. Undoubtedly, there are aspects of the dog's senses that remain unexplored, and unexplained.

Above: The German Shepherd, Bull Terrier and Elkhound all have pricked, erect ears, although size and positioning may vary.

Above: Button ears stand erect, but fold over in a V-shape, as in the Wirehaired Fox Terrier and the Jack Russell Terrier.

Above: Drop ears fall flat to the sides of the head or cheeks. Bloodhounds, Basset Hounds and Spaniels have drop ears.

Above: Rose ears fall back to expose the smooth inner portion of the ear. Bulldogs, Whippets and Greyhounds all have rose ears.

Scent & Taste

The nose ◆ *Nose shapes* ◆
*The importance
of taste*

A dog's sense of smell is highly developed. Indeed, it is now estimated to be one million times as efficient as that of humans. It is difficult to imagine just what information a dog may be able to determine through its sense of smell. Because of this uncanny ability, dogs have been trained to detect everything from truffles underground to certain types of tumors in humans.

HOW THE NOSE WORKS

Dogs' noses are known for being cold and wet. The moisture has a useful function: it helps to dissolve molecules in the air, bringing them into contact with the olfactory membrane inside the nose. Nerve impulses then convey this information to the olfactory center in the brain, which is more than 40 times bigger than ours.

The nasal membranes of the dog are dark, and it is thought that the usual black pigment of the nosepad may play some part in improving its sense of smell.

The dog also has a special organ in the roof of its mouth with which it can "taste" special smells. This is called the vomeronasal organ and it is used primarily for social scents, especially those concerned with sex. It transmits information directly to the limbic system – the part of the brain connected with emotional responses. Dogs can sometimes be seen using

Above: Puppies will smell and taste one another as a tool for learning about each other. They can gather information from another dog's scent.

Below: A dog's nose is at least a million times more sensitive than our own, and a huge number of its brain cells are devoted to scent recognition. The olfactory area of the dog's brain is much larger than ours.

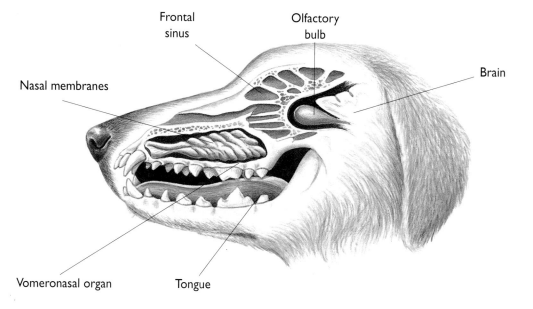

Frontal
sinus

Olfactory
bulb

Brain

Nasal membranes

Vomeronasal organ

Tongue

this organ when they find a really exciting smell. Typically, their teeth will chatter slightly and they may drool or salivate while they taste and smell the odor at the same time.

NOSE SHAPES

The large numbers of sensory cells contained in the dog's olfactory membrane need to be housed somewhere, and different breeds have developed differently sized and shaped noses. It is estimated that a Dachshund's nose contains 125 million sensory cells, while a German Shepherd may have up to 220 million. For the purposes of comparison, the human is thought to have 5 million. To accommodate this large area of olfactory sensitivity, the earliest dogs had a long nose like that of the wolf, though in some modern, more "artificial" breeds much shorter noses are evident.

TASTE

Of course, it is impossible to ask dogs what they taste when they eat. However, although there seems little doubt that dogs can detect bitter, sweet, sour and salty tastes, perhaps what is most important to them is whether they like a taste or not. Early experience counts for a lot here, and there is some evidence to suggest that dogs who have had a wide experience of different tastes and textures of food

Above left: Once hunters realized how single-minded the Basset Hound was at pursuing a scent, they quickly adopted the breed to accompany them on hunts.

Above right: A dog's nose is moist in order to help capture the scent and transmit it to the nasal membranes.

Right: Although there are fewer than 2,000 taste receptors on a dog's tongue, it can taste in conjunction with its sense of smell.

when young are more likely to be adventurous when they are older. Some dogs adore strong-tasting foods, such as raw onions and garlic, while others have a preference for a single type of food and will try nothing else.

HOW TASTE WORKS

Dogs have about one-sixth of the number of taste buds that we do. Most of these are clustered around the front part of the tongue. However, the senses of taste and smell are inextricably linked, and it may be that dogs gather more from the smell of food than from its taste.

As dogs' sense of taste is relatively poor, they require less variety in and fewer changes to what they eat than we do. Your dog is more likely to be indifferent to a food than he is to object to it because of its taste. Dogs that train their owners to pop down

to the supermarket to buy something different for dinner each night are probably playing power games rather than suffering from bored taste buds.

However, dogs do make rapid associations with tastes, in the same way that we do. This means that dogs who become ill after eating a particular food may not want to eat that kind of food again for some time. Such "taste aversion" is a sensible survival strategy, since it may protect an animal from eating toxic substances repeatedly over a period of time.

Movement

Walking ✦ Running ✦ Muscles and movement ✦ Special skills

A dog's movement is dependent on a number of factors. The first of these is the "conformation": the way that the dog's anatomy works. This means that a dog that has a well-angulated shoulder – for example the Golden Retriever – is likely to have a freedom of movement that is lacking in a dog with an "upright" shoulder. Indeed, such dogs may have an almost "hackney" step, but this may be quite correct for the breed, as with the Miniature Pinscher.

Movement is also dependent on age and fitness. A young, well-muscled dog is likely to show a greater range of

Above: The gallop is a very fast form of movement. Fit, healthy dogs can move at speed, but usually only for short periods.

movement than one that is old, unfit or overweight. As in humans, muscle tone needs to be built gradually, then maintained, if a dog is to remain in good shape. Unfortunately, there are far too many lazy canines in the world, and obesity in dogs is as common as it is in our species.

Excess weight has implications for the internal organs as well as the dog's overall flexibility and ease of movement. Many veterinarians now

run "diet clinics" for owners who need help in reducing their pet's weight and you should attend one if your dog is too heavy. Increased exercise, along with a controlled diet is as good for our dogs as it is for us.

TYPES OF MOVEMENT

Dogs generally move in four main ways: walk, trot, canter and gallop. The dog's walk is often characteristic of the breed or type. Large, powerful breeds may lope along, while small, sprightly terrier types may have a spring in their step. The trot seems to be the dog's favored gait. This is a

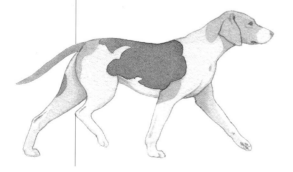

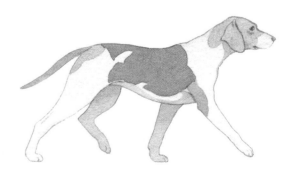

Above: Jumping is a good activity for lean dogs, but potentially dangerous for older, heavy dogs. If an overweight dog lands too heavily, it may damage himself.

Right: Unlike the skeleton and body shape, the musculature of a dog varies little between breeds. Muscles not only allow movement, they also protect vital organs and bones.

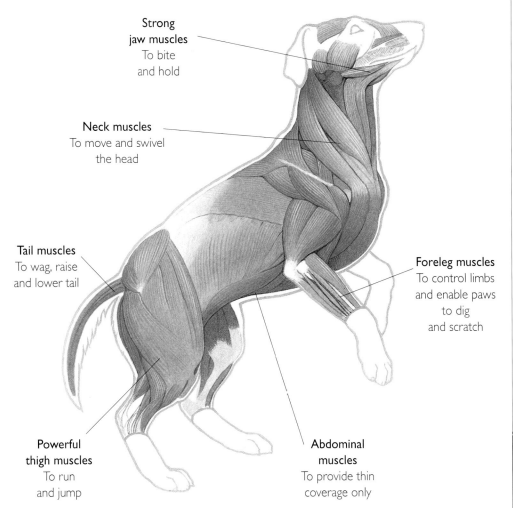

Strong jaw muscles
To bite and hold

Neck muscles
To move and swivel the head

Tail muscles
To wag, raise and lower tail

Foreleg muscles
To control limbs and enable paws to dig and scratch

Powerful thigh muscles
To run and jump

Abdominal muscles
To provide thin coverage only

steady pace, which maintains good speed but does not require a great deal of energy compared to faster, less sustainable speeds.

Galloping is used to cover short distances at high speed. It requires an enormous expenditure of energy, and although some breeds, such as Greyhounds and Lurchers, have been bred to be exceptional sprinters, they still lack the stamina to maintain high speed for prolonged periods.

Other breeds have been specially bred to enhance their flexibility. Border Collies and other herders, for example, can turn at high speed in order to redirect the flock, and can drop to the ground in a second on command from the handler. However, all the elements of these behaviors can be seen in the original "eye–stalk–chase" hunting sequence employed to great effect by the wolf.

MUSCLE POWER

Dogs have three types of muscle: smooth muscle controls movement of the large internal organs; cardiac muscle makes up the bulk of heart tissue; and striated or skeletal muscle makes up the rest. The dog can control all its skeletal muscles, which can be contracted or relaxed at will.

Muscles are made up of fibers that contract when stimulated by a nerve impulse. The ends of the muscles are attached to the bones by tendons. Contraction and relaxation of the muscle therefore causes movement in the joints, making them bend, extend, move inwards, move outwards or rotate. Each muscle is opposed by another that exerts the opposite force, making precise movements possible.

As well as the major movements, muscles also control less obvious functions such as shivering, breathing, defecation and giving birth.

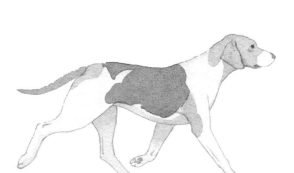

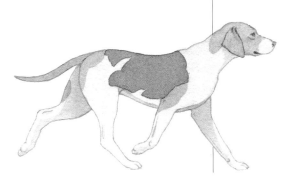

Movement

The dog's body is a miracle of natural engineering. As well as walking with perfectly coordinated movement and smooth gait, it can run, leap and swim. Its body is also impressively flexibile, enabling it to move easily from being curled up in a small ball to standing at full height on its hind legs. The dog's wide range of movement skills, combined with its versatility, has led humans to employ it in a variety of ways over the centuries, as rescue worker, hunter, draught animal, vermin controler and even as a fighter for "sport".

SWIMMING

While all dogs are able to swim, some breeds have been bred to work specifically in water. The Newfoundland, which has a thick coat for warmth, is an excellent swimmer, and even has webbed feet. This breed was originally bred and trained to help fishermen haul in nets, and then later to rescue people from water. It is even strong enough to tow a rowing boat out of the water if trained to do so. Stories also abound of Newfies who have made voluntary "rescues" of somewhat surprised swimmers.

Other breeds, such as the Poodle and the Portuguese Water Dog – which can be trained to retrieve lost fishing nets and swim with them to the shore – also owe their present shape to their swimming heritage. Both are clipped in a style that was traditionally thought to keep their joints warm while they swam and to increase their mobility in the water.

PULLING

Sled dogs have been used to transport people and loads across frozen land and ice for generations. Working as a team, the dogs pull the load behind them under the general control of the driver, or "musher". Sled dogs also participate in racing. Cornering – taking corners at high speed – may be easy for the dogs, but in relatively short races, of up to 20 miles (32 kilo-

meters), where the teams may reach speeds of up to 25mph (40kph), it may not be as comfortable for the musher who stands at the back. In longer races, speeds may not be as high, but the distances covered by sled dogs are astounding: the current record stands at over 1000 miles (1600km), traveled in less than 10 days.

Some types of dog have also been used to pull carts. Bernese Mountain Dogs were favored for this because of

Below: The ability to swim is one of the many physical skills dogs possess. This activity gives them both pleasure and exercise.

Above: Dogs need routine exercise to maintain their flexibility and muscle tone. Exercise should combine a range of movement, from walking to galloping.

their great power and flexibility. In central Asia, dogs are still sometimes used to turn water wheels.

HUNTING

The dog's natural instincts for hunting and retrieving have proved invaluable to humanity since domestication began (see pages 36–7). Among the earliest dog groups to emerge were the hounds that hunted by sight, such as the Greyhound, the Afghan Hound and the Deerhound. These long-legged hounds can run at great speed, and their suppleness makes them seem more akin to cheetahs than to other dogs.

Terriers have lithe bodies, capable of a considerable turn of speed. Many of this group were bred to hunt vermin and game in small underground holes and tunnels. This necessitated great speed of thought and movement, and the flexibility to be able to turn around in a very tight spot.

FIGHTING

Dog fighting has been portrayed in stone carvings dating back as long ago as the 6th century BC. Dogs that were originally bred by humans for fighting often have large and powerful

bodies. While size has reduced their speed of movement, they have retained considerable flexibility. The large Shar Pei has skin so loose and wrinkled that, according to legend, he is able to turn around in it if grabbed by an assailant from behind.

Overall, the sheer freedom of movement and athleticism of the average dog is outstanding. Dogs can usually out-run, out-jump and out-maneuver even the fittest human being. They can also curl into the smallest area of the car for a sleep on the way home.

The dog that's always on the go is better than the one that's always asleep.

IRISH PROVERB

Right: The compact and powerful body of this Boxer in motion vividly illustrates the athleticism of dogs.

Below: Dogs are not natural jumpers and climbers like cats because they cannot control their claws or legs in the same way. Although capable of the sudden muscle contraction required to jump, the dog's power is essentially developed for endurance running.

WHAT IS A
DOG?
Movement

35

Hunting & Retrieving

Highly developed senses ✦ *Hunting companions* ✦ *Special skills*

Left: A well-trained retriever will "mouth" the prey but not do any damage to it when picking it up and carrying it to its owner.

*E*very one of the dog's senses is well defined to assist in hunting. A highly developed sense of smell allows dogs to track the scent of quarry for miles, even hours after it has disappeared. Their eyesight, particularly in the case of sight-hounds, which rely on sight for hunting, is designed to detect the smallest movement over a wide area. Dogs also have excellent hearing and are capable of picking up even the tiniest sounds made by potential prey.

The bodies of dogs have also been developed by breeding to improve their hunting abilities. Greyhounds and Lurchers are the track athletes, capable of running at high speeds to catch rabbits and hares. Terriers are able to race down small holes after vermin, while herding dogs are fast and accurate, with a well-developed ability to stalk animals.

HUNTING PARTNERS

For centuries, dogs have accompanied humans while they have hunted, for food or for sport. Many of our present-day breeds have been formed through the selective breeding of dogs by humans to accentuate their natural hunting characteristics, so making them more effective on the hunt.

Hunting can be broken down into different areas. First, the quarry needs to be found, and there are many different dogs that specialize in this kind of work. Hounds are the obvious choice for this task. Bred to live in a world of scent, they usually work as a team to track down the prey, picking up particles of scent from crushed vegetation and even in the

air. Bloodhounds, Beagles, Foxhounds and Basset Hounds all come into this category, and many other more local breeds, such as Coonhounds, also operate in a similar way.

Sight-hounds, such as Afghans, Greyhounds and Whippets, find their prey by sight, while some dogs, like German Short-haired Pointers, also indicate that they have found prey by "pointing" towards it. Spaniels then flush out the quarry from the undergrowth, leaving it exposed to the hunter's gun or net.

Once a trail is located, large prey animals may need to be tackled, and this is where breeds such as the Irish Wolfhound and the Deerhound have come into their own in the past. After the kill, the prey animal needs to be carried back to the hunter and home, and this is where retrievers have the most valuable skills.

RETRIEVING THE SPOILS

Some dogs have been selectively bred to carry out the task of retrieving. The most common of these, both for work and as pets, are the Labrador Retriever and the Golden Retriever. Others include the Flat-coated Retriever, the Curly Coated Retriever, the Chesapeake Bay Retriever and the Nova Scotia Duck Tolling Retriever. These dogs are equally good at retrieving from the water or on land.

All of these dogs have one thing in common: they like to hold and carry things in their mouths and, with the correct training, will bring them to their owner without hesitation. Retrievers are known for being placid, obedient and good with people. Although there are always exceptions, it is mainly the submissive nature of these dogs that ensures that they want to bring the quarry gently back to the handler. A more dominant type of dog might be much more inclined to head off into the woods and eat the find itself.

HARNESSING YOUR PET'S HUNTING OR RETRIEVING ABILITIES

♦

Most of us live with dogs as pets, not as hunting companions, and this can lead to difficulties as they attempt to find an outlet for their natural hunting drives. While out for a walk, many pet dogs chase inappropriate targets, such as joggers, cyclists and squirrels, and this can get them into serious trouble. Equally, many retriever types will steal objects and run off with them if their natural skills are not directed into more appropriate activities. Channeling these instinctive behaviors through training, obedience and agility classes, working trials or simply through play, is essential. Working dogs without a job to do are likely to become self-employed: it is up to us to ensure that their skills do not become a liability. A busy dog will not need to satisfy its natural instincts elsewhere.

Scent & Defense

Scent skills ✦ *Guarding*

Although we can try to guess what it must be like to be a dog, there is one area of the dog's experience that humans find almost impossible to imagine, and that is the world of scent.

A dog's nose is designed to maximize the capture of scent particles and to interpret the chemical messages contained within them. While most humans are able to recognize certain smells, and may find that strong memories are triggered by them, it is thought that dogs can "read" scent and gather vast quantities of information from it.

Scent remains important to most dogs because it still provides a huge

Above: Smell is the dog's most advanced sense; a large part of the brain is devoted to interpreting scent. Below: Most dogs show great concentration when "on the scent".

amount of information about their environment, food and sexual partners, even though they no longer live in the wild.

SCENT SIGNALS

Dogs spend a great deal of time sniffing – each other, important "message sites", and even the air, which carries chemical "air mail" over long distances. The scent of a bitch in season, for example, can be carried on the air for many miles.

Dogs leave scent signals for other dogs to read, primarily through urine and feces. In an attempt to make these markers even more apparent, male dogs, or bitches in season, try to lift the scent as high as possible, by cocking a leg against an upright obstacle or even depositing feces on high objects.

SCENT SPECIALISTS

Some breeds or types of dog are much more scent aware than others. Bloodhounds and Basset Hounds, for example, live in an olfactory world, where smell is the most important sense, and hearing and vision less so. This is a direct result of the fact that these breeds have been selectively bred to work by using their noses.

Above: Dogs can be trained to sniff for nearly any substance, and can gather a great deal of information from the source. This dog has been trained to sniff for drugs.

Right: Urinating leaves a scent message for other dogs and probably contains information about the gender, sexual status and even health of the depositor.

Their highly developed scenting skills have been used to track down animals and even lost humans.

While it is impossible for us truly to appreciate the information that a dog gathers with its nose, the usefulness of the function has long been exploited by man. Dogs are regularly used to sniff out anything ranging from drugs to dry rot. They are able to locate truffles growing underground, or people buried in the aftermath of an earthquake or some other disaster.

DOGS AND DRUGS

◆

The greatest drug-sniffing dogs on record are a pair of Malinois called Rocky and Barco. These Belgian sheepdogs (whelped in 1984), are members of a stop-and-search team that patrols the Rio Grande Valley along the southern Texas border. In 1988 alone they were involved in 969 seizures of drugs worth $182 million, and they are so proficient at their job that Mexican drug smugglers put a $30,000 price on their heads. Rocky and Barco have been awarded honorary titles of Sergeant Major, and always wear their stripes when they are on duty.

The dog's heightened sense of smell can save human lives. Some dogs have even been trained to sniff out the early signs of cancer, while others can locate explosives and land mines.

KEEPING WATCH

From an early time, dogs have acted as guards for humans. In the wild, a dog would raise the alarm by barking if he saw a strange dog or predator approaching his pack's territory. Many pet dogs continue this practice, barking at visitors to the home and other intruders to let us know that the den needs defending.

In theory, dogs should only warn us that intruders are about. As pack leaders, only we have the right to decide when and who will enter our homes. However, some dogs, mainly the guarding breeds, may regard it as their responsibility to defend the inner sanctum of their den, and may even become aggressive to those they do not recognize, or whom they perceive as threatening, their domain. This can include visitors to the home and yard, and may explain why mailmen so often come under fire.

Outside the home, dogs are often thought to be defending their owners, particularly if they bark or lunge at passers-by or other dogs. This is, in fact, rarely the case. More commonly, dogs that behave in this way are

fearful. They have learned to put on a display of aggression to keep the other person or dog away from them as a means of defense. It could be argued that such dogs are protecting themselves in this way, and not their owner or their territory.

Below: One of the many ways in which dogs have served humanity is through guarding. Dogs use their excellent senses of smell and hearing to warn of potential danger.

Life Cycle of the Dog

Puppies ✦ Adolescence ✦ Old Age

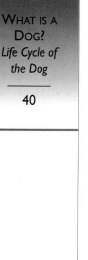
*F*rom the moment they are born, puppies begin changing and developing in a variety of exciting ways. From the first helpless days through to the delightful puppy behavior that characterizes the first 12 months, your puppy will grow and mature at a quite remarkable rate. He will discover a huge range of new experiences and will learn to play, to communicate and to understand the world around it.

THE NEWBORN PUP

Puppies are born unable to see or hear. Although they are covered in hair, they rely entirely on their mother for warmth and protection. At this stage, the primary sense a puppy has is that of smell. A newborn puppy's face confirms this, in that the nose and muzzle area seems to be disproportionately large compared with the rest of his body.

Very young pups have the ability to move, and they can drag themselves back to the warmth of the nest if isolated, and can also cry out to alert the bitch to their location when hungry.

Newborn puppies cannot urinate or defecate for themselves, nor regulate their own temperature. They rely entirely on their mother to lick them

Above: A newborn puppy is blind, deaf and entirely dependent upon its mother for food and protection.

to stimulate elimination of waste products and to keep them at the optimum temperature by sharing her body warmth with them.

Puppies are born with several basic abilities. The cranial nerves are well-developed at birth, allowing for feeding, facial sensitivity, balance and a "righting" reflex, which leads the puppy to right itself if it is tipped upside down. When held by the scruff of the neck, newborn puppies adopt a classical response, drawing in the limbs and remaining motionless. Yet, only four to five days later, they extend their limbs outwards when picked up in the same way. Very young puppies cannot see or hear properly, although they will react to loud noises. They can, however, make sounds of their own – and they may cry or yelp if they find themselves abandoned, which alerts the mother to their predicament.

Left: By three weeks of age, a puppy will be on its feet and exploring the area around the whelping box.

1 TO 3 WEEKS

Puppies begin to respond to noises as their ears open and they start to use their eyes to follow light and movement, although their vision will not clear fully until about four weeks of age. Most puppies are beginning to move around much more effectively by three weeks of age – starting to walk rather than crawl. Periods of activity are interspersed with long periods of deep sleep.

3 TO 6 WEEKS

By five weeks, a puppy has the fully developed hearing, sight and sense of smell of an adult dog, although his concentration span is a lot shorter. Weaning usually starts at about three weeks, and is completed by five to six weeks, as the mother's milk supply decreases and her tolerance of the puppies becomes limited. At this stage, the puppies have their first and most vital lesson in social behavior as they learn to cope with the frustration of not being able to suckle upon demand. Play with littermates and the mother also makes this an important time as the puppy learns that it is a dog. Many of the fundamental play postures and facial expressions are learned now.

6 TO 12 WEEKS

Human influence is most important at this time. Socialization – learning how to behave in a social context with both people and other dogs – must occur at this stage (see page 46). Habituation, or exposure to events and changes in the environment, is just as

Above: By three to four weeks, your puppy will start to show increasing signs of independence, exploring the environment.

important. Well-socialized and habituated puppies become confident, happy and obedient in a variety of situations and environments.

Puppies absorb a huge amount of information about their world from this point on. Their coordination and movement is well developed, allowing them to run, jump and roll. Play with littermates and with humans begins to take on the role of learning social behavior in earnest, and those sharp little teeth are in constant use, finding out just what is alive in the world and what isn't.

Most puppies are fully weaned from their mothers after about seven weeks and, by this time, puppies should be able to eat enough solid food to meet their nutritional needs. At eight weeks they are ready to leave their mother and littermates, although many remain with their mothers until the age of ten weeks.

Left: At six weeks your puppy will already have learned many vital social skills. It is up to owners to ensure this learning continues.

Life cycle of the dog

Above: Although puppyhood usually ends by six months, many dogs retain engaging puppy characteristics for much longer.

3 TO 6 MONTHS

Puppies build lots of bone and muscle during this time, in preparation for adolescence. At about 18 to 20 weeks, they lose their milk teeth and gain their permanent adult teeth. This marks the end of true puppyhood.

Experimentation with social behavior is constant and dogs of this age may even practice "sexual" behavior by mounting cushions, other animals and people. Finding out just who is "top dog" through games of strength and possession may occur. Through play, puppies learn about communication of emotional state and social standing. It is also quite normal for puppies to experience a "fear" period during this time, showing anxiety at the sight of objects or people with which they had previously been confident. How you handle these situations will determine whether or not your dog is fearful of that object for the rest of his life. Forcing a dog to be brave is confrontation and likely to result in further avoidance.

6 MONTHS TO 1 YEAR

This stage represents the "teenage" years of a dog's life. Bitches may come into season for the first time and dogs become sexually mature. This can be a trying time for dogs and owners, as social behavior can take on a whole new meaning. Some bitches seem to suffer from mood swings before, during or after a season, and may become intolerant of other dogs' advances.

Male dogs usually start to lift their leg when urinating at between 6 and 12 months of age. This enables them to mark territory and leave information through scent signals about their sexual and social status. Their encounters with other dogs may start to involve social challenge, usually without physical confrontation,

Below: A six-month-old puppy begins to progress towards sexual maturity and may exhibit difficult "teenage" behavior.

Right: By one year old, a dog can mate and produce her own puppies, although mental maturity may take somewhat longer.

although they may try to mount bitches and other males at this time in order to establish social rank. Adult teeth also set into the bone between 6 and 10 months of age. This can cause dogs to chew in order to relieve the pressure. It is sensible to have toys and chews available to prevent them from chewing inappropriate objects.

1 TO 4 YEARS

Although sexual maturity usually occurs between 6 and 14 months of age in most dogs, full growth and mental maturity may take much longer. Toy dogs tend to mature more quickly than large or giant breeds of dog such as Newfoundlands or Pyrenean Mountain Dogs, which may be three before they can be considered fully grown. Mental maturity can also take varying lengths of time, and owners of exuberant breeds, such as Boxers, may wonder if their dog will ever grow up. During this time, dogs

continue to learn and to establish roles within the household and in relationships with other dogs. It may not be until a dog or bitch is three or four years old that problems between dogs in the same household manifest themselves. In a few cases, a challenge for dominance occurs once the dog is mature enough to recognize his status and to attempt to change it.

OLDER DOGS

◆

Old age is a relative concept, dependent on the breed of dog, his or her overall health and fitness and the attitude of the owner. For a fit, healthy and active dog, the twilight years may simply be a case of slowing down slightly.

Most older dogs still enjoy going out for walks, playing with their owners and interacting with the family. They may sleep for longer and more deeply than previously, and may also need to relieve themselves more often, as the kidneys – along with the liver – are among the first organs to deteriorate. Loss of weight is also a symptom of kidney and liver failure and this should be monitored.

Other common physiological changes include arthritis and stiffness in the joints and spine. Excess weight will certainly exacerbate any geriatric changes, and should be prevented.

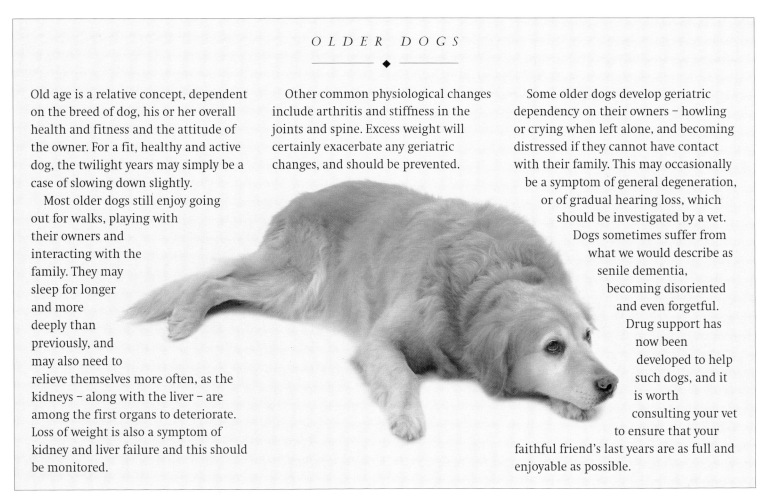

Some older dogs develop geriatric dependency on their owners – howling or crying when left alone, and becoming distressed if they cannot have contact with their family. This may occasionally be a symptom of general degeneration, or of gradual hearing loss, which should be investigated by a vet. Dogs sometimes suffer from what we would describe as senile dementia, becoming disoriented and even forgetful. Drug support has now been developed to help such dogs, and it is worth consulting your vet to ensure that your faithful friend's last years are as full and enjoyable as possible.

Dog Behavior

Packs and leadership ✦
Learning and
intelligence

Dogs are dogs! This may seem to be an obvious statement, but for many of us dogs become so much more that it is sometimes hard to remember their limitations, and their unique abilities. Dogs are a wonderful mixture of nature and nurture – of instinctive behaviors combined with learning. Nearly all the behavior a dog exhibits would have had a natural use or outlet in the wild, helping to promote breeding and the survival of their species. This means that in teaching dogs to live with us as a part of our social group and system, we have to teach them when and where they can use this behavior.

PACK BEHAVIOR

As a social species, dogs have a strong desire to fit in with a pack and to work as part of a team. In the wild, a single dog or wolf would not last long by itself, since it takes teamwork to bring down large prey. This is why a wild dog pack has a social order. This social order establishes which pack members breed and which usually eat first after the kill.

Naturally, disputes sometimes occur within the social system, but as it would be evolutionarily unsound for dogs to wound each other, they develop a series of ritual displays, including body posturing, staring and growling, to settle conflicts without causing bloodshed. This theatrical

Below: Dogs fight rarely and only when other ritualized forms of competition have failed to resolve a conflict.

form of body and facial language between dogs acts as a powerful system of communication that indicates both intention and response.

At one time, it was believed that the highest-ranking wolf was the biggest or strongest. However, it now seems that those with the best communication skills wield the most control and power.

Above: Dogs learn in a similar way to human beings. They can skilfully read body language and if a certain behavior is rewarding, they will repeat it.

LEADERS OF THE PACK

In a wild state, those dogs or wolves that get the best of everything are more likely to mate and produce healthy offspring than those that lose out. This means that those wolves who get the largest share of the kill also have the safest places to rest, enjoy being groomed by the others, and create allies within the pack for protection. They are more inclined to reproduce than those that go hungry until the others have eaten, sleep on the edges of the den and rarely get attention from others. We call dogs that get the best of everything – and that are therefore most likely to breed – "dominant", or "Alpha", dogs.

This social structure is familiar enough to humans. We do not have to look very far to see that the manager has a large office, his own desk and chair, a space in the car park and a company car, while the office junior has to make do with much less.

Indeed, the similarities between the social structure of the dog and that of humans have enabled our relationship with dogs to flourish. On the whole, dogs living in domestic environments understand that we get the best while they get the rest, and this avoids conflict between the two species. However, this understanding can be modified by experience in an animal as adaptable and intelligent as the domestic dog – and this is where "nurture" takes a hand.

CANINE LEARNING

Dogs are fast-learning opportunists. If they find a behavior rewarding, they are likely to repeat it; if not, they will probably not do it again.

This is the basis of learning theory, and the way in which a dog learns has many analogies to our own experience. We know, for example, that if a child tries a certain action, such as clapping his hands, and we give him a sweet for doing so, he is likely to do it again. After only a few tries, and a few more treats, the child is readily clapping his hands, showing that he has learned the behavior. Equally, a child that is punished for clapping his hands, or ignored for doing so, is unlikely to continue the behavior, and will stop repeating it.

It is important to remember that what appears to be a punishment to us, might in fact be a reward to a dog or a child. At times, any attention is better than none, and being told off or physically punished can sometimes encourage a behavior. This may explain why children are badly behaved in the supermarket and why dogs are rowdy when visitors arrive.

HOW INTELLIGENT ARE DOGS?

Domestic dogs sometimes appear more intelligent than other animals, such as cats, as they work out how to get what they want and repeat previously rewarded behavior. However, intelligence is difficult to quantify and it may be that dogs are simply very good at communicating with us in a way that we understand.

Other animals, like cats, pigs and even chickens, can be trained in the same way as dogs, but they require different motivation and a different system of communication. Cats are, for instance, more socially independent, and do not appear to have the same need for our approval as dogs.

Humans have externalized their wisdom — stored it in museums, libraries, the expertise of the learned. Dog wisdom is inside the blood and bones.

DONALD MCCAIG,

EMINENT DOGS, DANGEROUS MEN, *1997*

Below: Dogs learn through play to discover each other's abilities and weaknesses. This helps them to determine social status.

Socialization

What to expect at each stage ✦
What you can do to help

Socialization is a process through which a social creature learns how to cope and interact in the outside world. All parents know that children need to mix with others to learn about the world around them. Well-socialized children usually become well-adjusted adults, and puppies are much the same. Young dogs need to learn about their environment, about people, children and other dogs, so that they are not fearful of them in later life and know how to react to them socially.

Left: Puppies are keen to learn about their environment, and need their breeder's encouragement to do so.

EARLY STAGES
Neonatal period: birth to 2 weeks

Newborn puppies may appear to come into the world as tiny blank slates, awaiting key information about how to act and react to other dogs and the world outside their mother's womb. However, despite their total reliance on their mother for food, warmth and physical protection, the puppies' helpless appearance is deceptive.

Action: Despite their lack of sight or hearing, puppies of this age need to be handled by humans. They live in a world of scent and touch and can already begin to identify with the smell and feeling of human hands.

TRANSITIONAL PERIOD
2 to 4 weeks

This period represents extremely fast changes in the puppy's development. The ears open and the puppy will begin to respond to loud noises by becoming startled. The eyesight is also developing, and the puppy will quickly begin to respond to light and movement.

Action: As puppies head into the socialization phase, their environment must become more and more challenging and complex if they are to learn as much as possible about how to deal with variability in their domestic environment.

SOCIALIZATION
4 to 12 weeks

Puppies enter the socialization period at about four weeks of age, and the next eight weeks are the most formative and critical in the process of their development. In fact, research has shown that puppies raised in isolation from humans between the ages of 4 and 12 weeks subsequently avoid all human contact, are fearful of people and may be impossible to train without specialized help. By the end of this period, a puppy's thinking patterns and span of concentration are as fully developed as those of an adult dog.

Most pups stay with their mother until the age of seven or eight weeks. During this time, weaning occurs and the puppies have their first real experience of coping with conflict and frustration. Puppies also learn about social interaction through play with their littermates, learning to moderate how hard they bite each other, and where they stand in competing with others over resources. Emerging sexual and predatory behavior can be seen at this early age.

Above: A puppy's mother will teach her young about the world that she knows, and help provide confidence.

Below: Even before a puppy is old enough to walk, it will learn about its environment, listening, watching, smelling and tasting.

Puppies of four to five weeks – of either sex – may mount each other during play and pounce on objects and shake them as if killing prey.

Action: Given that a puppy usually remains with his mother until it is well into the socialization period, the onus for handling the puppies, for accustoming them to different noises, smells and textures, sights and sounds, rests with the breeder. This means that well before you pick up your puppy, it will need to have been exposed to a wide variety of different domestic stimuli. Before it even leaves the nest, a puppy needs to have seen and been handled by a range of different people. Ideally, it will also have been exposed to the movements, noises and smells of everyday human life – all before the time you take it home (see page 48). Puppies which have not been adequately socialized need help urgently.

CONTINUING SOCIALIZATION

Socialization must continue until at least 12 weeks of age, so if you bring your puppy home before this time, you must keep it on the crucial learning curve of its development. Even puppies that have been inadequately socialized will benefit from regular, gentle introductions to the outside world – a process that will help them to become familiar with people, objects and events in the home and in the world beyond it.

Puppies need to get out and about as much as possible before 12 weeks of age, yet most of them won't complete their vaccination series until this time, and cannot freely mix with other dogs until then. This means that compromise is required. Carrying your puppy is one option; another is to take your puppy to other people's homes, and to invite as many people into your home as possible. Allowing your puppy to meet sociable, vaccinated, adult dogs is also recommended. Do as much as you can before 12 weeks, then make up for any lost opportunies as soon as your dog is able to go out. Until that time, make sure that you introduce it to a range of stimuli within your home.

Socialization

Every second of the time that they spend awake, dogs are learning. We know that it is much easier to learn a new language at the age of five than at 50, and the same learning pattern applies to dogs. Enrolling your puppy in a good puppy socialization class (see page 85) will help you learn the techniques and understanding to be able to train your dog effectively, right from the start, but it is still no substitute for as much exposure to the outside world as you can manage.

Dogs don't suddenly stop learning after the age of 12 weeks. Indeed, as hormonal effects start to take effect during adolescence, the world starts to take on a very different perspective for some. Specialists have even suggested that a "secondary" socialization phase occurs between 5 and 15 months, depending on breed and maturity. During this time, dogs that previously adored other dogs may become suspicious around their own sex and somewhat flirtatious with the opposite sex.

This leads many "teenage" dogs to be reprimanded continually in the park by other dogs that they meet. This is a normal and useful part of

Below: Once a puppy's social life commences at four weeks, it needs to be introduced to a wide range of people, animals and noises.

growing up, but it can cause some dogs to become nervous or defensive. Maintaining socialization, and concentrating on humane training, helps to get you and your dog through this adolescent stage.

INTRODUCING YOUR PUPPY TO THE WORLD

Here are some of the key stimuli to which your puppy must be introduced during the socialization period.

People

All people look different, and your puppy needs to learn that individual appearance doesn't make a person any less human. It should meet men and women in all guises – wearing glasses, hats or crash helmets, using a cane or a walker, and carrying an umbrella. Make sure your puppy is exposed to people of different ethnic backgrounds, so he is as familiar with a black man as it is with a white woman. Children are something different for a puppy, and it will need to meet children of all ages, and of both sexes, including teenagers. Carry out these introductions in as wide a range of environments as possible.

Other dogs

Unfamiliar dogs can be as threatening to a young puppy as an unknown person, and you must expose it to other dogs in a variety of different situations, such as at the park, in the street, outside shops and in your

home. Expose your puppy to large and small adult dogs of all colors and hair types, and then to other puppies of different breeds. Color and size distinguish other dogs as being "different", so your puppy should be exposed to as many different types, colors, shapes and sizes of dog as possible from the very beginning.

Other animals

While a city dog may be unlikely to come across a chicken during its daily walk, it is important that it sees other animals, whether it does so outside a local city farm or zoo, or on a country walk. You never know what the future may hold, and your puppy may well end up living on a farm, or in the country. Expose it to all types of animals, including horses, cats, ducks, chickens, cows and sheep so as to prepare it for any eventuality.

Travel

Similarly, your dog may spend little time in the car or on a bus while it is a puppy, but its situation may change, and it should be accustomed to all modes of transport, both public and private. Ensure that your dog has trips in a car (strapped in or housed safely, see page 100) early on. Take your dog on a bus, on a train and on a boat, if possible, while it is young.

Environmental experiences

We become accustomed to the things that other people do in public, and to

the amazing variety of things that we see on a daily basis. To your puppy, everything is new, and it will need to be exposed gently to the new stimuli and situations. Take it to the shops, and let it see strollers, baby carriages and shopping carts.

Your puppy will also need to see and hear a tractor and a large truck in action. Open spaces such as the park or a local field as well as busy pedestrian areas and shops are also important experiences. It should

> *You may catch the glance of a dog sometimes which seems to lay a kind of claim to sympathy and brotherhood.*
> RALPH WALDO EMERSON, ESSAYS, 1847

become familiar with other people's homes and backyards, and learn that the rules in your household will apply elsewhere. Similarly, it should learn to cope with, and how to behave in, a busy environment, such as outside a shop, or crossing a busy street.

Inside the home
The stimuli inside the puppy's own home is equally important, and it will need to become familiar with all different types of noises and movements.

Let your puppy see and hear a washing machine and a tumble dryer, the vacuum cleaner, a telephone and the lawn mower. If you are a cook, the food processor or juicer will need to be included in your list of items to

Above: Supervised meetings with other dogs in the park will teach your puppy social skills and help it to make friends.

which your puppy must be exposed from an early stage. Look around your house and try to imagine what it would be like to be a small puppy with no experience of the world.

Domestic situations
People laugh, cry, argue and can occasionally have too much to drink. Make sure your puppy comes into contact with people in all of these situations, while it is still young. Similarly, a puppy needs to become accustomed to the daily traffic of a normal household: people coming and going, ringing the doorbell, running back for a forgotten item, and even slamming the door.

Left: Introduce your puppy to children on their own, and then to other pets. Teach your children to be gentle with your puppy, and it will become confident with them.

Intelligence & Communication

Social behavior ✦ Learning ✦
Body language ✦
Vocal communication ✦
Teaching rewards

*I*n the wild, familiar dogs would relate to one another as members of a social pack. The hierarchy determined each dog's individual place and role within that pack, and pack members would rarely be faced with a canine that they did not already know. Indeed, meeting a member of another pack would be likely to cause suspicion, with a great deal of body posturing and attack behavior if the pack members felt threatened by the intruder.

CANINE COMMUNICATION

We expect our domestic dogs to react quite differently to one another. Dogs of both sexes, of all ages and sizes, from many different "families", are expected to meet and mix freely every day on streets and in parks – without confrontation or conflict.

This is only possible for two main reasons. The first is that during their development from the wolf domestic dogs probably underwent a process of natural selection that left them in a state of neotony, or permanent reliance on juvenile behavior. A dog

Right: When dogs first meet at close range, they sniff each other. This is one of the social rules dogs follow in order to avoid conflict.

Above: Dogs have a rich communication system based on body language and a refined ability to read the visual signals of others.

never gains the full behavioral repertoire of an adult wolf, but remains pliable, and even rather playful, in his attitude to other dogs.

The second reason why we manage to mix dogs from so many different groups together without conflict is that we socialize them early on. We teach puppies that even though another dog may not look or smell like his or her litter mates, they are still friendly and pleasant to be with.

However, vestiges of wolf behavior are still to be found in the activities of dogs when we take them for a walk to the local park. Dogs may mix and meet, but they usually do so by following a recognizable set of social rules. These rules emphasize the fact that dogs are willing to introduce themselves and to attempt to establish a social relationship with other dogs, albeit a transient one.

Dogs also announce their existence and intentions in a number of other ways, not all of them face to face. Leg cocking, urine marking and the careful location of feces are good examples of this (see page 30).

SCENT SIGNALS

Dogs use their scent to mark what they consider to be their territory or area of usage. They probably "read" urine marks left by other dogs a little like we read the morning paper. The scent marks may contain information about the marker's sex, health, social status and even hormonal state.

Below: One of the ways in which dogs communicate with one another is through scent signals left in urine, which define their territory.

Dogs can also smell fear in other animals. It is thought that fearful dogs release chemical substances known as pheromones, which act as a warning to other animals that danger is present. This may explain why so many animals are frightened of visits to the vet, when in reality they may never had a traumatic experience there themselves. Such sensitivity to scent signals probably allows dogs to know exactly which dogs are, or have recently been, in the park and whether they are familiar or not.

VISUAL SIGNALS

Visual signals take over from scent signals as soon as dogs are within visual range. When they are off lead and free to behave naturally, most domestic dogs that are strangers will take some time to sum one another up. Initially, they may stand still, then approach the other slowly and cautiously, often using an indirect, circling approach rather than straight on, which could be regarded as threatening. Once in close range, most dogs attempt to sniff each other, starting with the head and face, before moving on to the genital area, where the scent glands are most productive.

BODY LANGUAGE

Sometimes dogs use body postures to indicate dominance and submission when they meet other dogs. One dog may attempt to place his paw or paws on the other dog's back, or may try to mount the other dog. More rarely, a dog attempting to exert dominance over another dog may put his head over the other dog's back or neck.

In most cases, dogs sort out their differences easily and the interaction ends either in play or in a peaceful parting. Indeed, most dog fights occur when owners try to get involved and disrupt the complex pattern of communication that the dogs quite clearly understand.

After this, one or both dogs may walk past, then lift a leg, or simply keep moving, and the interaction is over. Other dogs may attempt to initiate play, perhaps by pawing in the air, by using an obvious body posture such as the "play bow", where they drop down on to their front legs, or by barking. Although play fighting may look rough, it is also usually conducted by dogs abiding by clearly understood social rules, with no hard biting and little overt dominance.

Intelligence & communication

Like that of most mammals, the dog's brain has evolved to be capable of thought, learning and memory. The cerebrum controls learning, emotions and behavior, while the cerebellum controls the muscles. The brain stem is connected to the peripheral nervous system, which runs throughout the body. Chemical messengers known as neurotransmitters carry information within the brain, and these are regulated and affected by many other factors in the body, including hormones, and even diet.

LEARNING AND MEMORY

Dogs' brains function in a way that allows them to learn either through basic association, called "classical conditioning", or by learning which actions produce which results; this is known as "instrumental" or "operant" conditioning.

The work of Russian physiologist Ivan Pavlov (1839–1936) is probably best known for demonstrating the potential of the dog's conditioned reflexes. His discovery of conditioning was accidental. For his research on

digestion, Pavlov needed to collect saliva from his laboratory dogs. He stimulated saliva flow by placing meat powder in the dog's mouth; soon he noticed that the dog would begin salivating at the sight of the researcher, in the expectation of receiving meat powder. Pavlov tried to

Above: When approaching other dogs for the first time, dogs may circle one another tentatively in a non-threatening manner.

pair other stimuli (such as the sound of a bell) with the meat, and found that the dog soon began salivate to the other stimuli itself. Any owner of a domestic dog will know that such associations are formed all the time, particularly in the kitchen.

Perhaps more importantly, the work of American behavioral psychologist B. F. Skinner (1904–90) proved beyond doubt that dogs could learn to alter and adapt their own behavior, depending on past experience and the consequences of their actions. This discovery has allowed training to become increasingly sophisticated, based on the understanding that dogs can make decisions, have a memory for events and recognition, and can communicate their intentions, albeit in a non-verbal manner.

Left: This Golden Retriever is attempting to make itself appear large, confident and therefore dominant, yet it avoids direct eye contact with the younger dog.

Dogs that are fearful, anxious or attempting to show submission keep their bodies low to the ground. The ears are likely to be flat to the head and the mouth may be drawn back into a submissive "grin". The eyes may become narrow slits and the tail is usually kept low, or even tucked between the legs. Dogs showing total submission may roll on to their sides or backs, and may leak a small amount of urine in an attempt to appease another dog.

BODY LANGUAGE

The body language of dogs and wolves is extraordinarily similar. However, facial features, length of coat, body size and body structure have all been modified in the domestic dog, so that recognition of their complex body language is more difficult.

Generally, a dog that is relaxed and calm will show this clearly with a relaxed body position and neutral facial expression. The ears will be held in a normal position for its breed, the tail will hang low, and the body will be neither crouched nor elevated. The dog's eyes may be slightly closed and the muscles of the muzzle and neck relaxed.

A dog that is confident and attempting to exert some authority, or show its dominance over another, will look quite different. This dog will try to appear as large and powerful as possible, with ears up and alert, neck and head raised and its whole body slightly arched, ready for action.

IMPORTANCE OF THE TAIL

The dog's tail is an important guide to his mood and his intentions. A raised tail normally means that the dog is confident, excited or even dominant, although there are some breeds that have permanently raised tails.

On the whole, a wagging tail means that the dog is either pleased or excited. However, a tail that is upright and stiff, wagging with small, high-frequency movements, may indicate a dog showing dominance. A tail that is held low and wagged in slow, rhythmic swings may indicate that the dog is more uncertain. Indeed, owners of aggressive dogs often note that the dog was wagging his tail as he bit them.

Tails say so much about a dog's emotions that docking the tail removes a major part of a dog's

Below: A dog's howl can communicate different messages. For example, it can convey its location to others, as well as communicating loneliness or distress.

communication system; it should be avoided unless required medically.

VOCAL COMMUNICATION

Dogs express themselves vocally through a wide a variety of sounds: infant cries, warning growls and deep barks, attention-seeking barks and howls, painful "yips", yelps and screams, and moans of pleasure.

Some dogs "sing" by howling, a throwback to their ancestor, the wolf. Each wolf has his own individual, characteristic howl. Dogs bark more than wolves and use this method of communication in a wide range of circumstances to get their point across.

WHAT IS A
DOG?
*Intelligence &
Communication*

53

Intelligence & communication

The fact that dogs are quick, intelligent learners has undoubtedly been their greatest asset in establishing themselves in our lives and hearts. Fast learning, of both simple associations and more complex behavioral consequences, means that dogs are usually easily trained and sociable, and that we can communicate with them.

Their intelligence does, however, lead many owners to assume that their pets are little people, and that they can communicate as we do. Beware of assuming that your dog understands every word that you say. Dogs are intelligent, but they do not speak our language, and they rely on our body movements and a series of intonations and key words to understand our communication.

THE ALL-SEEING EYE

Dogs are masters of observation. They know when we are happy, sad, angry or tired just by watching our body language and facial expressions. They soon learn what brings them rewards and what does not. The sound of the key in the door or the sight of a certain pair of walking shoes can make

them ecstatic with pleasure, while the sight of a briefcase or suitcase can send them into decline.

This skill allows us to train dogs to behave in a way that we want. In time, dogs come to make associations between the signals that we give and their own actions. Nonetheless, this is a foreign language to a dog, and requires patience, practice and good motivation on both our parts.

ESSENTIAL STEPS TO GOOD COMMUNICATION

✦ Be patient! Remember that it takes us years to become fluent in

Above: Show your dog what you want it to do, and reinforce it with reward signals and praise. Never expect it to understand only spoken instructions.

a language; dogs need time and practice to learn the consequences of our words.

✦ Provide your dog with sufficient motivation. Dogs need to be motivated to work, just as we do.

✦ Give your dog clear signals of reward and non-reward (see below). Dogs feel more secure with boundaries, providing that they are consistent and fair.

✦ Use your body language and facial expression to aid communication. Most dogs learn more through visual signals than auditory ones.

Dogs sometimes need a reminder of what is an appropriate behavior and what is not, but this can be achieved through thought and understanding. Ask yourself why your dog is behaving in an appropriate way, and try to repeat the reward process. If he behaves inappropriately, do not reward him. He will learn that certain actions reap rewards and will therefore repeat them. For most dogs,

Left: Dogs learn through observation, and their behavior will be based on repeating acts that gained them rewards. Offer plenty of praise and encouragement for a job well done, and your dog will repeat it in future.

Above: While dogs can usually learn to respond to simple commands, they are more likely to understand what you want if you back up your requests with appropriate body language and facial expressions.

being ignored or isolated from social contact is the most effective way of eliminating unwanted behavior.

Dogs work hard for attention, even negative attention, and this means that they learn fast if their behavior is non-rewarded.

THE IMPORTANCE OF SIGNALS
Signals of reward and non-reward, often (but not always) sounds, should be introduced in training. If a reward, or the withholding of a reward, for particular behavior is accompanied by the appropriate signal, the signal itself will become a powerful sign for the dog of what is expected of him.

Teaching your dog a signal of non-reward is one of the most effective ways of interrupting inappropriate behavior, without confrontation, punishment or aggression.

NON-REWARD SIGNALS
A signal of non-reward can be a voice command such as "Ah-ah", a unique sound produced by a set of special training discs, or even a visual signal such as a flat hand with the palm down, held out to the dog. It can be taught as follows:
✦ Find a reward that your dog likes – small pieces of food are usually best.
✦ Give the dog a couple of pieces of food, then place a piece on the floor.
✦ As the dog goes to take the food, say "Ah-ah", or use your desired signal, then pick up the food quickly.
✦ Repeat this until your dog is backing off and avoiding the food when you give the signal. This usually takes four to six repetitions.
✦ Finally, repeat the whole procedure with a different reward that your dog likes, such as a favorite toy or access to the backyard, to reinforce the meaning of the non-reward signal in your dog's mind. You can now use this signal of non-reward to interrupt behavior that you do not find acceptable (see also pages 86–7).

MOTIVATION
The word "discipline" conjures up images of strict school teachers and parents. While dogs need to be shown what is appropriate behavior and what is not, physical punishment has no place whatsoever in dog training. A dog should want to work with you through trust and good motivation, not feel compelled to do so out of fear.

Sadly, dogs have been punished in many inhumane ways over the years, and it is only the dog's huge loyalty to us that has allowed us to retain his friendship. Even shouting is unacceptable for most dogs, since it can cause fear and anxiety.

When working with your dog, you must motivate him with rewards, and offer plenty of praise and encouragement. Always remember that he is a dog, and must be communicated with in ways he will understand.

If you are experiencing difficulties, or your dog is beginning to develop behavioral problems, ask your vet to refer you to a canine behavior or training specialist.

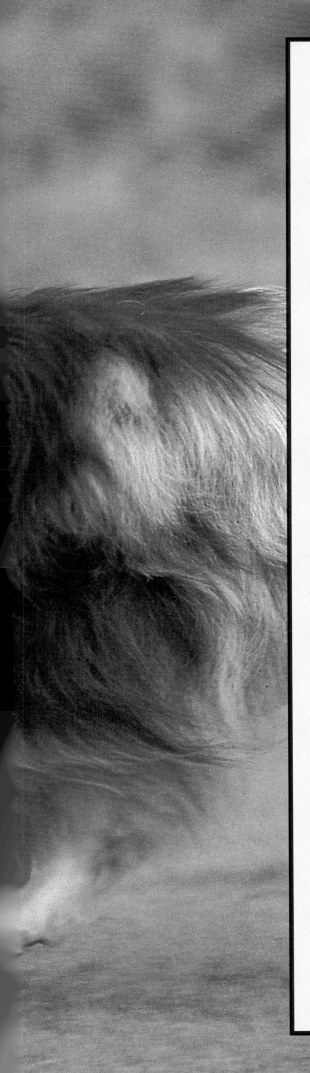

PART 2

CARING FOR DOGS

Dogs have lived with people for thousands of years, cohabiting in our homes and resting by our hearths as companions, working partners and friends. There is no doubt that this most rewarding of relationships is based on mutual understanding and trust. To achieve this, you'll need to take time to learn about your new pet and its individual temperament, personality and idiosyncrasies. Welcoming a new dog into your home creates a new set of responsibilities, including careful handling and training, choosing the right equipment, satisfying your dog's exercise needs and ensuring that he or she is emotionally and physically healthy, through proper diet, veterinary care, grooming, play, companionship and respect. With loving, responsible and consistent care, your dog will have a happy and secure future.

Why a Dog?

Protection and companionship ✦ *Health benefits* ✦
An important decision

Why a dog? For some people, the reasons for owning a dog are obvious and the prospect of living without one is almost unimaginable.

Dogs suit all kinds of people, for all kinds of reasons. For some – such as visually or hearing impaired people – a dog is a lifeline and a source of confidence, security and protection. Highly intelligent in many cases, dogs can be trained to help their owners and make their daily lives easier. They can find lost or dropped things, perform tasks that may be difficult for their owners, recognize sources of danger and take action accordingly – not crossing a road if traffic is approaching, or barking at an intruder, for example. For other people, such as farmers, dogs are a supplier of labor, without which many tasks might be considerably more difficult.

AN IDEAL COMPANION
For people with less specific needs, a pet dog can be just as important. Dogs are loyal, generous creatures. They provide company, friendship and a non-judgemental listening ear. There is nothing quite like coming home to a dog at the end of a hard day and being met enthusiastically by a friend who loves you unconditionally. Dogs are always pleased to see you, always willing to play, and are content just to be near you. Many dogs seem to pick up on the moods of their owners – quietly sitting and listening to the woes of the day, then cheerfully running and jumping when their owner feels more inclined to join in with their *joie de vivre*. For people who love them, dogs can enhance the quality of life and boost confidence with their

Above: All dog owners benefit physically and emotionally from the regular exercise necessary to keep their dogs fit and healthy.

Below: With plenty of free time on their hands, children often become constant companions to their dogs and are able to build up a special relationship with them.

unquestioning loyalty and constant companionship; they can even help to teach children how to play and communicate without shyness.

BENEFITS OF OWNING A DOG
Extensive research has been carried out into the emotional and physical benefits of keeping a pet. Stroking a dog has been proved to reduce human blood pressure and heart rate – and dog owners have been found to be generally more healthy than people who do not own one, suffering fewer minor illnesses like colds, infections and backache. Interestingly, owners of dogs also seem to be happier about life in general, reporting a lower incidence of depression. And for people who live alone, dogs provide not only company, but also a structure to the day through the routine of caring for their needs.

DECIDING TO HAVE A DOG
Having a dog can enhance the quality of your life, and becoming a dog owner should add to the pleasures of

day-to-day life, not to the stresses. But if you are already suffering from the usual torments of modern life – too much work, too little money, too few hours to yourself – then a dog may not be the pet for you. All of the benefits of owning a dog need to be weighed against the reality of the responsibilities: if you are in any doubt about owning a dog, stop and think again. A dog is a commitment.

You are responsible for your dog's health and happiness, and if you either can't spare the time, or do not have enough space in your home or access to open ground, you may be making the wrong decision. Perhaps another pet would be a better choice? Otherwise, there is a variety of ways to enjoy canine company without actually owning a dog. Animal shelters often need volunteers to walk dogs, socialize puppies or assist in training. Charities also appreciate fundraising and event organization by people who love dogs but cannot keep one of their own. Alternatively, it may be possible to get involved with a local training class or group. Learning as much as you can about this wonderful species will stand you in good stead when the time is right for you to have a dog of your own.

Left: No dog will benefit from being shut away when you are too busy to see to its needs.

Far left: All dogs need plenty of outdoor play and exercise. If you are unable to make time for these essential activities, a dog may not be the ideal pet for you.

DOG DAYS

In the Northern Hemisphere, the hottest days of the summer, extending from about 3 July to 11 August, are known as dog days. The term originated in the Mediterranean region, where from ancient times the weather during this period was regarded as unhealthy and uncomfortable. It was a time of year when dogs were thought to have spells of madness, and when Sirius, the "Dog Star" in the constellation Canis Major, rose with the Sun and supposedly added to its heat.

What's Involved?

Commitment ✦ Choices ✦ Factors to consider ✦ Training

The decision to become a dog owner is such an important one that it is worth taking the time to weigh up the advantages and disadvantages in a little more depth.

First of all, remind yourself that your new family member will be a huge commitment. It will mean spending time and money, and will involve a great deal of effort and sometimes frustration. In return, you will be rewarded with pleasure, companionship and loyalty from your dog – but this doesn't happen overnight.

There are more safeguards in buying a new car than there are in obtaining a new dog. Prospective dog owners are not tested for suitability, the puppy or dog does not arrive with an instruction manual, and there is no warranty if anything goes wrong. When buying a car, we select one that suits our needs, lifestyle and budget. We can anticipate how much it will cost to maintain, insure and repair.

These are the issues that the prospective dog owner also needs to consider: is the breed you have in mind suitable for your home, lifestyle and financial situation? Is it more susceptible to health problems than others? Some breeds or types also need huge amounts of maintenance – dogs with long coats, for example, such as the Afghan Hound or Lhasa Apso, need extensive daily coat care if they are to be kept in peak condition. Other types may simply be expensive to keep – big dogs need large amounts of food, and some breeds or types are more expensive to insure. Some dogs have a greater need for exercise.

RESPONSIBILITIES

Although dogs offer wonderful company, they need company in return. They also need the right food and good veterinary care – no matter what other claims there may be on your finances. They need grooming, exercise and mental stimulation on a daily basis, regardless of the weather or a busy schedule. These responsibilities simply cannot be ignored, even if they seem like a chore.

If you have a busy lifestyle and are unable to make alternative arrangements for your dog's care, you will have to think very carefully about whether a dog is the pet for you. Dogs need to be allowed to be dogs. Would you be able to tolerate all the things that they do? Sometimes they roll in smelly things, leave hair all over carpet and clothes, chew your shoes and dig up the yard.

Finally, and above all, you must be prepared to give your dog a great deal of your time. A dog needs to be trained to fit in with your lifestyle, which can

---

FACTORS TO CONSIDER BEFORE BECOMING A DOG OWNER

✦

If you have already decided to buy a dog, but are unsure about what kind of breed or type would suit you, ask yourself the questions below.

- ✦ How much time do you have to devote to training, walking and grooming?
- ✦ Do you travel a great deal?
- ✦ How much space do you have at home?
- ✦ Is your backyard securely fenced?
- ✦ How active are you as an individual or as a family?
- ✦ How much exercise are you able to give a dog, in terms both of time and of distance?
- ✦ How much money can you spend on buying a dog and looking after it?
- ✦ Are your children and their friends comfortable with dogs and able to cope with the responsibilities and occasional upheaval?
- ✦ Are you house-proud?
- ✦ Are you a keen gardener?
- ✦ Do you have any allergies?

Below: As attractive as it may be, a large puppy will eventually become a large dog, with all the responsibilities that this entails. Size is an important consideration when deciding on the type of dog for you. Large dogs can be both expensive to buy and to feed, and will not be suited to homes in big cities, or houses or apartments with small backyards. Smaller dogs need far less exercise, but may not take kindly to the rough and tumble of family life.

be expensive and time-consuming, and played with so that they grow to be happy, well behaved and sociable. Without this type of care, on a regular basis, they are likely to develop behavior problems. Many dog owners find these responsibilities a pleasure; others are surprised by just how much is expected of them.

PET-TRAINING CLASSES

Learning to communicate with your dog will take time and commitment, but brings much more freedom for both dog and owner. Like any new language, your communication with your dog will be stilted and strange initially, as you watch each other's body language and facial expressions, trying to understand what the other is saying. With practice, however, communication will become fluent. Dog-training classes offer owners the opportunity to get to know their dogs, but think hard about whether you will be prepared to drag yourself out of your armchair on a cold, windy night to attend them.

Below: Dog training, whether simply for the purposes of control, or obedience-style training for competition, can be very demanding.

Below: Play is a vital element in the development of a puppy (and in the training of an older dog) and requires time and commitment.

Choosing a Dog

Which breed? ✦ How old? ✦ Pedigree or mixed breed? ✦ Which sex?

Dogs come in all shapes and sizes, and you will have to consider carefully which breed is right for you. Obviously, it would be unwise to buy a giant breed of dog, such as a Great Dane or Mastiff, if you live in a small apartment. Equally, it would be nothing short of disaster if you bought a herding breed, such as a Border Collie, knowing that you have very little time to devote to training and exercise. Perhaps you have young, boisterous children who might upset a highly strung breed like a Chihuahua.

Some other considerations may not be quite so apparent, however. For example, some breeds of dog shed hair almost constantly, while others such as Poodles or Chow Chows shed very little or not at all, making them more suitable for those with allergies or intolerances to dander or hair. Some dogs, such as the Doberman, require less grooming than others, which is important if your time is at a premium. Think about the list of considerations on page 60 and look carefully through the different types of breeds described on pages 164 to 241 of this book, assessing which dog is most likely to fit in with your needs and lifestyle.

PUPPY OR ADULT?

As well as deciding which breed is most appropriate to your needs, household and lifestyle, you will have to consider whether you should get a puppy or an adult dog. Buying a puppy has the advantage that you will be able to mould its behavior through all the stages of development to suit your own lifestyle. You can ensure that his upbringing, from training to socialization, is as good as it can possibly be. However, buying a puppy also

Right: By choosing a pedigree dog, you'll know in advance its potential size and energy requirements, and have a fair idea of its temperament.

means that you really do need to start from scratch, and that takes time. House-training can be frustrating, time-consuming and involve giving your dog a great deal of attention. Socialization is equally important, and will mean interacting with your puppy and teaching him on a daily

Below: Dogs are social animals and should be treated as one of the family. You'll need to train your dog from an early age to be trusting, even-tempered and sociable with people and other dogs.

Left: Consider other pets when choosing a dog. Some breeds maintain the vestiges of a predatory instinct and are more likely to object to another pet than others. Most puppies, however, will bond well with cats and other pets if they are introduced when the dog is younger than 12 weeks old.

Below: The amount of exercise needed varies according to the dog's breed, age and state of health, but all obedient dogs should be let off their leads daily and allowed to run in a safe place. All active breeds revel in daily physical exercise.

HEREDITARY DISEASES

◆

Many breeds suffer from hereditary defects, including hip dysplasia, heart and eye problems and deafness (see pages 130–31); you need to ensure that your puppy's parents have been checked and cleared of having, or carrying, these problems. Many breed clubs now run checks to ensure that breeders test their dogs for hereditary diseases before breeding, and it is vital that you look at any certificates held and are able to interpret the results. Your vet or local Kennel Club will be able to offer advice on breed scoring.

Choosing a dog

Right: Puppies are undoubtedly appealing, but if you are considering a puppy as your first dog, you must be prepared to take the place of its mother until it has become less dependent and is able to cope on its own.

basis, from the moment it arrives in your home.

Obtaining an adult dog instead of a puppy often means that the dog comes ready house-trained. Many older dogs will have also learned how to be sensible with people, children and other animals. However, adult dogs may have behavioral idiosyncrasies or problems that need to be dealt with carefully in a new home. Retraining an older dog is perfectly possible, but may take longer than starting out with the blank slate of a young puppy.

BREED OR MUTT?
Whether you have chosen a puppy or an adult dog, the next decision to make is whether to buy a pedigree dog or a mixed breed. Again, the advantages and disadvantages of each need to be considered.

There are now literally hundreds of breeds of dog to choose from – all with differing appearances and behavioral characteristics. There is little doubt that with most pedigree dogs "what you see is what you get". This means that it is easy to predict how large a puppy of a certain breed will grow, what color it will be, and what coat length it will have. To a certain extent, you'll even be able to predict how it will behave.

Right: Whether you choose an adult dog or a puppy, you must be prepared for your new pet to exhibit typical pack behavior, which can include some types of aggression.

Right: Pedigree dogs, such as the Whippet, may be beautiful, with a shape and proportion that will be widely admired. However, many pedigree dogs are heir to unwelcome hereditary problems. It is wise to consider the special characteristics of any breed before buying.

Choosing a mixed-breed dog does not afford these advantages, although crosses between breeds are often thought of as combining all the best characteristics of those breeds. It is sometimes claimed that this makes mixed-breed dogs stronger, healthier and even more intelligent than many pedigree breeds. It is often possible to determine roughly how large a mixed breed puppy will be by looking at its likely ancestors. And its behavior can be predicted in this way, too. For example, mixed breeds that show strong Collie characteristics are quite likely to have an innate desire to herd other animals, or to chase toys.

If you are considering getting a dog of a certain breed, but have had no previous experience of owning a dog like this, it is a good idea to find out as much as possible about them and even "test drive" one first. Most caring breeders will be only too happy to allow you to interact with adults of their breed, and discuss their needs with you. Borrowing a dog from a friend for a weekend, or volunteering to walk dogs every day at a local animal shelter, may also help you to make your decision.

DOG OR BITCH?

Whether to buy a dog or a bitch is often a personal decision. Generally speaking, female dogs are easier to train and can be less demanding in a family environment than males. Males can sometimes be naturally competitive, squaring up to other males, so arranging early interactions with other dogs is very important. Females are more likely to be good natured with other dogs. Unless neutered, a bitch usually comes into season twice a year, during which time it is important that you keep her away from other dogs to prevent unwanted pregnancies. However, both sexes will require the same amount of veterinary treatment, socialization, exercise, training and general care.

Right: Some people consider male dogs to have a more even temperament than bitches, but their competitive behavior might be problematic, especially in a family situation.

Making the Right Choice

A new puppy ✦ *What to look for* ✦ *Which puppy to choose*

If you have decided to buy a puppy, finding the right breeder and choosing the right dog out of the litter is very important. Always buy a puppy from a responsible outlet. Do not be tempted to buy a puppy from an advertisement in a newspaper, particularly where more than one breed is included for sale, or from a pet shop. Sadly, puppies bought from these sources may have had terrible experiences or be harboring infections, and they quite often make completely unsuitable pets.

Although the Kennel Club keeps lists of breeders with puppies, a Kennel Club registration is no guarantee of either the quality or health of the puppy being sold.

WHAT SHOULD YOU LOOK FOR?

Always insist on seeing the mother, and, even better, both parents, when choosing a puppy. The temperament and behavior of the mother have an enormous influence on her puppies. A bitch of good temperament should be happy to see visitors and children, and will be confident enough in her environment and owners to allow you to handle, play with and pick up her puppies. Any mother that backs away, growls, snarls or appears in any way nervous, aggressive or subdued may have passed these traits on to her puppies. Do not take the risk – these puppies could already present a potential behavioral problem.

Of course, the father is responsible for 50 per cent of a puppy's genes and characteristics, but very often a breeder may take a bitch to be mated to a stud dog that lives some distance away, and the dog will not be available for viewing. Never buy a puppy spontaneously, and never be tempted to buy from anyone who offers to

deliver the puppy to you. These puppies can come from many different sources, often unlicensed breeders keeping too many bitches in unsuitable conditions. The dog you choose could be with you – for better or worse – for well over the next decade. That's a long time to repent at leisure.

Do not be tempted to take two puppies at the same time, even if your heart is breaking at the thought of leaving one puppy behind on its own.

Top: Recognized breeders are the best source for purebred puppies, and you will be able to see the puppy, with his mother, in its rearing environment.

Above: Whenever possible, arrange to see the puppy with its mother, as this will tell you a great deal about its temperament.

Two or more puppies of the same age, particularly litter mates, are a recipe for disaster. If you have already decided that you would like two dogs, be patient and wait until you have formed a relationship, socialized and trained one dog through to adolescence, before you get another. Two puppies together are rarely double the pleasure – only double trouble.

Finally, never be tempted to buy a puppy that has not been exposed to a domestic environment. Puppies need to have experienced the fundamentals of everyday human life, and to have been in contact with people, children and a range of domestic stimuli, such as the vacuum cleaner, the TV and the general hubbub of family life. They should also have seen something of life outdoors – depending on their age – including busy streets, cars and other animals. Good breeders ensure that their puppies have contact with all of these things. If you buy a puppy from the home of someone other than the original owner, you'll have no idea of what contact he has had with the outside world.

WHICH ONE FOR YOU?

The best puppy to choose is usually the most average of the litter. Many people report that their puppy chose them, by running up, pushing all the other puppies out of the way, and demanding their attention. This may well be the puppy to choose if you are an experienced owner, or if you want to work with him when he is older, but in the wrong hands this pup may rule the roost within a few months.

Equally unsuitable is the puppy that does not approach you, sitting at the back of the litter, or hiding behind its mother or litter-mates. The puppy that is happy to see you, content to be picked up and played with, is not scared by a sudden sound such as a hand-clap, and plays well with its litter-mates, is likely to become the most well-balanced, all-round pet dog.

CHOOSING A DOG

◆

PUPPIES

Choosing a healthy puppy is not difficult – unless you allow your heart to rule your head. Too many puppies are bought out of pity, and not because they will make a suitable family pet. Make sure you check any puppy thoroughly before buying.

◆ It should have bright eyes, with no discharge or cloudiness.

◆ The ears should be clean – look right down inside the ear flap and check that there is no brown wax or smelly discharge.

◆ Any odor from the ears may indicate the presence of an infection or mites.

◆ A puppy's coat should look clean and shiny. Running your hand against the grain of the coat allows you to look at the condition of the skin.

◆ The coat should be free from any signs of parasites, such as fleas and lice, and any scaliness or dandruff.

◆ Overall, the puppy should look well fed, firm and rounded, but with no stomach distension

◆ Breathing should be quiet and with no hint of a cough.

◆ Any breeder who tries to tell you a puppy is just getting over a bout of diarrhea, a cold or any other "minor" ailment needs to be treated with suspicion.

◆ Have the puppy checked by a vet before you buy.

ADULT DOGS

If you are buying an adult dog, check its medical history if possible.

◆ Has the dog been neutered?

◆ Is the dog up to date with vaccinations and has it had proper veterinary care?

◆ Is there any history of digestive disorders or other complaints?

◆ Take the dog out of the home or kennel and walk it in an area that closely resembles the park or the street. This may enable you to determine what the dog's behavior would be in similar circumstances.

◆ Handle the dog gently around the head, neck and mouth areas. Use a food treat to make the experience pleasant.

◆ Many animal shelters will insist on a home check for all prospective owners before re-homing a dog. Most also offer after-care, so that any queries you have can be answered.

Supplying the Basics

Feeding ◆ Bedding ◆ Collars and leads ◆ Playtime ◆ Grooming

Any new dog will need a certain number of items to make him feel at home. These need not be expensive – until you know whether your new pet is a compulsive chewer, there is little point in spending money on a new doggie comforter.

FEEDING YOUR DOG

All dogs need feeding dishes and a water bowl of their own. These should be washed and kept separately from your plates. Bowls can be plastic, ceramic or made of stainless steel. Breeds that have particularly long ears, such as Cocker Spaniels, may need a specially designed deep dish so that they keep clean while eating. Giant breeds may also benefit from having their dinner fed to them in a special raised bowl – to help prevent gastric problems and air-gulping.

Like people, different dogs have different nutritional requirements and different reactions to various ingredients or elements in their diet. Dog food is usually available as either moist food (in a can), semi-moist (packed in sealed bags), or dry food (available in various size pieces in a sack lined with plastic). Price and con-

Below: Your dog's bed will make an important contribution to its sense of security. Every dog needs a bed, even if it is not elaborate.

venience will influence most people's choice, but it is essential to make sure that you understand the feeding instructions that come with each type of food. Dog food is divided into two categories: complementary and complete. Most canned foods are described as complementary – this means that they require an additional biscuit or mixture to add bulk to the diet and balance their components. Many of the dried foods, on the other hand, are complete. This means that additional food is not required. In fact, adding anything to it may cause the nutritional balance of the food to be altered (see pages 110–11).

A COMFORTABLE BED

Every dog needs a bed to call his own. Some owners now prefer to use a crate (or indoor kennel), which is basically a cage, made comfortable and secure inside. Many dogs love these once they get used to them. They become a sanctuary, providing the dog with total security and comfort, as well as a den in which to get away from the kids, or other dogs or pets in the household. Indoor kennels also serve as a portable "home away from home", which is useful for travelling and for transporting the dog safely in the car. Only humans regard them as cages because of the way they look.

A SUITABLE COLLAR OR LEAD

A collar and lead are essential pieces of equipment. Choose a comfortable, lightweight, leather or nylon collar and lead. Though once regarded as standard training equipment, choke or check chains are now considered outdated and even harmful. For dogs that really pull on the lead, other safer and more humane options are now available. Look for a head-collar or harness. An extending, or

Below: Your dog should become used to wearing a collar from as young as eight weeks. When it is old enough, leave the collar on, together with its identification tag.

retractable, lead may also be useful, particularly in the early days of your relationship with your dog, when you want to be able to give it some freedom outside in safe areas, without letting it run free.

You will also need to be able to restrain your dog while it is in the car. Use your dog's traveling crate or "indoor kennel"; as an alternative, dog "car safety harnesses", which are both comfortable and effective, are now available .

PLAYING

Dogs of every shape, size and age need to play (see pages 120–1). Play offers a dog mental stimulation, and a chance to bond more closely with his owner. Toys can be a useful training tool, or can simply keep your dog occupied when you are not available. Ideal toys are those that provide some interactivity – in other words, they maintain the dog's interest without having to have a human on the other end. Hollow, sterilized bones and rubber toys are ideal – especially if you stuff them full of interesting food morsels. Beware of small balls, which may become lodged in a dog's throat and cause suffocation.

Throwing sticks for a dog is also highly dangerous: vets have to treat too many cases of puncture wounds from sticks to dogs' mouths or throats. Balls on ropes, tug toys and rings make safe, fun alternatives.

GROOMING YOUR DOG

You will need some basic grooming equipment (see page 118). The exact design will depend on your dog's coat and condition, but nailclippers, a brush, comb and a good pet shampoo are usually sufficient. A soft toothbrush and dog toothpaste will also be required for dogs of all ages. On-going dental care prevents the building up of tartar and tooth decay in later life.

Right: Most dogs enjoy grooming sessions, and they can help develop mutual trust and the sense of companionship between you and your dog. They will also help you to keep tabs on your dog's health.

Left: Balls should be large enough to ensure that your dog does not choke on them.

Below: An indoor kennel or traveling box can act as an ideal "home away from home", which can be useful if you plan tc travel with your dog. Many small dogs enjoy sleeping in a travelling box, which provides safety and security.

Early Days

Getting to know your dog ◆ *Patience and understanding* ◆
Body language ◆ *Establishing house rules*

Even if you have been a dog owner before, getting a new dog really is like starting out on an adventure. All dogs are different, and even members of the same breed can have personalities, characteristics and behavior that differ widely. It usually takes several weeks or months before a human and a dog can sum up each other's characteristics and begin to predict how the other will behave. However, many problems and misunderstandings can be avoided if you plan the development of your relationship with your dog.

Of course, unexpected challenges and surprises are bound to occur on both sides during the first weeks, but thinking ahead can save tears and trauma later on.

WELCOMING A NEW DOG

If your new dog is a puppy, the chances are that it will have come straight from being with its mother and litter-mates to a house where it is effectively alone. Everything about the new environment will be strange and different. Even if you already have an older dog, it will smell strange and behave differently from the dogs that your pup has known before. If your new dog is an adult, and is accustomed to living in a domestic environment, the surroundings may seem more familiar to it – but you, its owner, certainly are not.

At this stage, both for puppies and for older dogs, calmness and consistency are of utmost importance. It may be tempting to move quickly, shout or even run if you catch the newcomer doing something you find unacceptable, but stop, wait and think. It is going to take time for your

Right: Don't be surprised if your puppy adopts a secluded spot of its own in which to settle down. All dogs need a quiet, draught-free place to sleep in.

dog to get to know you, and to understand the rules of your household – even to learn the different tones of your voice. Patience is essential if you are going to avoid frightening a new puppy or dog in your home – and avoiding anything that may make it fearful or uncomfortable should be the number-one priority.

THE BODY LANGUAGE OF DOGS

Dogs cannot tell you that they are feeling insecure, helpless and alone. They cannot send you a letter saying that they don't like some of the new smells, sights and sounds that they

are experiencing. Dogs can only demonstrate their emotions and fears through body language, sounds and facial expression.

A puppy that is frightened by suddenly meeting a larger dog may

Below: Smell is part of any greeting between dogs, and dogs will assess each other by circling and sniffing.

show submissive body posturing – creeping as close to the floor as possible, with its ears back and its tail tucked between its legs. It may also urinate or even defecate in fear. Not the best introduction to your new housemate! Equally, an older dog may react badly to being cornered in a strange environment – grabbing an adult dog to put it outside or prevent it from doing something may seem logical to us, but to the dog it may signal punishment. In this situation it may choose to use paws or jaws to defend itself.

Right: Approach your new puppy slowly and speak in a gentle, reassuring voice, taking care not to startle it.

HOUSE RULES

Although it is vital not to scare or intimidate your new dog, some basic house rules, established at the start of the relationship, mean that you can maintain consistency and give the dog security. Dogs, like children, need to know where the boundaries are. Some dogs do push their owners to find out if they can budge the boundaries that have been set, while others happily accept our rules with no challenge at all. Whatever rules or boundaries you establish, remember that the philosophy of those first weeks with a new dog needs to be: start as you mean to go on.

It is much easier to set house rules that will prevent problems arising than it is to try to correct problems at a later date. Writing down the rules may seem excessive, but if you have a busy household, with a number of people all interacting with the dog, this is sometimes the only way to ensure that everyone is treating the dog in the same way. If a dog is disciplined and rewarded inconsistently, it will never learn what is acceptable and what is not. A cuddle on the couch with one member of the family brings smiles and attention, while the same activity sets another family member into a tearing frenzy: no dog will ever understand that different rules apply for different members of the family.

Right: Your dog will respond to play with energy and enthusiasm. Help it to learn acceptable behavior during playtime.

HOUSE RULES FOR THE FAMILY

◆

✦ Turn away and ignore the dog when it jumps up; reward it when it greets you without jumping.

✦ Don't feed the dog from the table; it only encourages it to beg.

✦ Put things away. Puppies find dirty laundry, children's toys and papers irresistible.

✦ Play with the dog with appropriate toys, not with shoes or slippers.

✦ Train the dog – little and often – every day of the week.

✦ Make the dog sit before feeding, being groomed or cuddled and before going out of the house or car.

✦ Everyone in the family must help with training, feeding, grooming and exercise – and discipline.

✦ Make the dog sit on the floor; only humans sit on furniture.

✦ Decide where the puppy is going to sleep and stick to it.

✦ Distract or stop the dog if it begins mouthing or chewing things.

Understanding Your Dog

Inherited characteristics ✦ Experiences and influences ✦ Personality traits

*A*dog's personality is formed and influenced by many different factors. The nature versus nurture debate will always be a controversial one, but it is fair to assume that your dog's character will be formed partly through the characteristics it has inherited from its mother and father, and partly through the experiences it has had or will have during the early, formative weeks of its life.

Inherited characteristics are highly influential. Puppies born to a mother who is nervous, aggressive or fearful are much more likely to show these behavioral characteristics than a dog whose mother is calm, confident and friendly. However, this may not be related to bloodlines or genetics – the first few weeks that puppies spend with their mothers are a critical learning time and they are very likely to copy her behavior and responses and then employ them later on.

INFLUENCES ON BEHAVIOR

The kinds of experiences that a puppy has during the first few weeks of life will also mould its behavior during adulthood. Of course, a negative experience may mean that a puppy develops fears of a particular object or person in a given environment, but studies show that even a few negative experiences are better than an entirely sheltered early life. This may be due to an effect known as "stress immunization": the more experiences a puppy has – even if they are not all pleasant – the greater its abiliy to cope with what later life has to offer. This does not mean that puppies should not be protected from bad experiences (this is

Left: Dogs are very good at detecting subtle signals from humans, and you can expect your dog to relax and enjoy your company when you are in the mood for a quiet moment together.

Below: Like people, dogs use their voices to express themselves, and can produce a wide range of sounds to get the message across.

essential, of course) but it does mean that the effects of bad experiences and even the effects of inherited characteristics may be minimized by lots of early exposure to the outside world.

PERSONALITY

Puppies are born with a set of characteristics that make them more likely to be confident, shy, pushy or quiet. Your dog's personality will determine how easy it will be to train, socialize and live with. As a general rule, confident puppies and dogs rarely need to behave aggressively in conflicts, so building the confidence of your dog is crucial. Some dogs can be pushy in a home environment and will try to take liberties. In this way, dogs are like people – some are born leaders, others prefer to follow, but all need good social skills if they are to survive modern-day life.

Dogs often seem to reflect the behavior and characteristics of the people they live with. Certainly, raising a puppy in a household of boisterous children is more likely to result in a noisy, energetic dog, used to competing for attention. Equally, a dog living with a quiet, elderly couple is more likely to reflect their way of life. We should not underestimate the effect that we, the dog owners, have upon our dogs. There is, perhaps, an art in balancing the two – at times, we want our dogs to be energetic and fun, while appreciating that calm behavior is sometimes required. It is no accident that people who have had a problem dog in the past often find that they have another with the same problem at some point in the future. All dogs are different, but the extent to which we influence them with our attitudes, beliefs and behavior should never be underestimated.

Left: Your dog will express itself with a variety of different body signals. The play bow is usually a request to play.

Your Dog's Needs

Basic requirements and needs ◆
Intelligence ◆ *Emotions*

Above: Strong retrieving instincts mean that most dogs enjoy playing ball. Such games provide both exercise and stimulation.

Below: All dogs love to play. Toys that are safe for your pet vary according to the size of the breed: an active Collie, for example, will enjoy a game of frisbee, and will often prove adept at catching the toy.

*T*o most of us, it is obvious that dogs have certain basic requirements: food, water, a place to rest, exercise and veterinary care. However, we want our dogs to do more than simply exist: we want them to live contented, happy lives – while enriching our own. To ensure this, we need to do a lot more than simply satisfy a dog's physical needs – his emotional and social needs should also be met. All dogs need affection, social interaction and mental stimulation, and they deserve understanding and empathy, too.

Understanding your dog depends to some extent on its breed or type. For example, a dog that for centuries has been bred to herd sheep or cattle will almost certainly try to herd other things too – joggers or cyclists, for example – if given the chance. Much of your dog's behavior can be traced to his genes and to inherited behavioral characteristics. The behavior typical of any breed can, of course, be modified in individual dogs, but such modification is mainly made by channelling the characteristic behavior into appropriate outlets, rather than by attempting to suppress it outright.

Above: Puppies in particular require affection and attention, and protracted loneliness can lead to behavioral problems.

As the eminent British behavioral psychologist John Rogerson once noted: "Genetics load the gun, but it is the environment that fires it."

SIGNS OF INTELLIGENCE

As a species, dogs cannot comprehend the concepts of right and wrong. They may learn to adapt their behavior to our responses, but they do not share our values or judgements.

Right: Dogs are essentially pack animals, and their close rivalry can lead to fights.

They do not recognize that walking all over the carpet with muddy feet is "wrong", or that taking the Sunday bagel off the kitchen counter and eating it is "forbidden". Unfortunately, dogs often look as though they understand our values by appearing "guilty" when their owner comes in or reprimands them. Many owners will say, "He knows he's done something wrong", because the reaction from the dog appears to be an admission of guilt – a recognizable human emotion. Instead, what the owner is usually seeing is a display of submission – the dog is trying to deflect his owner's anger by using submissive body postures. After all, from the dog's point of view, keeping your ears back, tail down, body low to the ground and slinking away to bed seem like sensible social signals when your owner is showing irrational and unexplained aggression.

EMOTIONAL SIGNALS

Dogs are emotional. They can be roused to aggression or anger, and certainly experience stress and frustration. However, although these states appear similar to those experienced by human beings, we have no means of telling whether dogs really feel the same way as we do. Canine language, although rich and varied, is very different from our own; fundamental communication problems between humans and dogs lead some owners to brand their dogs as "stupid" because they cannot teach the dogs to understand even basic words. We have the ability to learn new languages,

Extraordinary creature!
So close a friend, and yet so remote.
THOMAS MANN, "A MAN AND HIS DOG",
STORIES OF THREE DECADES, *1919*

master new ideas and develop new skills, but dogs have very different abilities; it is pointless to measure their intelligence directly against ours. Ask yourself this: which dog is more intelligent – the dog that hears its master's call in the park and comes rushing back to be put on the lead and taken home, or the dog that hears its master's call, but carries on sniffing and running, enjoying itself, while its master leaps up and down, trying to get its attention? Perhaps, like beauty, intelligence is relative, and emotional sensitivity is just as

DOG DEPENDENCY

✦ A newborn puppy is totally dependent on its mother for food, warmth and protection. It cannot even eliminate waste without help.

✦ Your dog is now dependent on you for its basic needs: food, water, shelter and veterinary care.

✦ Your dog cannot tell you when it feels ill. Learn to notice any changes in behavior or appearance.

✦ Dogs are emotionally dependent on social interaction. They need contact, play and company from you.

✦ Your puppy's future behavior is in your hands. Socialize it properly to prevent behavior problems.

✦ Training will teach your dog how to behave in different situations – you are entirely responsible for this.

✦ Some dogs become too dependent on their owners – meaning that they cannot cope when left at home alone. This is not "spite" or being "naughty", but real distress.

✦ If you have two dogs, make sure they spend time apart. Dogs can become over-dependent on each other as well as on you.

Basic Practicalities

Preparing your home ✦ *Backyard safety* ✦ *First needs* ✦ *Bringing your dog home*

Becoming a dog owner marks the beginning of a relationship that may last for the next 10 to 15 years. It's important to remember that your new friend is a living, breathing being, requiring love and respect, and will need to be treated with care. Also important, however, are practical considerations.

Before bringing your pet home, take some time to prepare, so that its introduction to your home and family go without a hitch.

MAKING YOUR HOME SAFE

Take a look at the interior of your home from a puppy's view. Bear in mind that your dog will have no sense of personal safety in a domestic environment. Ornaments and plants may be beautiful and decorative to us, but to your new puppy or dog they could hold a deadly fascination.

Every year, vets remove thousands of unlikely objects from the stomachs of enthusiastic puppies. Objects as seemingly harmless as elastic bands,

Above: Your new dog is likely to feel disoriented and probably frightened when it is first brought into your home. Take some time to offer reassurance and security.

paperclips, pens, childrens' toys and hair elastics are easily picked up, played with and then swallowed.

Imagining that you are having a small toddler to stay will probably help you to decide which objects are potentially dangerous, and from which range. You may even want to consider putting locks on cabinets that your dog may be able to reach. Household products, such as bleach, rat poison and detergents can be lethal to dogs if consumed, and human medicines may also pose a considerable threat.

Other household items can spell disaster for your dog. Many house plants, for example, are poisonous, and even some cut flowers can cause problems if eaten. Chocolate is also responsible for causing serious illness – dogs have been known to die after eating small amounts of human chocolate, since their bodies simply cannot tolerate some of the chemical ingredients. For more advice on household safety, see page 78.

SAFETY IN THE BACKYARD

Having inspected your home thoroughly and locked away any potential hazards, take a walk around the backyard. First of all, this needs to be absolutely escape-proof. Puppies can squeeze through surprisingly small holes or weaknesses in perimeter fences and may become traffic casualties, or lose their way and never be seen again. Next, check carefully for any possible chemical hazards. Slug pellets, insecticides and cleaning chemicals can all be harmful, if not fatal. Dogs and puppies of all ages also like to chew garden plants from time to time, and some can be toxic. Fence off any plants that may represent a danger.

BASIC CANINE NEEDS

Before setting off to bring your new pet home, make sure that you have a basic kit ready and waiting for its arrival. All puppies or dogs should have a collar and lead. A name tag, bearing your name, address and telephone number, is a legal requirement in many countries, and is a sensible safety precaution in any case.

Make sure that the dog's bowls are ready – with one already down on the floor filled with water. Dogs need to locate their water supply very quickly, so it is a good idea to choose a place and keep it in that spot. Your breeder or animal shelter should already have

provided you with information about the types of food that your puppy or dog is used to eating. Ensure that you have a supply of the same food on hand for its arrival. Even if you intend to change your dog's diet later on, it is important that you stick with what it is used to for several days after bringing it home. Stress may cause stomach upsets in puppies and dogs, and it is

vital that this is not exacerbated by a sudden change to a new type of food. Your dog will also need a place to sleep (see page 96) or a den to call its own. It is a good idea to have one ready, so that you can introduce the dog to it as soon as it arrives.

A few toys or treats may also be awaiting your dog, to help encourage it to feel at home – and don't forget newspapers to soak up any accidents.

B R I N G I N G   Y O U R   N E W   D O G   H O M E

◆

Before setting off on the journey to pick up your new dog, think about how you are going to restrain it on the way home. If you are driving, it is safer to have another pair of hands to help you – while one person drives, the other can concentrate on the dog. Do take some newspaper, paper towels and plastic bags with you, as many dogs are sick on their first few journeys in the car. Most dogs feel calmer in the dark, so it may help to cover the travel box. Your dog may also feel more comfortable on a firm surface, rather than a lap or a soft back seat.

Introducing Your New Pet

Family members ✦ Other dogs ✦ Cats and other pets

Bringing a new puppy or dog home is exciting for all concerned. However, to a young puppy or an adult dog, which will be feeling a little insecure, this excitement can be overwhelming. Try to make the first introductions as calm and quiet as possible. Take the puppy outside to your yard at once to relieve himself. After this, allow it to explore one room at a time, with careful, but distant, supervision. Make it a rule that children are not permitted to try to pick up the puppy, and that they do not run around too much or crowd him into a corner.

MEETING OTHER DOGS

If you have another dog at home it is a good idea to let the two dogs meet for the first time on neutral territory.

Right: An older dog may be suspicious of the new arrival, and both dogs should be given time to get to know each other. It is best to let them get accustomed in a safe environment, under supervision.

Above: Most cats and dogs can develop a good relationship, but their first meeting is crucial. Ensure that the dog is restrained, and that the cat can jump up to a high shelf or table to escape the puppy's attentions.

Ideally, you should take your adult dog with you to the breeder to pick up the puppy. Once the two dogs have travelled home together, allow them some time in the yard or a suitable, safe, outdoor spot, before walking with the puppy into the house, and encouraging the older dog to follow. Remove any items that your older dog may feel the need to defend, such as toys and bones. If you are concerned that your established dog may be aggressive to the new arrival, keep both dogs on the lead, or put the puppy in a playpen or an indoor kennel for frequent protected introductions until you can judge how they both will react.

In the next few months you will need to maintain your established dog's status as top dog, by greeting him first, feeding him first and generally giving him priority for attention and affection. This may be difficult, since puppies can be hard to ignore, but it will help prevent competition.

CATS AND DOGS

Dogs and cats can be great companions, if introduced correctly. Most difficulties occur when a puppy or dog has been permitted to chase – which erodes the cat's confidence and gives the dog a taste of how exciting chasing a cat can be. If you are using an indoor kennel, put the puppy inside and close the door. Bring the cat into the room, but allow it to move away and escape to a high vantage point if it wants to. Cats have a very strong flight instinct and always need an escape route or a safe place to which they can retreat. Most cats will initially glare indignantly at a new puppy, but feel confident enough to come down to the floor quite quickly. When you next introduce them, restrain the puppy or dog, and give it a treat to distract it.

Controlled introductions need to be repeated in order to form acceptance on the part of both animals. You'll need to put the cat's food and water out of the puppy's reach, and to prevent the puppy from ambushing the cat when it is most vulnerable – for example, on the litter box.

Although occasional problems do occur with those breeds or types of dog that have a strong drive to chase, such as Lurchers and Greyhounds, cats are excellent dog trainers. Indeed, they rule the roost in most households.

OTHER PETS

Puppies can be taught to regard other kinds of pets as part of the family if they are introduced at an early age.

Above: Give your dog a guided tour of the house and yard when it first arrives. Family members should try to meet the dog on an individual basis, so that it doesn't feel overwhelmed. Approach it slowly, and crouch down by its side to greet it, before stroking it and perhaps offering a treat.

For a puppy to consider creatures such as guinea pigs or rabbits as part of its "pack", it will need to meet them before it is 12 weeks old.

CHILDREN AND DOGS

◆

Children benefit enormously from the responsibilities of caring for an animal – but it is questionable whether children under the age of seven or eight can really manage. Once the novelty wears off, it will be down to Mom or Dad to cope with all the hard work of looking after an addition to the family.

◆ Involve children at feeding times. They can put the bowl on the floor, and can add extra "delicacies" to the dish while the puppy is eating. This helps to prevent food-guarding problems later on.

◆ Children often make excellent trainers. Find a local puppy class where children are encouraged to attend.

◆ Help your children to interact with the dog in a way that makes it clear they have some human authority. Teaching children and dogs to play hide and seek with a toy, learning new tricks and grooming are all useful.

Settling In

Supervision ◆ Safe areas ◆ Night-time routine ◆ Welcoming older dogs

Most puppies that have been well socialized by the breeder will come into a new home full of confidence. They will have seen many of the trappings of domestic life already and simply want to explore. If this is the case, then allow your puppy to do so, but supervise it all the time. It only takes a couple of minutes spent on the telephone or loading the washing machine to discover that puppies can chew through electric cables, climb out of windows and swallow dangerous objects when you have your back turned. As no one can possibly watch a puppy every second, it is sensible to create a safe place where your new dog can go to rest or play when you are busy elsewhere.

A SAFE HAVEN

A special indoor kennel or "crate" is an ideal way to keep tabs on your puppy, but, if you don't have one, a baby gate erected at the kitchen door can be useful. Puppies tend to have fairly short bursts of activity, followed by periods of deep sleep. In order to accustom your puppy to being alone in this safe place for short periods, wait until it starts to look tired, or falls asleep after exploring. Then carefully pick it up and take it to its bed in the designated "safe haven". Leave it to sleep in this area and enjoy the short time that you will have to yourself before it wakes and is ready to go adventuring again.

PUTTING YOUR DOG TO BED

If you have managed to put your puppy in this area several times in the course of a day, the night-time routine will be very much easier. Where you decide to let your puppy sleep is up to you, but do bear in mind that small, cute Labrador puppies turn into large,

Above: If you make a decision to allow your dog to sleep on your bed, be prepared to allow it to do so as it grows older. It won't understand a change of rules once it has become accustomed to a routine.

Below: A pen can keep your puppy safe when you are unable to supervise it, and can act as a "den". The pen or crate should never be used to punish your puppy with isolation, but should remain a happy place.

The first few hours in a new environment can be quite traumatic for an older dog. Allow your new dog to go straight out into the yard when you get home. Encourage it to relieve itself, then bring it inside and calmly allow it to look around, one room at a time. This prevents the dog from rushing madly around the living room, up the stairs and back to the kitchen in wild excitement. If your new dog refuses to relieve itself at first, supervise it very carefully, and give it frequent opportunities to go outside until it is calm enough to do so.

The most common problem that re-homed or "rescue" dogs present is being unable to cope with being home alone. Short periods of being left alone in a safe area with a bed and some toys during the first few days in a new home are essential and, along with patience and gentle encouragement, will help to foster the sense of security that your dog needs.

heavyweight dogs when they want to share the comforter later on.

Dogs are social creatures, and it can be hard for some pups to cope with being alone at night during the first few days in their new home. This may result in some crying for reassurance. Try to contain your puppy in a crate or high-sided cardboard box with a blanket in the bottom, so that you can have it in the bedroom with you without having to worry about what it is getting up to when you are asleep. Puppies will not usually soil their beds, and if they are confined, will normally make a noise when they need to relieve themselves – which gives you time to make the appropriate arrangements, quickly if speed is necessary.

If you would prefer not to have your puppy in the bedroom with you, make a cosy nest in the kitchen or resting area, and leave it. Try not to return to every little whimper he makes, or your puppy may "train" you to come when called. Very few pups can manage a whole night without relieving themselves. You will need to set your alarm clock to take it out during the night, or be prepared to clean up in the morning, which will delay its house-training.

Below: Your puppy may feel overwhelmed and insecure in the first few days, and you can expect a number of "accidents" until toilet training is complete. Lay down plenty of newspaper, even if you do plan to train it to go outdoors. It takes a human baby months to become toilet-trained – puppies require time and patience, too.

Handling Your Dog

Contact ◆ Holding a puppy ◆ Lifting a dog ◆ Meeting unfamiliar dogs

With communication skills similar to those of human beings, dogs usually enjoy the same tactile contact that we do, but there are some clear distinctions. While many of us enjoy being held close, and having our faces close together or even touching, this is often alien to dogs. To a dog, being held tightly may indicate that it is being threatened by another dog or predator, and is in danger. It may even appear to the dog that it is being mounted – which is inappropriate, and can be interpreted by the dog as dominating social behavior. Although dogs do lick each other around the mouth as a gesture of submission, the appearance of a face very close to their own may lead to an aggressive response. It is important that children in particular are taught how to touch dogs, and that everyone knows how to pick them up and to handle them properly.

Below: Every family member should be taught to hold the dog properly, for the safety of all involved. Children are notorious for inappropriate handling.

HOW TO HOLD YOUR PUPPY
Place one hand around the dog's chest and support its weight with the other hand under its bottom. Bring the puppy in close to your chest to give it security. Never lift a puppy under the armpits, by the tail or hold it in midair.

LIFTING ADULT DOGS
Adult dogs often object to being lifted – partly because it feels slightly uncomfortable and partly because it often prompts unpleasant associations, such as being placed on the vet's examination table. It is sensible to use the "calf lift" when picking up a medium- to large-sized dog. With the dog standing sideways, place both arms around its body and legs and scoop it up gently, in one movement. This lift minimizes any uneven weight distribution and prevents the dog from attempting to struggle.

Practicing the calf lift with a dog will help to prepare it for the time when it needs to be lifted for real. Simply supporting the dog's weight in your arms as if you were going to lift it, on a regular basis, then giving it a treat or a game, helps to create positive associations with what can otherwise be an unfamiliar and frightening experience.

HANDLING
It is absolutely essential that you are able to touch every single inch of your dog's body without it objecting. Practice doing this when there is no

Above: Always hold your dog gently but firmly; this will give you control, but ensure that it does not feel threatened in any way.

Below: Introduce your dog to its collar and lead early on in its life, and it will not object to having it put on and removed. Every dog should have a collar with identification.

discomfort, to prepare your dog for the day when you have to treat a painful ear infection or look at a sore paw. Handling should be a daily occurrence, and can be combined with grooming or massage. Eyes, ears, teeth, gums and feet are all sensitive, so treat these areas gently. Don't forget that your dog cannot tell you if there is a part that it doesn't like you to touch, so if it starts to object, begins to wriggle or tries to mouth you, don't get angry or aggressive. Stop, get a treat or toy and go back over the area very gently; if it does not object, give it the reward for accepting your handling.

UNFAMILIAR DOGS

Always ask if you may pat or stroke someone else's dog. If the owner is happy about it, check that the dog is too. Keeping your body sideways, and your eyes averted, offer your hand for the dog to sniff. This is usually a good indicator. If the dog comes forward to sniff or greet you then all should be well. If the dog backs away, puts its ears back or looks unhappy, then stop. It can be threatening to place your hand directly on the dog's head or neck – always tickle the dog's chest and under its chin as an initial greeting. Many dogs will then elicit more attention by moving closer or turning, hoping for a scratch on the rump – a friendly signal in dog language.

Right: A pat on the head can appear to be a "dominant" gesture to a dog. Always greet a dog with a scratch under the chin and leave head-patting until your dog feels comfortable with the action.

Left: Always talk to your dog to reassure it before trying to pick it up. Always lift a small dog by supporting the chest with one hand, keeping the other under its rump. This method prevents it from jumping out of your grasp. A dog should become used to being picked up from an early age, and should learn not to struggle in an effort to get down.

Training a Puppy

Home training a puppy ✦ *Unwanted behavior* ✦ *Puppy classes*

Thankfully, training has come a long way in the last ten years. Gone are the days when it was believed that puppies needed to be over six months old to cope with the rigors of training. New methods and behavioral understanding has meant that training can begin the day after you bring your puppy home.

Most owners think of training as teaching the dog to sit or lie down. However, these are behaviors that your dog is already capable of doing. Training is really about teaching the dog a foreign language – ours – so that he complies with our requests through understanding what we want and when we want it.

Training a young puppy is also about teaching him which behaviors are acceptable and which are not. From a very early age, all puppies have an admirable set of teeth. These are needle sharp, and, prior to the age of 18–20 weeks, are designed to play an important role in the puppy's education. Play biting is normal and, in fact, essential for all puppies. Dogs, like toddlers, explore their environment by taking objects in their mouths. Objects that do not

Above: If your puppy jumps up, gently push it down and say "No". All puppies will want to share in household activities, but will soon learn the rules if you are consistently firm.

Below: Finish training exercises by praising the puppy and offering a reward. Stroking and food are powerful rewards, as is an encouraging, positive tone of voice.

react to pressure exerted by these incredibly sharp teeth must be lifeless: anything that reacts when bitten is clearly alive.

BITING

Play biting teaches the puppy just how hard he can bite other living beings. Watching young puppies play together makes this apparent. Biting each other is entirely friendly – unless one of the pups bites the other a little too hard. When bitten, a puppy will give a really loud yelp, and refuse to play for the next few seconds. We should adopt the same response with our puppies, to teach them that we too feel pain and object to it.

Humans need to communicate that they are hurt when their puppies mouth them, not that they are angry – which puppies regard as irrational aggression. If your puppy is mouthing you, yelp loudly, or give a shout, then turn away as if to nurse your wounds. The puppy should look a little surprised when this first happens, but do not expect the biting to stop straight away. Gradually, over the next few weeks, the biting should become increasingly gentle, until you are yelping at the slightest pressure.

Finally, you can show pain if the puppy touches you at all with its

Above: Encourage children to take part in training, but ensure that they know the rules. Dogs bite in play and will not understand an angry or over-excited reaction.

Above: Offer encouragement and praise your dog constantly when training, to let it know you are pleased with what it is doing. Your dog will rely on you to train it from an early age to have an even temper, and to get along with other dogs and people. A well-mannered dog will obey commands from its owner, and feel more secure.

teeth. Its biting should soon cease altogether. Puppies must learn that dogs never bite humans, even in play.

SEEKING ATTENTION

For some puppies, getting a reaction to their mouthing is very exciting. This is often related to attention-seeking, and seems to occur particularly in households where there are small children who scream and flap their arms if the puppy starts to bite their clothes. Of course, this brings Mom running in from the yard and great excitement ensues all round. The puppy probably thinks it has won the jackpot – even negative attention is better than no attention at all. Distracting the puppy with toys and not letting either dog or child become over-excited will help. Time-outs, with the puppy put in its crate, pen or the kitchen for a short while, also allow things to calm down.

TAKING A PUPPY TO CLASSES

Playing with members of the same species is one of the quickest ways for a puppy under 18 weeks old to learn good bite inhibition. Attending a well-run puppy socialization class can speed up this process, and also helps owners with beginning all the other essential basic training. Finding a good class can be as difficult as choosing a good school for your children and it is worth taking time and effort to select the right one.

Most importantly, try to be as calm and patient as possible as with your puppy during training – he will learn quickly, given the right circumstances and guidance, and you will both be rewarded by the results.

---

*FINDING A GOOD PUPPY
SOCIALIZATION CLASS*

◆

◆ Both puppies and people in the class should look relaxed and happy.
◆ Punitive methods or equipment should not be in use.
◆ Noise should be kept to a minimum – shouting is not necessary. Lots of barking can indicate that the dogs are stressed.
◆ Methods should suit the dog and handler in question. Food and toys are excellent motivators. Not many dogs work for praise alone.
◆ A good puppy class will offer a sensible combination of gentle training and controlled play.
◆ If puppies are permitted to come off lead to play they should all be under 18 weeks old at the start of the course.

Continuing Training

Rewards ✦ Calling your dog ✦ Sitting and lying down ✦ Food lures ✦ Socialization problems

The more you can teach your dog and the more he experiences before he reaches adolescence, the better. But dogs, like people, need motivation to learn. Not many humans would go to work for a pat on the head or praise from the boss alone. For many dogs, puppies in particular, food is the equivalent of a salary – it can act as the ultimate reward and is also useful as a lure in the initial stages of training.

SIGNALS

Most dog owners do not want to rely on food rewards indefinitely, so the use of a "conditioned reinforcer" is essential. This means that you give the dog a signal that it has done the right thing and that a reward is on its way, instead of giving it the actual reward each time. The dog will soon come to treat the signal itself as a reward. Common signals include a single sound or word, such as "yes", which you initially pair with a food reward. A small "clicker" can also be used to create a sound signal that your dog will learn to recognize. Make the sound, then give the pup a food treat. Repeat this until it instantly looks round for its reward. You are now ready to begin your puppy's training.

---

*S O C I A L I Z A T I O N
P R O B L E M S*

✦

Act quickly if your puppy seems fearful, or aggressive, either towards other dogs or people. It is essential that puppies learn life's lessons before they are 18 weeks old. Find a good puppy training class, or ask your vet to refer you to a behavior specialist. Leaving it too long can lead to behavioral problems later in life.

Come when called!

✦ Stand directly in front of your dog and call it in a friendly voice, with just two words, such as, "Ben, come!"
✦ Wave a piece of food in your outstretched hand and start moving backwards. If the dog shows no response, clap your hands or make a noise until it looks at you.
✦ If the dog moves just one step towards you, make the signal sound, "Yes" or click, then offer the food.
✦ Gradually increase the distance it has to come to get the food. Practice by calling your dog to you at unusual moments in and around the house.

Right: A dog that is well behaved can be let off the lead and allowed to run free in appropriate areas. If your dog reliably comes to you when it is called, and is prepared to walk by your heels when you request it to do so, you can confidently offer it more freedom in more places.

Left: Hold the food bowl above your puppy's head so that it will sit in order to keep its eye on the bowl.

Sit!

✦ Hold a food treat close to your dog's nose. Now lift your hand up and back so it has to look right up to follow your fingers. When a dog looks up, there is a physical chain reaction – its rear end has to go down. If the dog's front legs come off the ground, your hand is probably too high.
✦ As soon as your dog's rear touches the ground, give the signal and then offer it the treat.
✦ Once your dog is sitting reliably, you can add the word "Sit", just before its bottom hits the ground. Ask your dog to sit before it gets anything it likes – such as its dinner or being let out into the yard – it should soon become its way of saying please and thank you.

Down!

✦ Hold the food lure above your dog's nose. Then lower your hand right down to the floor, directly between the dog's front paws. Hang on to the treat by turning your palm down, with the food hidden inside your hand.

✦ Be patient! As your dog tries to get the food, the head and body must lower to the floor. As soon as it flops down, signal, then offer the treat. If it does not catch on quickly, pass the food or toy under a low chair or table, so that it follows the lure underneath it by dropping down to floor level.

✦ Remember that practice makes perfect. Don't add your word command until your dog is offering the required behavior fluidly and reliably when requested.

PHASING OUT FOOD LURES

Gradually ask more and more from your puppy before giving your reward signal and the food treat. This means keeping the pup in a "sit" or "down"

Above left and above: Some breeds of dog are natural retrievers and can be trained to fetch virtually anything. Finish every training session with a reward or a game.

position for longer sessions, and lengthening the distance and amount of distraction when you call it. When all three exercises are executed reliably, reward the dog only for its fastest responses, sometimes with food, and sometimes with praise or a toy. This will keep it guessing what it's going to get for a job well done.

Below: When walking with you, your dog should always be under control, both as a courtesy to others and for its own safety. Learning to walk on a loose lead is one of the foundations of training.

Training an Adult Dog

Home training an adult dog ✦ *Training classes* ✦ *Walking on the lead*

Left: As a puppy, your dog should have learned to accept its collar and lead. Walking to heel may take some time to master, but keep training sessions short and frequent to ensure quick success.

Training a dog is an ongoing, day-to-day task, not something that takes place once a week in a class environment. Training classes are designed to teach you how to train your own dog, to allow your dog to socialize with other canines, and to set up a "support group" for owners who may need help and advice. Like people, dogs can react badly to stressful situations, and this makes a good choice of training class imperative. The days of repetitive, boring and compulsive classes may at last be gone. Modern training methods, using food or toys to motivate the dogs, are fun, informal and enjoyable. A good class should offer advice on all of the practical aspects of dog care and training.

BEGINNING AT HOME

Much of your training with an older dog needs to be done in your home and during walks. The "sit", "down" and "come when called" techniques (see page 86) can be mastered in the same way as for puppies, and need to be practiced regularly. Walking calmly on the lead is an important skill for dogs of all ages to learn. Despite the danger of choking themselves, many dogs appear to find pulling on the lead very rewarding. They pull all the way to the park, then get the biggest reward of the day for doing it – a chance to run free.

It is impossible to start to teach a dog not to pull when you're on the way to the park. The dog will be excited and not interested in your commands. Instead, start by encourag-

Left: Training sessions should be enjoyable. Take the time to praise your dog, and offer rewards. Just like people, dogs will work harder when they feel valued.

◆ It is important to watch a class before enroling.

◆ The venue should be large enough to allow dogs to be spaced well apart.

◆ There should be no more than eight dogs per instructor – preferably no more than 12 dogs in the class.

◆ Outdoor classes are often useful, providing training in an environment where obedience will be crucial.

◆ Methods should be kind and gentle, and owners and dogs should enjoy the experience.

◆ Instructors should be well versed in problems associated with adult dogs.

ing your dog to follow you around the house, with the lead off. Lure your dog into the right position with a treat, and give your signal (see page 86), and then reward it when it is in the right place by your side. Keep sessions short and fun, and offer constant praise when it stays by you.

Training your dog on the lead

Once you have mastered off-lead walking in the house and yard, attach the lead. If your dog is a persistent puller, a head-collar or a body harness may assist training. Make sure that it is properly fitted and does not chafe. Begin training your dog to walk on the lead in the house.

◆ Keeping the lead slack, move off slowly, and signal then treat the dog when it is in the right place.

◆ Stop if you feel tension in the lead. Only move off again when your dog has slackened the lead – no matter how long it takes.

◆ Once you have mastered this in the house, graduate to the yard, then larger spaces, such as parks. If your dog begins to pull on the lead, stand still. It'll soon realize that walking calmly will get it to the park faster.

"Leave it!"

"Leave it", means "Don't touch until you are told you can". This is a very useful command if you have children

who eat away from the table, and for dogs who may be tempted to chase.

◆ Hold a piece of food tightly between your fingers and show it to the dog, without saying anything. If it goes to take it, say "Leave it" in a quiet voice.

◆ Hide the food in your hand, making a fist around it.

◆ As soon as the dog pulls its nose away from your hand, even for a split second, give your signal of reward, say "Take it", or "Thank you" and give it the treat. Your dog will soon learn what you want it to do.

Above: Positive reinforcement is an effective way to shape a dog's behavior. A food reward and verbal praise will give the dog a clear message of approval. Vary the reward to make learning fun for your dog.

◆ Practice several times until your dog takes its nose away instantly when you say "Leave it".

◆ Gradually lengthen the amount of time that your dog is expected to keep its nose from the food. This can be developed into all sorts of games, with plenty of appropriate rewards.

Establishing Roles

The pack instinct ✦ *Rank* ✦ *Power games* ✦
Taking the lead

Dogs are pack animals, which means that they are quick to learn social skills within a small group. To a pet dog, your family is his pack, and all humans need to be recognized as "pack leaders" for the dog to feel secure and safe. Dogs do not denote rank structure or leadership by physical force, or aggression. Instead, they use subtle signals that all dogs recognize as indicators of rank. Dog owners can usefully learn many of the signals outlined in this section, and imitate them to ensure that peace and harmony reign in their home "pack" structure. It is, of course, unnecessary to enforce every "social signal". Use them to ensure that your dog maintains good "manners" and does not attempt to challenge you when he sees something he would like to have.

THE PECKING ORDER

Canine social order is quite simple to understand. In basic terms, the higher up the "rank ladder" you are, the more privileges you are allowed. When you look at the main features of life that a dog may view as a privilege, it is not difficult to see why some dogs may begin to take advantage of the system – and their owners.

Getting attention

To your dog, it's the higher-ranking individual that demands attention, affection and games. Many dogs are masters of getting attention when they want it, but quite willing to deny it to their owners. In this situation, boost your rank by giving attention when you decide it's appropriate, or ask your dog to respond to a request, such as "Sit", before it gets attention.

Above: Dogs that fit harmoniously into the family "pack" are a joy to live with, and are easily trained. A happy dog will enjoy pleasing you, and will respond well to guidance.

Below: Routine training exercises, like making your dog sit before you feed it, will help to reinforce your dominance and establish your pack leadership.

Freedom of movement

Many dogs enjoy total freedom of movement around the house, with no problems whatsoever. However, if your dog consistently lies in your way, stops halfway up the stairs to block your path, pushes you off the sofa, or won't move from the middle of the bed, it may be time to rethink your relationship. Creating no-go areas where you can sit or walk, but your dog can't, is a good idea. Teaching the dog to get off the furniture when requested, or discouraging it from getting on from the very beginning, is also sensible, since height seems to reinforce rank and may give your dog a feeling of authority over you.

Establishing status

Some dogs may use toys and games as tools with which to control their owners, while others play happily and never cause difficulties. If your dog pesters you to play, then runs off with the toy when it gets bored, or won't let you have the toy when requested, work out a program of structured games that gently puts you back in control. Many dogs like to play tug games with a toy. These are fine as long as you can take the toy away from your dog at the end of the game, without a struggle. Simply swapping

Above: Some dogs are easier to train than others, depending on their individual characteristics, but most dogs will pull on the lead until they learn to do otherwise. Finding the right motivation is the key to success.

the toy for a tidbit or another toy is an excellent way to teach your dog to drop the item without confrontation. Alternatively, play games that avoid contests of strength, such as "hide and seek" with the toy.

Leading the hunt

Most dogs consider a walk to the park as a hunting expedition, and are justifiably excited. As pack leader, you should lead the "hunt" from the moment you leave the car or the front door. Insisting on respect at doorways is a vital part of training, and one that also reinforces your leadership. If your dog tries to go through the door in front of you, shut the door quickly and gently, taking care not to hit the dog's nose, to block its path. Repeat this until it takes a step backwards to allow you right of passage.

All of these measures are intended to give your dog predictable boundaries in his life. If you feel that your dog is challenging you over resources or attention in the house, ask your vet to refer you to a behavior specialist who can offer expert help based on your dog's individual needs. Until you can arrange assistance, be cautious and avoid confrontation. Dogs can and do use their teeth to win a battle if they are confronted.

Below: Pets will establish between themselves which roles they play within the household, and are usually able to forge a good relationship.

Below: Your puppy may chew almost anything. Offer a treat as a distraction, and he will soon leave things alone on command.

Dog Discipline

Playing fair ✦ *Physical punishment and aggression* ✦
Non-rewards for bad behavior

Although dogs are extremely good at reading our body language, learning basic words and predicting our behavior, there is no doubt that they find our values and actions confusing.

PLAYING FAIR

From a dog's point of view, there is no difference between jumping up to greet someone who is wearing old trousers and someone who is wearing a skirt and stockings. We, however, tend to be more discerning. Disciplining a dog for being a dog is nearly always unfair, and unless it has been specifically taught that its behavior is inappropriate, we cannot expect it to differentiate between days of the week and dress codes.

PHYSICAL PUNISHMENT

Physical punishment is almost always counterproductive. There are a few times when physical action becomes necessary to prevent a dog from continuing with a specific behavior, but it should never be done with

Above: A dog that is aggressive towards other dogs may not have been properly socialized. Socialization (see page 86) needs to occur early in life. Later rehabilitation requires time, patience and commitment.

great force or aggression. Smacking or hitting a dog can have a number of negative consequences. Dogs that are slightly anxious in nature may learn to associate punishment with the punisher. Dogs that have been physically threatened may refuse to come when called or be "hand shy" – cowering when a hand is raised.

Even worse, a nervous dog may learn to make a false association between punishment and people, dogs or another aspect of the environment. These types of associations can cause a dog to defend itself against children, other people or strange dogs, which they believe to be the source of pain or fear. On the other hand, a dog that is assertive and self-confident may become aggressive when threatened physically.

AVOIDING AGGRESSION

It is not unusual for dogs that have been punished to behave aggressively in return. There is a much higher incidence of dog owners being bitten by their own dogs than of dogs biting strangers. Inappropriate punishment is usually the cause.

Not many owners want to punish their dogs physically, and can understand that this is likely to make unwanted behavior worse. Instead, they attempt to teach the dog as they would a child – giving instructions and explaining clearly when things go wrong. Unfortunately, this type of training can be equally ineffective.

Dogs simply do not understand human speech, and are more likely to

Left: A well-behaved dog will feel happy and secure with other dogs and people. Kindness and consistency help to achieve these aims.

Above: Barking is often unintentionally rewarded by owners. If you shout at your dog, it may assume that you are barking encouragement, and come to think that its behavior is acceptable.

respond to tone of voice. Many dogs interpret shouting as encouragement to bark. It is also possible that the behavior of some dogs is fuelled by the simple excitement of having enraged their owners – to this type of dog, negative attention is better than no attention at all.

PREVENTING BAD HABITS

There are several different humane and effective ways to interrupt or prevent unwanted behavior and to stop your dog forming bad habits. The first of these is called "non-reward". This type of discipline involves ensuring that the dog does not receive any type of reward for its bad behavior. When behavior is not rewarded, it is unlikely to be repeated.

For example, many dogs jump up when they greet people. This type of behavior is primarily a friendly greeting, but it can be considered inappropriate. Instead of rewarding the behavior by making a fuss when the dog jumps up, turn away and ignore it until it has all four feet on

the ground. Offer the dog plenty of praise when it greets you appropriately, and make sure that it is consistently encouraged to behave in this manner by withholding attention until it is calm at greetings.

Direct aversion is another method commonly used to discourage unwanted behavior. With this technique, an interruption is created by something that the dog doesn't like – a squirt of water, perhaps, or a loud noise. Care must be taken if you

Above: The most serious problem that a dog can develop is to show aggression. Seek help early if you suspect that your dog is unusually aggressive or out of control.

choose to use this type of discipline however – some dogs learn to make unpleasant associations with such actions. Good training prevents bad habits, but if they do occur, they can almost always be remedied with patience and the advice of a behavioral specialist.

House Hygiene

Errorless learning ✦ Toilet training ✦ Submissive urination

*I*t is a mistake to expect young puppies to have full control over their bodily functions, and the occasional accident will undoubtedly occur. The approach known as "error-less learning" will, however, guarantee that toilet-training problems are quickly overcome. This method ensures that puppies quickly learn what is expected of them, and learn to relieve themselves from the beginning in an appropriate place. Errorless learning simply involves making it impossible for your puppy to relieve itself in the wrong place.

TOILET TRAINING YOUR PUPPY

It is important that you can predict when your puppy will need to relieve itself – for instance, after playing, upon waking, after any kind of excitement (such as the children coming home from school) and after meals.

The following guidelines will help you to train your puppy to relieve itself appropriately.

✦ Take your puppy to the same place outside and wait there with it – even if it is raining. Gently repeating a word, such as "quickly" will help your puppy to remember why it is there. As soon as your puppy starts to sniff around, or circle, give it encouragement.

✦ Once it has relieved itself, lavish praise on it and offer a special tidbit as a reward. Play with it afterwards, then bring it indoors.

✦ Between these events it is wise to take your puppy outside on an hourly

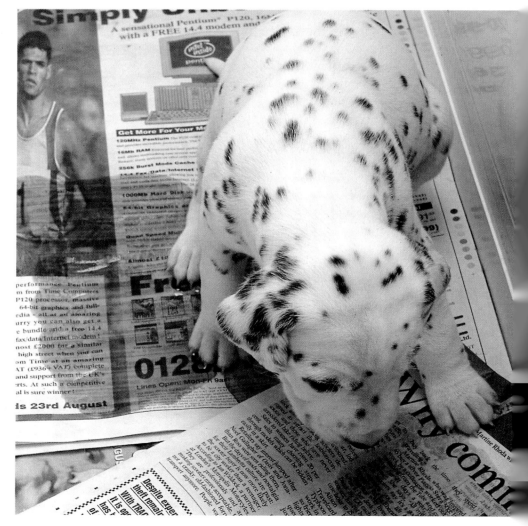

Right and above: Paper-training can confuse your puppy about whether or not it is acceptable to relieve itself indoors. Newspaper provides a useful standby for accidents, but your puppy should not be encouraged to use it.

Far left: Puppies normally sniff and circle before relieving themselves, and are more likely to urinate in a place they have used before.

Left: If your dog needs to relieve itself on walks, ensure that it does so out of the path of passers-by, and always clean up afterwards. Carry a plastic bag or a "pooper-scooper" with you, and place the mess in a dog bin, or take it home for disposal.

Below: When adult dogs urinate, they also leave a scent message, which marks the area they consider to be their territory.

basis, and to watch it closely for signs that it might need to relieve itself, such as sniffing or circling.

✦ If you wait outside with your puppy and it does not relieve itself, bring it back inside. You should supervise the puppy constantly until your next trip outside. If you are unable to keep a close eye on your dog, put it in an enclosed area, laid with paper.

✦ If you catch your puppy in the act of relieving itself indoors, or about to do so, at any other time, say "outside" in a gentle voice, then take it to a familiar outdoor spot. Accidents may happen, but move quickly and get the pup outside, even if it is halfway through the act. If your puppy gets even one drop in the right place, you should still praise it.

✦ If you confine your puppy to its sleeping area, it will be more likely to hold on until it needs to go out again, or call you when it is ready. Most puppies will not soil their beds.

Staying calm

Becoming angry with your puppy for making a mess is pointless. Dogs soon learn to associate the mess with your anger – not with the act of relieving themselves – and simply show fear when you find it. It takes years for a child to be fully toilet-trained, but no one would consider punishing a baby for having any accidents along the way. Old-fashioned punishments, such as rubbing the dog's nose in its own mess, are counterproductive and abhorrent, and should not be used.

Many people use sheets of newspaper to teach their puppy to relieve themselves in a particular place, but this approach is harder work than the "errorless learning" method. Paper training involves training your puppy twice – once to use paper, and then again, to go outdoors.

PROBLEMS WITH URINATION

Dogs that leak urine when meeting people or other dogs are not showing a lack of house-training, but are communicating their deference. Puppies may also roll over, sit with a hind leg heldout to the side, or squirm along the floor when meeting someone or something they think is dominant.

If your puppy urinates when it greets you, ignore it until it is outside, and only greet it when it has urinated there. Alternatively, crouch down and greet the puppy sideways, without looking at it directly. This will reassure your puppy that you are gentle and friendly, and pose no threat.

Living Areas

Sleeping areas ✦ *Preventing fleas and other insects* ✦ *Feeding areas*

A bed or kennel is an important part of your dog's surroundings, and provides it with its own territory. Not all dogs choose to sleep in their beds, but every dog will benefit from the security offered by his own domain. Just as important is a designated feeding area, where your dog knows it will be fed.

SWEET DREAMS

Where your dog sleeps is largely a matter of personal preference – but this preference should be yours, not the dogs. Many people enjoy having their dog in the bedroom with them at night – either under or on the bed, or perhaps on the floor – and there is nothing wrong with this. Traditional wisdom claimed that allowing a dog to sleep in the "center of the den", or in a privileged position, would encourage dominance, but there are two ways to ensure that your dog knows who is in charge.

First of all, if you choose to allow your dog to sleep on the bed, its behavior should be impeccable. Any refusal to let you in or out of the bed indicates a problem, and your dog should be taken out of the bedroom while you address it. Second, however comfortable your dog is in the bedroom, when you ask it to move, it must do so. These are "house rules" that should be established early on, and adhered to strictly, in order to avoid problems in the future.

For those with white sheets and an aversion to snoring, a dog bed may be a better idea – and obviously hygiene is also an important issue. All dogs

Left: Whatever bed you choose for your dog, whether it be a basket, a bean bag or a plastic bed, make sure that it will be comfortable and warm and that it is the right size. It should be a little bigger than the dog and allow enough space for it to turn around in.

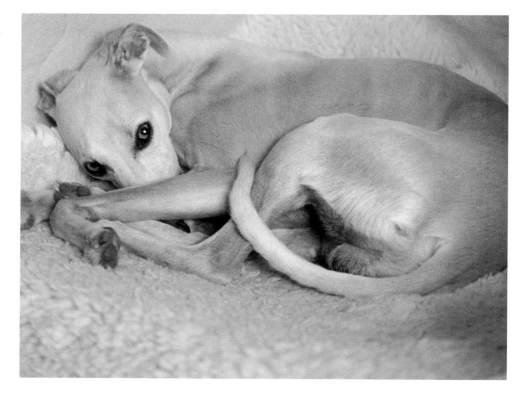

Right: A bed lined with soft and comfortable material will provide warmth and a feeling of security. For puppies, who may chew and wet their bedding, an expendable lining is best.

should have a small area to call their own, and a bed is usually the best way to achieve this. Dog beds come in all shapes and sizes – from those filled with pea-sized polystyrene balls, to proper comforters. Even heated under-blankets are available for dogs that are sensitive to the cold.

Whatever bed you choose for your dog, ensure that it is easy to clean, and that you clean both bedding and bed regularly. Wicker baskets are the traditional dog bed, and they look lovely when new, but they are almost impossible to clean and are easily chewed. A plastic dog bed, with a comfortable, washable blanket is probably the best option for long-term use. A cardboard box is a good idea for growing puppies, who have a tendency to chew anything in sight while their teeth are growing.

A FLEA-FREE HOME

Fleas are the great menace for any dog owner. Contrary to popular belief, fleas spend very little time on their host animal, and more time in their surroundings. They love our centrally heated homes and breed prolifically if preventative measures are not taken. This is one reason for washing your dog's bedding regularly.

There are many preparations now available to rid your dog of fleas.

Below: Fleas are the most common skin parasites that affect dogs. Effective treatment involves the regular use of insecticides, shampoos or powders.

Although it may be tempting to buy the cheapest powder or shampoo from the pet shop, be warned: fleas are hardy creatures that have evolved and adapted for at least as long as mammals have. They have survived our attempts to eradicate them by becoming immune to the various chemicals in anti-flea products. It is therefore always sensible to buy flea spray, drops or shampoo from your veterinarian, who should have the most up-to-date products that are available (see page 139).

WHERE TO FEED YOUR DOG

A dog likes to have a regular feeding place, and eating in the same place each day encourages it to learn and stick to a routine. To ensure good hygiene, always use separate bowls for your pets and keep them apart from your own. Flies may be attracted to unwashed dog dishes, so removing and cleaning bowls after each meal is a sensible precaution. Unless you are free-feeding your dog a complete, dry food, never leave uneaten meals on the floor for too long. It is sensible to choose a feeding area that can be cleaned easily, like the kitchen floor – particularly if you offer large pieces of food, which are likely to be dragged to the floor for intensive chewing!

Above: A dog should have its own bowl, from which it alone eats – and it should be discouraged from eating from other places, such as your plate! Always placing the bowl in the same place helps encourage a routine. Long-eared breeds should have deep bowls that keep their ears clear of the food.

BURYING BONES

Before the days of domestication, and regular feeding, dogs and wolves would bury surplus food in the ground, to protect it from scavengers and, in hot weather, from flies. Typically, the burying took place near the kill. A hungry dog will, like its wolf ancestors, eat everything it can. Only leftovers will be carried to the yard and buried. Commercial foods are impossible to carry and bury, so most dogs never have the opportunity to store food in this way. Given a bone, however, many dogs will attempt to bury it – no matter how hungry they are – a legacy of the days when food that could not be broken up and eaten immediately was buried for retrieval in leaner times.

Dog-proofing Your Home

A safe environment ◆ Chewing ◆ Retrieving ◆ Digging ◆ Kennelling

Having a dog around the home is similar to having a toddler. Both want to touch things and put them in their mouths, and both are able to reach to surprising heights if they are determined to do so. Although both can be taught to behave, it is still wise to take some precautions about the house.

CHEWING AND TYPES OF CHEWS

Dogs need to chew. They have teeth designed to chomp through everything from vegetation to bones. Unless they are given appropriate outlets for this behavior, they may turn to the interior of your home to find a suitable substitute. There are hundreds of different types of chews and bones available commercially that will help to prevent your dog from chewing your belongings.

Rawhide chews: These are cheap and are useful for temporary distraction, but only when you can supervise. The chew becomes soggy after a while, which means it can get stuck in a dog's throat if you don't take it away.

Below: A pen can keep a dog safe while you are introducing it to your yard.

Cooked bones: Bones are tasty and satisfying. Always choose large marrow bones. Chicken bones should never be fed to dogs because they can splinter and cause terrible injuries.

Rubber toys or nylon chews: These are probably the safest and most durable type of chews. Hollow toys can be made more interesting by stuffing them full of food which the dog has to work hard to remove.

Puppies chewing

A home can seem to offer a paradise of chewing opportunities for a puppy. In reality, it presents a catalog of dangers and potentially serious accidents. Prevention is always the best course of action, so unless you are prepared to join a queue of patients at the vet's, it is wise to minimize the risks.

Puppies in particular seem to have a tendency to pick up and chew socks, underwear and small items such as hair scrunchies and pencils. If your puppy starts to chew on something dangerous or unsuitable, it is advisable to stay calm. If the article is potentially harmful, such as a stone or a pair of scissors, offer it an immediate swap for something tasty to eat. Above all, do not panic. Like toddlers, dogs will be keen to hold on to something that provokes a reaction.

Bear in mind that your puppy will enjoy "stealing" things that guarantee instant attention. If the object is forbidden but unlikely to cause injury to the puppy, walk away and ignore it. Create a distraction elsewhere, such as rattling the dinner bowl or ringing the doorbell. As soon as the dog has dropped the item, you can go and pick it up and put it out of reach. Do not make a fuss, or your puppy will

know exactly what to pick up the next time it is beginning to feel bored.

RETRIEVING TENDENCIES

Some types of dog have been bred especially to "retrieve" things and bring them back to you. Golden Labrador and Flatcoat Retrievers fall into this category, and you may find that they feel the need to have some particular item to present to you every time they greet you.

Unless you are happy for your underwear or the dish towels to be paraded around the house on your arrival, it is best to provide toys that your dog can find quickly and bring to you as a "present". Scolding or punishing gundog breeds such as Retrievers or Spaniels for doing what comes naturally to them can lead to severe behavioral problems.

Many dogs that naturally retrieve things are now taken to dog behavior specialists for "possessive aggression" treatment. Such

Below: All dogs enjoy chewing, so provide an object you do not mind being chewed.

Above: Although outdoor kennels may be suitable for robust dogs, few dogs cope well with being housed outdoors. Dogs need company and the security of living inside.

Below: Set aside part of your yard where digging is allowed, and ban digging elsewhere.

behavior usually begins with some confusion over what they are allowed to pick up and what they are not.

SUPERVISED DIGGING

Some dogs love to dig. Curing this type of behavior can be almost impossible. It is a good idea to provide a place where your dog can dig – and then encourage it to dig there and there only, by burying exciting toys, biscuits and chews. Alternatively, do not allow your dog unsupervised access to the yard.

OUTDOOR KENNELLING

Dogs are social animals that need company as well as food, water and shelter. Many behavior problems occur when dogs are not provided with adequate stimulation or companionship, and those that are kept outside can become bored far more quickly than dogs living in a home environment. Most of us now live with neighbors close by, and a dog that barks for several hours a day will soon provoke complaints from neighbors, environmental health or animal welfare officers.

Although it was once considered more natural to keep a dog outdoors, that thinking is now outdated and unacceptable. If you want to have a dog in your life, you should also be prepared to share your space and time generously with it.

Traveling

Car and air travel ◆ Public transport ◆ Traveling abroad ◆ Kennels

As a member of your family, your dog will want to take part in all your activities and to accompany you on your trips. He will therefore need to become accustomed to traveling with you, experiencing as many different types of transport as possible. Traveling with your dog should be enjoyable, but you will need to plan your journeys.

BY CAR

Traveling by car is not an experience that most wild dogs would ever encounter, so your dog has no set of "natural behaviors" to fall back upon when traveling by road. It is therefore important to teach your dog that car travel is a pleasant experience, and that certain behavior is expected.

Introduce your dog gradually to the car. Encourage it to sit quietly while the car is stationary. Next, drive the car, keeping the dog as still as possible, as motion sickness can be exacerbated by additional movement. Many dogs are car sick on the first few journeys, so do not worry too much.

Keeping your dog still when in the car is also vital for safety reasons. If the dog is free to move around the car it may interfere with your driving. The dog itself will be safer, too, if it is properly restrained. It will not be thrown forward if you brake sharply, nor will it be able to escape from the car when the door is opened and risk running into heavy traffic.

Using a crate is ideal, particularly if your dog has been accustomed to using one in the home. Alternatively, you can place your dog behind a dog guard that separates the back of the car from the passenger seats. If your dog has to travel on a car seat, use a special dog seatbelt – a harness that clips into the seatbelt holder.

A WORD OF
WARNING

◆

Dogs should never be left in a car on a hot day and should never, ever be placed in the trunk of a sedan. Dogs quickly overheat and can die of heatstroke in a matter of minutes. Do not take the risk.

Some dogs bark continually in the car. This is usually because they have learned to associate the journey with a walk in the park or a visit with friends, and so become overexcited. If your dog is noisy while in the car, vary your journeys as much as possible, even when traveling back home, thus ensuring that the journey does not always end as he expects.

Above: When traveling with your dog, you should stop to allow it to exercise, relieve itself and have something to drink (the last is especially important in hot weather).

Below: Special seatbelts are now available to help keep your dog safe in the event of an accident or a sudden stop.

AIR TRAVEL

Rules and regulations for traveling abroad with a dog vary from country to country. Some rabies-free countries such as Great Britain, Australia and Japan have strict quarantine regulations governing the importation of pets. Other countries will require a "pet passport", declaring all necessary vaccinations, and identification by microchip or tattoo. Always check the regulations before departing with your pets to foreign countries: it may be that taking them with you is no problem, but bringing them back again can be fraught with difficulties.

BY TRAIN AND BUS

Your puppy needs to become familiar with bus and train travel at an early age. If it is introduced later in life, it may have trouble coping with the movement and sounds.

Always obey local regulations concerning dog control, and keep your dog on a lead at all times. It is also important to be considerate to others when traveling on public transport. You may be required to transport your dog in a carrier; also, there may be a fee to have him ride with you.

LEAVING YOUR PET BEHIND

If you have decided to go on holiday without your pet, you must ensure its well-being while you are away. Rescue shelters are always full during the summer months, when irresponsible

dog owners turn their pets out of doors to fend for themselves or pass them on to the kennels to avoid paying boarding-kennel fees.

A good boarding kennel is worth its weight in gold. Personal recommendation is usually the best way to find a reliable one – you could ask a friend, your vet or trainer – but always take the time to inspect the boarding kennel yourself. Many dogs do not find kennel life easy, so it is a good idea to introduce your dog to

Above: A dog carrier or traveling box will ensure that your dog stays safely in its place during car journeys. Most dogs prefer the security of their own environment and regard their crate as a "portable home".

the prospect by giving it occasional short stays early in its life.

House sitters have become popular with dog owners who have more than one pet, or who prefer to leave their dog in the comfort of its own home. Ask your vet for a recommendation.

Below: In some countries dogs are allowed to travel along with their owner on buses, trams or trains.

CHOOSING A GOOD KENNEL

◆

◆ You usually get what you pay for. Kennels may be basic or luxury "dog hotels": the choice is yours.
◆ Kennels should offer a safe, warm place to sleep and an outside run for exercise and natural functions.
◆ All kennels should ask to see your dog's vaccination certificate.
◆ Ask if the dogs are walked individually and whether your dog will be fed its usual diet.
◆ The noise level should be kept to a minimum. Excessive barking indicates

that the dogs are bored or stressed and that the kennel is poorly designed.
◆ Ensure that you give the kennel a name and number to contact if there is a problem while you are away.

Problem Dogs

What is normal? ✦ *Dog defense strategies* ✦
Aggression ✦ *Consulting expert help*

Most types of behavior that we tend to regard as problems in our dogs are, in fact, absolutely normal. Barking, digging, chewing and even biting are all typical dog activities – the problem is that humans do not always appreciate their timing, intensity or context.

A dog's behavior is, therefore, only a problem if it is seen as such by its owners. If you are worried about your dog's behavior for any reason, act quickly. Ask your vet for a referral to a pet behavior counsellor and get help as soon as possible.

However, some types of behavior are so anti-social, or even dangerous, that they clearly have to be addressed at once. Understanding what motivates undesirable behavior is the first step to solving the problem.

Below: Some dogs will growl and display their teeth to warn strangers or other dogs that they feel threatened or insecure. It is usually wise to back away from such threat displays.

DEFENSE STRATEGIES

If threatened, a dog will adopt one of four main defense strategies in order to cope. These are: Flight, Fight, Freeze or Flirt. For example, a dog may try to run away, use aggression, stay perfectly still and hope that the threat goes away, or use an appeasement gesture, such as rolling on its back or picking up a toy. Which of these it chooses will depend on its breed, its previous experience and the situation itself.

These defense strategies are used throughout a dog's life. Generally, what we consider to be a behavior problem occurs when a dog uses any one of these strategies excessively. Constant aggression (too frequent use of the Fight strategy) provides the greatest cause for concern.

Stages of aggression

The average dog turns to aggression only when it feels threatened. Before actually attacking, the dog will usually go through a process of escalating threat and bluff:

Growling: A growl is a warning. In a situation where a dog feels threatened, it is likely to stand very still, even if only for a second. People do not usually recognize this first warning to back off, so the dog escalates its aggression by growling to get the message across.

Snarling: Quite clearly, this is the next stage of the warning. If the dog has failed to remove the threat by growling, it backs this up with a visual display of teeth. Generally, a fearful dog will have its ears held back and down, its lips drawn right back to

Above: All dogs bark as a form of communication, usually when feeling positive or playful. However, dogs can be taught when and where it is appropriate to bark.

show as many teeth as it can, and its tail low to the ground, or even tucked under its body. An assertive or confident dog may have its ears pricked forward, its tail up and only its front

Above and right: Dogs "play fight" with each other in order to learn social rules about aggression, and it is essential that your dog understands and abides by these rules. Dogs that display aggressive behavior towards other dogs may not have been properly socialized with others at an early age.

teeth showing, with the nose and lips wrinkled to reveal them.

Snapping: A common third stage of aggression, snapping involves a move towards the source of the threat to try to make it go away. Typically, a dog will snap, then retreat.

Biting: When all else has failed to remove the threat, a dog may bite. The damage that a dog will do in biting depends on the number of warnings given before the bite, the breed or type of dog, the circumstances in which the bite is given and whether or not it has been trained not to bite (see page 84).

AGGRESSION TOWARDS HUMANS

Aggression towards human beings is guaranteed to cause trouble. If your dog growls, snarls, snaps or bites you, or anyone else, then you clearly have cause for alarm. You must be particularly careful if the dog is likely to meet children; if so, you should consider restraining it with a muzzle or in a crate while you seek help. Quite clearly, a dog that growls at you wants

> *The small percentage of dogs that bite people is monumental proof that he is the most benign, forgiving creature on earth.*
> W. R. KOELHER, THE KOELHER METHOD OF DOG TRAINING, *1997*

you to back off for some reason. As the dog has the teeth, it is always prudent to forget your dignity and do so. Too many dog owners have been the victims of bites because they felt they had to win a confrontation. Think carefully about why the dog is behaving aggressively. Perhaps he feels threatened in some way. If your dog displays such behavior, it is best to consult your veterinarian or a canine behaviorist without delay.

AGGRESSION AND OTHER DOGS

Dog-to-dog aggression can take many forms. Some of these are perfectly normal. For example, it is quite acceptable for an adult dog to chastise or discipline a boisterous puppy for

Above: Although dogs will bite one another in play, really aggressive behavior is not acceptable. Seek professional advice if your dog shows signs of aggression.

overstepping the mark. As long as no blood is drawn, the adult dog is probably doing you a favor. The odd scuffle between male dogs to test the pecking order is also not unusual. However, serious or repeated fighting with other dogs requires expert help.

Problem dogs

BEHAVIORAL PROBLEMS

Some basic behavioral problems can be overcome by first asking yourself why the dog is displaying them, and then finding a way to ensure that any "rewards" for the behavior are removed. This is the opposite approach to punishment, which is nearly always counter-productive.

Jumping up

Why do dogs jump up? In dog terms, this is a friendly greeting. The dog is trying to get close to your face.

Prevention: Teach puppies to sit when greeting you, or to find a toy to bring at greeting. Never reward jumping up by giving attention.

Solution: Ask visitors to turn away and ignore the dog if it is jumping up. Only give attention and affection when the dog's four feet are on the ground, or it is sitting down.

Scavenging

Why do dogs scavenge? In the wild, dogs find much of their food by

Below: Scavenging is natural behavior, but can lead to health problems for the dog and may upset neighbors. Dogs that tend to scavenge should be closely supervised.

Above: Your dog will naturally want to jump up when it is excited, but it can be trained to greet you properly. If your dog jumps up, turn away, and do not give it attention.

scavenging from carcasses or the kills of other predators, and the behavior has persisted.

Prevention: Do not leave food lying around, especially when you cannot supervise your dog. Just one successful, stolen mouthful will reward it sufficiently to try again and again.

Solution: If your dog scavenges regularly, teach it to leave the item on command. To do this, follow the instructions on page 89.

Food guarding

Why do dogs guard food? Possession is the whole of dog law: if dogs have something, they have the right to defend it.

Prevention: From early on, accustom the puppy to eat when you are around, but do not take the bowl away from it. Occasionally place extras in the bowl while it is eating. This confirms that you are the giver of food – not a threat to its dinner.

Solution: The solution will depend on the level of aggression shown. If your dog growls when you are simply standing next to it, keep well away and seek expert advice. If your dog only guards its food when you go near the bowl, place the dog's empty food bowl on the floor. Then put its dinner into it one spoonful at a time, allowing it to eat each spoonful in between. You will be confirmed as the giver of food, not a threat, and it should become more tolerant.

Pulling on the lead

Why do dogs pull on the lead? It can be a demonstration of rank – top dogs lead the hunt. Alternatively, it may simply be because they are rewarded for it – getting to the park faster and being let off the lead after pulling all the way there.

Prevention: From day one, never allow your dog or puppy to put tension on the lead. If it does pull on the lead, stop moving until it stops and

Below: If your dog guards its food, it may feel threatened. To prevent this happening, offer extra bits of food when it is eating; do not remove its bowl until it has finished.

the lead becomes slack again. Reward it for doing so by moving off or offering it a treat when it is not pulling.
Solution: For confirmed pullers, time and effort are required. Are you a clear pack leader (see pages 90–1)? Using a head collar or an anti-pull harness may help to restrain it.

Over-excitability with visitors

Why do dogs become overexcited when visitors arrive? Over-excitement usually guarantees lots of attention.
Prevention: Teach your puppy to be calm and quiet when visitors arrive. Give it a special chew or toy to keep it occupied when you do not want to give it attention. Invite as many people as possible to the house in the early days to practice "meeting and greeting" behavior.
Solution: Practice calm greeting behavior with people known to your dog – even family members – at the doorway. Teach your dog to sit well back from the door by opening the door and closing it again carefully if it surges forward, and reward it when it gets to the right place.

When "real" visitors come, ask them to ignore the dog if possible and give it a really special toy or chew to distract it. It is advisable to consult a behavior specialist if your dog is defensive or aggressive, rather than simply overexcited.

WHEN TO GET HELP

◆

Training your dog to behave in an acceptable manner from an early age should prevent the development of many behavioral problems. However, even the best-trained dog can develop habits that may prove annoying or unpleasant to the most tolerant pet owner. Seek professional advice from a vet, a dog-training club or a pet behaviorist if your dog shows signs that it is not always under your control, or persists with any behavior that you find unacceptable.

Above: Pulling on the lead is a common problem. When your dog pulls, stop walking and stand still until it stops straining. Only begin walking again when the lead is slack.

Repeat this measure every time your dog pulls, and it will soon understand what is required of it. Remember to praise it when it obeys.

Your Dog's Well-being

Feeding ✦ *Exercise* ✦ *Cleanliness* ✦ *Regular checks*

Your dog's individual needs will depend largely on its breed or type, its age and general health. On the whole, dogs that are provided with a nutritious diet, daily exercise, regular health checks and sensible social interaction should live long and happy lives.

FEEDING YOUR DOG

When and what your dog eats is ultimately your choice, but you will need to assess carefully both its individual needs and the nutritional requirements of dogs in general.

The type of diet that you choose for your dog needs careful consideration (see page 110).

Most dogs appreciate being fed twice a day, rather than only once. This encourages the effective working of the digestive system and helps to balance your dog's blood sugar levels, avoiding the sudden peaks and troughs that can cause mood swings.

Avoid giving human food to dogs. Biscuits and sweets produced for people pile on the calories and add to the risk of tooth decay. In particular, chocolate made for people should be avoided, because it is toxic to dogs. Special dog biscuits, treats and chocolates specially made for dogs can be given as training rewards.

Always ensure that clean, fresh water is easily available for your dog.

EXERCISING YOUR DOG

Exercise is important to a dog's well-being. Adult dogs need to burn off excess energy to prevent weight gain. Also, if dogs are denied the level of physical and mental activity they need, their energy may be channeled into unwanted behavior. Two walks a day are usually sufficient for most adult dogs, but the length of the walk may need to be varied according to the breed and age of the dog.

Varying your routes on walks to take in different sights and sounds can increase your dog's confidence and interest. Visiting different places can make your outings as exciting for your dog as they are for you.

Below: All dogs benefit from unrestrained exercise and you should ensure that your trained puppy or dog has ample opportunity for exercise through frequent walks and runs outdoors. When your dog can be trusted to come obediently when it is called, it can be let off the lead to enjoy its freedom.

Right: Regular, varied exercise and, most importantly, play, are essential to your dog's physical and emotional well-being. Some breeds, such as these Irish Setters, love water and will plunge in at the first opportunity. Retrievers and Newfoundlands were bred to work in water and enjoy swimming regularly.

Below: Occasional baths will keep your dog's skin and coat healthy. Only use specially formulated dog shampoos and always follow the instructions supplied by the manufacturer.

Above: Dry your dog carefully after bathing, and take the opportunity to check its body carefully for any signs of ill-health or parasites.

KEEPING CLEAN

Dogs are generally clean creatures and many do a reasonable job of grooming themselves. However, some dogs may not be able to keep themselves as clean as nature intended, and they may need help. Most dogs roll around on the ground sometimes and their coats become dirty or smelly, so they often require brushing or bathing (see pages 112–17).

Dogs that are kept together will often groom each other. Regular examination and routine grooming of your dog also serves a social function.

A FULL EXAMINATION

You should be able to inspect every part of your dog's body, including eyes, ears, mouth, feet and genital area, looking for any physical changes or injuries. Teaching your dog to stand still is essential, and should be done through rewards and kindness (see pages 84–9).

✦ With your dog standing in front of you, start by looking into each eye to check for redness or inflammation.

✦ Move on to your dog's ears, gently lifting the ear flap away from the head and peering right down the ear canal to look for obstructions.

✦ Moving on to the mouth, lift the lips, first one side, then the other, to inspect both sides of the teeth for plaque. Then open your dog's mouth very gently to inspect the tongue and the back of the mouth and throat.

✦ Next, move on to the neck and shoulders. Feel every inch of your dog's skin and coat, checking for tenderness or inflammation.

✦ Move gently down each front leg. Lift the front feet in turn to check the length of the nails, then tuck its foot under to inspect the pads for cracks. Gently probe between each toe to check for foreign bodies.

✦ Move back to the shoulders and run your hands along the spine to the hips, then down the ribs.

✦ Feel down each hind leg, then lift the rear feet in turn to inspect them.

✦ Finally, stroke down your dog's body, from the head to the tip of its tail. Hold the tail up firmly but gently at the base, and inspect the anal area for signs of parasites. Then slip your other hand underneath to check the belly and, in males, the genital area.

✦ Praise and reward your dog for being calm and patient during this detailed examination.

The Healthy Dog

Signs of a healthy pet ✦ When to get help

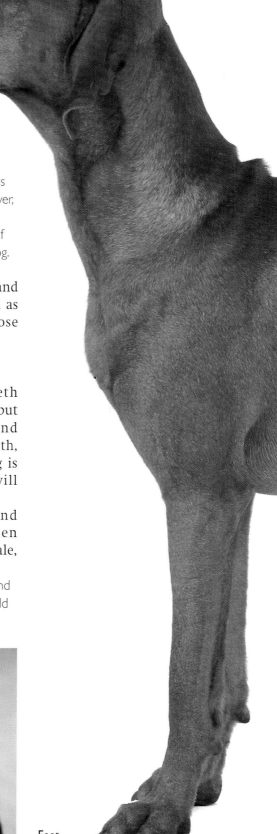

Nose

Eyes

Ears

Mouth

Feet

Whether you are thinking about buying a dog or simply want to make sure that your own dog is perfectly healthy, it is important to know the signs of good health. A healthy dog will show clear signs of vitality and well-being, while possible health problems are often indicated by warning signs: these are discussed here. Specific diseases and other health problems are discussed in detail on pages 128–31 and 134–45.

discussed in detail on pages 128–31 and 134–45.

EYES
The eyes should be clear and bright, with no discharge. Any cloudiness, permanent changes in the pupil size, or redness should be assessed promptly by a vet. Like us, dogs can suffer from conjunctivitis. This needs treatment from your vet, but is usually cured relatively easily.

Dogs have a "third eyelid" – a membrane that is sometimes partially visible across the eye. The appearance of the third eyelid usually indicates that the dog is unwell, or is recovering from an illness.

Some breeds are prone to a condition known as entropion, where the eyelashes turn inwards and irritate the eyeball. This may require surgery.

EARS
The inside of a dog's ear canal should appear as clean, pink skin. If there are any brown deposits, or if there is an odd smell, this may indicate either an infection or ear mites.

NOSE
A dog's nose should not show any kind of discharge. Traditional wisdom says the nose should be cold and wet, but this is not always the case, since

Right: It is sometimes clear when a dog is unwell. A listless attitude, dull coat and loss of appetite are clear warning signs. However, careful and regular inspection of potential trouble spots can reveal the early stages of disease in an otherwise healthy-looking dog.

the nose varies with the weather and the dog's level of activity as much as with its health. However, the nose should not be very dry or hot.

MOUTH
As with human teeth, dogs' teeth deteriorate in condition with age, but ideally they should be clean and white. Occasionally, dogs break teeth, so regular checking and cleaning is essential. Routine dental care will also help prevent gum infections.

The gums should be pink and smooth, with no bleeding. When pressed gently, they should turn pale,

Below: Your dog's teeth should be clean and white, and free of decay. The tongue should look pink and unblemished.

then flush pink again straightaway when pressure is released.

Although there is no such thing as pleasant dog breath, you should not be able to detect it from across the room. Any persistent unpleasant smell from the mouth may indicate a dental or dietary problem.

Skin and coat

A dog's skin should be pink, showing no signs of scurf or dandruff. Some parti-colored breeds or types of dog may have pigmented patches on their skin. This is perfectly normal.

The coat should be free of fleas and other parasites. Fleas can be difficult to spot – but their tell-tale dirt is not. Fleas defecate on their host's coat – leaving tiny black specs of dirt. If you are in any doubt, comb some dirt from your dog's coat on to a damp piece of white paper. The flea dirt dissolves into small red blotches, since it is chiefly made up of dried blood.

Feet

The pads on the bottom of a dog's paws are generally quite robust but, like humans, they can suffer from

blisters and cuts if they have been walking and running too much.

Many dogs have retained the "dew claw" on the inside of the front legs – and a few breeds, such as Pyrenean Mountain Dogs, have them on the hind feet too. Dew claws can be injured accidentally during exercise and may become infected as a result.

Stomach

If the stomach is distended, this may indicate gastric upset or worms, so have your dog checked by a vet.

All dogs have eight nipples in pairs on the abdomen. To the uninitiated these can look like skin tags or even ticks. If you have a bitch, it is a good idea to examine this area regularly for lumps or bumps under the skin. Mammary tumors are all too common and need to be given prompt medical attention if they occur.

Like us, dogs also have a navel, where the umbilical cord was attached. It is not uncommon for puppies to have a hernia around this site, so keep an eye on this area for any abnormality.

Anal area

In many dogs, the anal area is completely covered by the tail. This means that you need to lift the tail to examine the area, checking for dirt or soreness. If your dog rubs its bottom on the ground, or repeatedly licks this area, its anal glands may need attention or it may be trying to pass worms, so seek veterinary advice.

Genitals

Finally, your dog's genital area should be inspected regularly. Although this may seem strange to some people, it is important to detect changes here as soon as they occur. The testicles of an unneutered male dog should be fully descended – if one or both remains permanently in the body cavity, surgery may be necessary.

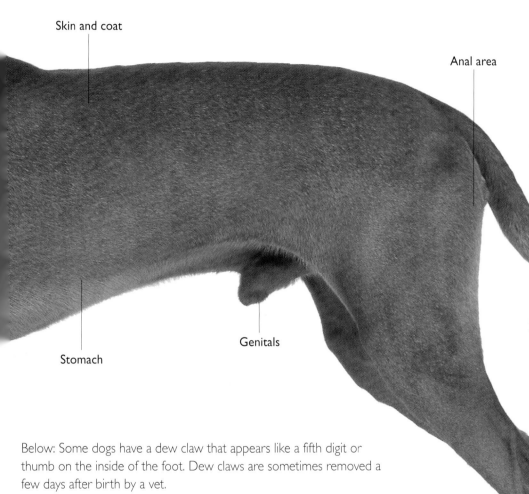

Skin and coat

Stomach

Genitals

Anal area

Below: Some dogs have a dew claw that appears like a fifth digit or thumb on the inside of the foot. Dew claws are sometimes removed a few days after birth by a vet.

Nutrition & Diet

Nutritional requirements ✦ *Types of food* ✦
What's in the food ✦ *Reading the labels*

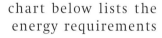

A nutritious, well-balanced diet is vital if you want to have a healthy dog. This is as important for adult dogs as for puppies, although a dog's nutritional and dietary requirements vary according to age and breed.

There are now countless brands of dog food on the market to choose from, and what you feed your dog is up to you. However, it may be useful to ask your breeder what to feed a new puppy or, if you have an older dog, to seek advice from your vet.

WHAT YOUR DOG NEEDS

Like people, dogs need good, healthy food in order to grow and maintain their body functions.

Above: If you have a fussy eater, prepare small quantities of food at frequent intervals and gently encourage your dog to eat.

Too much food, however, leads to obesity. This is a common problem; to prevent it, you need to be aware of both the nutritional content and the calorific value of the food. The chart below lists the energy requirements and ideal weights for various breeds. Use it and the dog food label to check that all the necessary nutritional components are present.

Dogs should have a varied diet that includes each of these elements: proteins, fats, carbohydrates, vitamins, minerals and fiber. In addition, it is very important for dogs to have fresh water at all times. Fluids are essential, ensuring that nutrients are carried through the body effectively and that wastes are eliminated.

A dog's nutritional requirements vary according to weight, lifestyle and age. For example, a working dog that is getting plenty of exercise will require more food than a pet dog that is more sedentary. Puppies and pregnant bitches also have special needs.

Normally, a dog's nutritional needs can be estimated using weight and age as a guide. Most dog foods come with suggested servings that are based on the dog's weight. Special cases would include: a dog with a high metabolic rate (it may seem constantly hungry and slim, although fed the recommended amount of food); a puppy (buy a food specially designed for puppies); a pregnant bitch (multiply the quantity by about one and a half); and a bitch in lacta-

IDEAL BREED WEIGHTS

WEIGHT (LB / KG)	CALORIES (KCALS) PER DAY	BREED EXAMPLE
4½ / 2	230	Papillon, Chihuahua
11 / 5	450	Toy Poodle
22 / 10	750	Corgi, small Terrier
33 / 15	1010	Beagle, Staffordshire Bull Terrier
44 / 20	1250	Basset Hound
55 / 25	1470	Collie, Samoyed
66 / 30	1675	Labrador, Airedale Terrier, Boxer
77 / 35	1875	Old English Sheepdog
88 / 40	2070	Greyhound, Irish Wolfhound

tion (multiply the normal amount by three to four).

DIFFERENT TYPES OF FOOD

There are so many different types of dog food that it is best to experiment with them to see which ones are most appropriate for your dog.

Dry foods: These are among the cheapest ways to feed your dog and take up little storage space. They are high in bulk, and may be useful if your dog has digestive ailments.

Semi-moist foods: Many owners prefer these types of food because they look "meatier" and more natural. They normally come pre-packed in individual servings and can be stored for a fairly long time. They can be quite expensive, but fussy dogs tend to prefer them. A high sugar content in some semi-moist foods may make them unsuitable for diabetic dogs.

Canned foods: There are two main types. One is a complete food (see below) with a balanced cereal component. The other is meat only, and you will need to supply roughage and carbohydrate in the form of mixture biscuits. Each brand has a different formula, and you may need to try out a few to find the one that suits your dog best. Cans can be expensive, and take up a lot of space, but they come in a variety of flavors and textures, one of which is guaranteed to suit your dog.

Below: These days it is not recommended that you give your dog meat bones. A synthetic bone is a much safer option.

Above: Every dog needs to have a diet suited to its breed, weight and age.

Biscuits: If you are feeding your dog an "all-meat" canned food, you will need to supplement the diet with biscuits to provide the necessary fiber and carbohydrates.

WHAT'S IN THE FOOD?

In recent times, emphasis has been placed on healthy eating for humans, and this trend is now being extended to pets. This increased awareness has led to claims that added dyes or preservatives may have a long-term impact on health. Even in the short term, some foods may exacerbate, or even cause, behavior problems.

Protein types and levels have also come in for criticism, and it is worth discussing diet with a nutritionist or your vet if you are worried. If your dog suffers regularly from one or more of the following, it may indicate the need to alter its diet, so try experimenting with other foods:

✦ Inconsistent digestion – sometimes constipated, sometimes loose.
✦ Flatulence.
✦ Irritations or allergic reactions to external factors such as fleas or grass.
✦ Smelly, frequent, large motions.
✦ Lack of weight despite eating well.
✦ Over-activity or under-activity.

✦ Eating soil, grass, plants or tissues.
✦ Eating own feces.
✦ Rubbing, nibbling or scratching at the feet, stomach or base of the tail.

READING THE LABELS

Some dog food manufacturers make a variety of claims that can be bewildering. Consider your dog's individual needs carefully, and talk to your vet if you are in any doubt about the food that is right for it.

Look at the label on the food. If it states that the food is complete, this means it can be fed to your dog without anything else being added. Dog food labelled as complementary means that another element, such as biscuits, a mixture or meat, needs to be added to the food in order to provide a balanced diet.

Check the ingredients list to ensure that a good, pure source of protein is listed. Chicken, poultry, egg, lamb or turkey are all excellent and easily digested sources of protein. If the food contains meat and animal derivatives or cereals, you cannot tell what is really in the food.

It is worth checking if the dog food is described as being for the average pet dog or if it is designed for working dogs. Those for working dogs – often called performance, field or premium foods – are unsuitable for a pet dog, since they provide excess energy and may induce overactivity.

Below: Biscuits can be part of your dog's diet, providing minerals and vitamins. But they can be high in calories, so do not overfeed.

Grooming

Your dog's requirements ◆ *Bathing* ◆ *Cutting and thinning hair* ◆
Anal glands ◆ *Nail clipping* ◆ *Brushing teeth* ◆ *Cleaning ears and eyes*

Although dogs are, up to a point, able to groom themselves, they often need help. Grooming maintains the condition of your dog and keeps him looking good.

Some breeds of dog have coats that require frequent brushing, stripping or clipping. The lifestyle of the average pet means that nails do not get worn down and so need clipping. Whatever your dog's needs, you will soon become used to the steps necessary to ensure that his coat and skin stays clean and healthy.

TOY DOGS

This is a varied group, with breeds ranging from those with short coats, such as the Chihuahua, to the luxurious long-coated and time-consuming Yorkshire Terrier and Maltese.

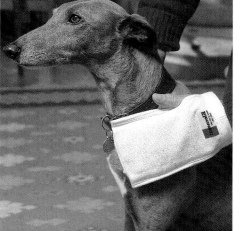

Above: A grooming glove is useful for short-haired breeds, for polishing the outer coat and removing the dead undercoat.

◆ The Yorkshire Terrier and the Bichon Frisé have become popular, which has necessitated an easy-care version of the coat, and many are clipped short to prevent tangles.
◆ The Cavalier King Charles Spaniel has a silky, medium-length coat that needs extensive brushing, but requires no trimming.
◆ The Chinese Crested Dog may be born with or without a full coat. Those with full coats are known as 'powder puffs', as they are covered in light, fine, fluffy hair. Those without hair are bald, apart from the top of the head, the tail and feet. Skin care is more appropriate than hair care.

GUNDOGS

Most gundogs require good amounts of brushing, combing and, in some cases, a little trimming.
◆ The Labrador is the most easily kept gundog in terms of coat care. However, it has a dense undercoat that falls out in handfuls during moulting, so extra grooming is required at this time.
◆ Hungarian Vizslas, Weimaraners, English Pointers and German Short-haired Pointers are short-haired and require no trimming.
◆ Most of the Retrievers, Setters and Spaniels have silky, medium-length coats and need moderate amounts of brushing, combing and raking to remove dead hair. All benefit from a little trimming to tidy the feet and, in some cases, such as the Golden Retriever, also need trimming around the neck and to shape the tail.

Left: Brushing your dog's coat will remove dirt and any dead hair that may become matted, keeping the coat clean and shiny.

HOUNDS

Hounds frequently have the most easy-care coats, requiring sensible maintenance, rather than long hours spent grooming.

✦ Breeds such as the Basset Hound, the Beagle and the Greyhound have smooth, short hair, that needs relatively little care.

✦ The more wiry-coated breeds in this group require a moderate amount of care: the Irish Wolfhound and the Deerhound, for example, both need regular brushing, but very little trimming or bathing.

✦ The Afghan Hound stands out as requiring considerable time and preparation. This breed's fine and silky hair is its trademark, and takes hours of meticulous bathing and brushing to keep it in peak condition.

TERRIERS

Most of the terriers have easily cared-for coats. They are usually harsh and wiry, designed to withstand the rigours of the countryside, and are water-resistant and dirt repellent.

✦ Some terriers require 'stripping' – the removal of dead undercoat – as they moult very little. An alternative to this is clipping, and many Westies and Scotties respond well to this grooming method.

✦ The Soft-Coated Wheaten Terrier and the Skye Terrier both have long, silky coats that need regular brushing and combing, and caring for these can be hard work.

✦ The Bull Terrier, Staffordshire Bull Terrier, Smooth Fox Terrier and Manchester Terrier stand apart as having short, smooth coats, which require the use of a soft-bristled brush or grooming glove to keep them in good condition.

UTILITY DOGS

Poodles of all sizes – Toy, Miniature and Standard – are included in the Utility group. These are probably the breeds best-known for requiring extensive clipping and trimming.

✦ Poodles need only a short clip all over to keep them in good condition, but combing is still required. They shed little hair, making them ideal for

allergy sufferers or for those worried about hairs on the furniture.

✦ Smooth-coated breeds that need minimum care are the Boston Terrier, Dalmatian, Shar Pei and Bulldog, but the latter two need attention around the face to ensure that no dirt becomes trapped in the facial folds.

Below: Grooming is a social occasion enjoyed by many dogs. Early practice will accustom young dogs to this experience.

Above: Dogs with wiry coats, such as Schnauzers and Terriers, need to have their coats 'stripped' every few months. It is best to have this done by a professional groomer, or ask one to show you how it is done.

WORKING AND HERDING DOGS

The working and herding group contains breeds with a wide diversity of coat types and grooming needs. At one end of the scale is the Great Dane, with its smooth, short coat, and at the other, the Komondor, with its long cords of hair, like dreadlocks, which hang to the floor.

✦ Many of the working breeds are sheepdogs, often used for herding purposes in farming. Border Collies, Rough Collies, Bearded Collies and Old English Sheepdogs all need quite extensive brushing and combing to keep the hair free of tangles and matts and the coat clean.

✦ All the smooth-coated dogs in this group present relatively few problems in coat care. The Dobermann, Bull Mastiff and Boxer are all good examples of low-maintenance coats, but with these breeds regular nail care is important since the shape of the foot means that the claws tend not to get worn down by routine exercise.

Grooming

BATHING YOUR DOG

How often you will need to bath your dog will depend on the breed, whether you show your dog, and the individual dog's behavior. If it rolls around in smelly substances twice a day, it will need a bath twice a day.

It is important to gather all your equipment before you start. Once the dog is soaking wet and covered in shampoo, running off to get the towels may not be such a good idea. You will need:

✦ Absorbent cotton
✦ Dog shampoo, plus a container in which to dilute it
✦ Large sponge
✦ Bath, sink or large container if in the yard
✦ Rubber mat for the bottom of the tub to prevent slipping
✦ Dog towels
✦ Brush and comb
✦ Hairdryer

You do not have to take every step in the following order, but this sequence usually give the best results:

✦ Insert a piece of absorbent cotton in the top part of your dog's ear canal to prevent water from getting into it.
✦ Lift your dog into the bath and give it a couple of minutes to become accustomed to its new surroundings. Reward it with praise and treats for calm behavior.
✦ Soak the dog all over with tepid (not hot) water. Do this either by using a shower attachment, by pouring jugs of water over the dog or by using a large sponge.
✦ Dilute the shampoo and then apply it to the dog, lathering as you go. Pay particular attention to grubby areas.
✦ Rinse well, then rinse again.
✦ Wrap your dog tightly in a towel and lift it out of the bath. Towel dry, or use a chamois cloth to remove most of the moisture.
✦ Brush and comb your dog, while using the hairdryer if appropriate, or allow it to dry naturally – but not outdoors in cold weather or the dog may catch a chill.

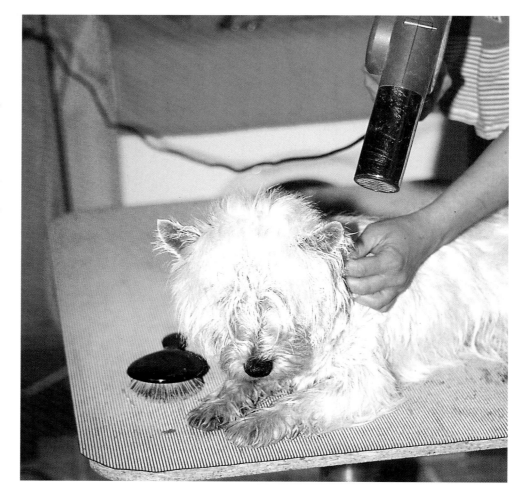

Above: In the winter, you may need to blow-dry your dog after bathing to ensure that it does not catch a chill. Introduce it to the hairdryer at a young age. Hold the dryer some distance away, and use a low setting.

CUTTING AND THINNING HAIR

Once your dog is thoroughly dry and brushed, you will be able to see the areas that need to be trimmed. Most pet dogs can be safely clipped at home, using a pair of sharp, specially designed scissors. Longer-haired breeds, or some of the utility dogs, for example, may need professional grooming on a more regular basis.

With some breeds of dog it is a good idea if the hair between the pads of their feet is clipped out to prevent dirt from lodging there. Others may need some trimming under the tail to stay fresh and clean.

Any trimming should be done with the dog calmly standing or sitting. Take off a little hair at a time. You can always trim more hair later, after you have seen the overall effect. You may wish to get advice from a groomer on your dog's individual needs.

Below: Hair around the ear is very sensitive and many owners prefer not to strip or pluck this area. If necessary, use scissors to trim hair here, but take care not to cut too close to the skin. Take your time and be gentle.

EMPTYING THE ANAL GLANDS

Some dogs need to have their anal glands (see page 139) emptied on a regular basis. Symptoms of blocked or infected anal glands are the dog dragging its rear along the ground or licking the anal area persistently.

Anal glands should empty each time the dog passes solid motions, to act as a scent marker. If your dog's glands need emptying frequently, it may be worth speaking to your vet about a diet change. If the glands are infected, antibiotics may be necessary.

To empty your dog's anal glands, follow these steps:

✦ With the dog standing, hold the tail up by lifting firmly at the base.
✦ Wearing a rubber glove and using a large wad of absorbent cotton or paper towels, place your whole hand over the dog's anal area.
✦ The anal glands lie either side of the anus at four and eight o'clock. Press firmly at this "twenty to four" angle, upwards and inwards.
✦ The contents of the anal glands will then be expelled. They are usually grey-brown in color and smell awful.

If you feel at all uncertain about performing this procedure by yourself, ask your vet for advice.

NAIL CLIPPING

Most dogs hate to have their nails clipped. The foot is a sensitive area, and many dogs feel vulnerable when their feet are handled. Unfortunately, it is actually easy to hurt a dog when clipping its nails, and one bad experience can put it off for life.

The dog's claw has a blood supply known as the quick. If this is cut it bleeds profusely, and hurts. Great care must be taken not to cut the quick, so only a tiny amount should be clipped off the nail (see page 116).

Many owners have so much trouble clipping their dog's claws that they take the dog to the vet or a groomer to have it done. This adds extra stress for most dogs and can build negative associations about both the vet and having their feet handled. If a dog becomes accustomed to its owner clipping its nails from an early age, the procedure is much less stressful.

FINDING A GOOD GROOMER

If you have a type of dog that needs professional clipping, stripping or grooming, or you are short on time to do this yourself, you may prefer to find a professional, qualified dog groomer. Some are established in large salons, while others will bring their mobile service to your home. You should look for these qualities in a groomer:

✦ The groomer must always be kind and patient with the dog.
✦ The groomer should use sedatives only in exceptional circumstances, and only under the direction of a vet.
✦ The groomer should understand your needs and the particular requirements of the breed to which your dog belongs.
✦ The grooming environment should be clean and calm. Lots of barking or noise will inevitably increase the stress levels all round.

Below: Use scissors to trim the hair between the pads of the paws in long-haired breeds, to avoid matting. Before trimming, you will need to inspect the area between the toes for any dirt or debris. This should be cleaned gently away, using pieces of damp absorbent cotton or a thin flannel washcloth. If you plan to trim your dog's nails yourself, use specially designed clippers and be very careful to avoid the sensitive quick.

Grooming

CLIPPING NAILS

◆

Take care to trim the nails without cutting the quick, or nail bed. The quick is the pink area inside the nail (below) and contains the blood supply and nerves. If you have any problems, ask your vet or dog groomer to cut the nails for you.

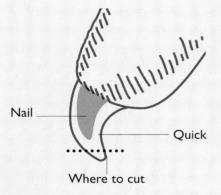

Nail

Quick

Where to cut

◆ First of all, accustom your dog to having his feet handled. Offer him a food treat and pick up each foot in turn, then give him the treat. Repeat this several times a day for three or four days.

◆ Repeat the process, but this time hold the paw firmly and extend each nail for inspection.

◆ Now get the clippers, but do not try to cut any nails. Show the dog the clippers and give him a treat. Do this several times so that he looks forward to seeing the clippers.

◆ Hold each foot in turn and extend a nail. Tap the clippers on the nail lightly, then give the dog a treat. Do not cut the nail. Do this for each nail and repeat it until your dog is confident with the procedure.

◆ You can now cut the nails. Cut about one millimeter off each nail. You can always cut more off later, but you cannot undo the pain and damage to your dog of severing the quick.

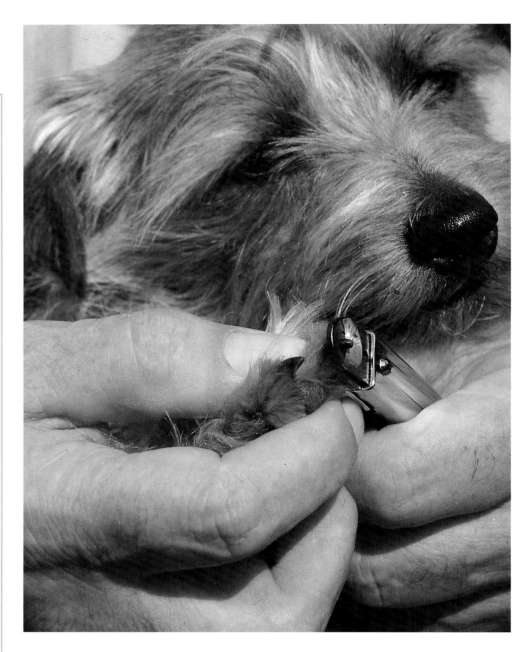

Above: Trimming your dog's nails should be included in your grooming routine. It can usually be done at home or by a professional groomer, but in either case requires great care. The best clippers to buy are those that actually clip the nail rather than crushing it.

Below: Check regularly between the toes for dirt and other embedded objects, especially grass seeds, which can cause infection.

Below: Accustom your dog to having his teeth brushed daily, and use a toothbrush and toothpaste specially designed for dogs.

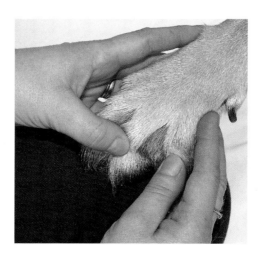

BRUSHING TEETH

Just like humans, dogs suffer from tooth decay and gum disease if their teeth are not kept clean. You should check your dog's mouth to inspect the teeth for plaque (see page 107) and you should establish a regular dental cleaning regime. Some toys, such as raggers and hard chews, may help to "floss" the surface of the teeth, but this cannot be a substitute for regular cleaning.

To clean your dog's teeth, follow these simple steps:

✦ Use a specially designed dog toothbrush and toothpaste. Do not use human toothpaste.

✦ Put a little paste on the brush and, lifting the lips one side at a time, work from front to back, sweeping the brush from the gum down the tooth, to dislodge any remaining food and to massage the gums gently.

✦ Most dogs take some time to adjust to regular toothbrushing, but special liver flavour toothpaste seems to help. Persist, and make it part of your daily routine.

CLEANING THE EYES

Some dogs' eyes weep, causing a brown stain to develop under their eyes. Ensure that you keep this area clean by gently wiping the dog's face with damp absorbent cotton, tissue, or eye wipes specially manufactured for dogs. Never touch the eye itself, and never put any drops or ointments into your dog's eyes unless they have been specially prescribed by your vet.

CLEANING THE EARS

You should also check your dog's ears regularly. Lifting the ear flap and gently manipulating it outwards and upwards should allow you to see right into the ear canal to check for any brown wax or infection. Using a damp tissue, absorbent cotton or a special ear wipe, gently remove any dirt on the ear flap or outer parts.

Never push anything into your dog's ear, such as cotton swabs, since these can damage the ear drum. Deeper wax or dirt may indicate that medical treatment is necessary, so ask your vet for advice.

Above: Try to keep the hair in the anal region short to avoid matting. Always use round-ended scissors for safety. You may also need to clip the hair around your dog's genital area to ensure that this area stays clean and free of infection.

Below: Always clean from the inside corner of the eye outwards, with moist, absorbent cotton, using a separate swab for each eye.

Below: Check the ears for hair plugs and remove excess wax with a cleaning solution and a piece of absorbent cotton.

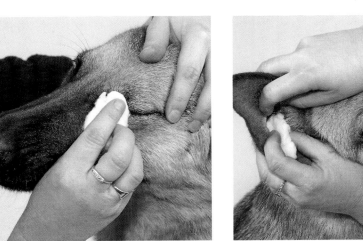

Essential Equipment

What you'll need ♦ *Little luxuries*

Detangling comb

Pin-brush

Wide-tooth comb

There are many products now available for dogs – many of which are expensive and are largely unnecessary. The following equipment can be considered essential for the average dog.

BRUSH

Brushes may be made of traditional bristle, pins or even rubber. Rakes are useful for long-coated breeds with a thick undercoat, such as Golden Retrievers, particularly when they are shedding. Some very thin-skinned and fine-coated breeds, such as Dobermans, may benefit from a grooming glove to shine the coat.

A good rule of thumb in choosing a brush for your dog, particularly for a puppy, is to try it out on your own head first. Many owners who wonder why their dog does not like being groomed are quite surprised to find out just how uncomfortable it can be to have a pin-brush dragged through their own hair.

COMB

Metal combs are probably the most popular, and come in fine-tooth or wide-tooth versions, some of which have rotating teeth.

NAIL CLIPPERS

Nail clippers with guillotine or scissor action are available. You should always use a pair with a safety guard to ensure that you cannot clip too much off the nail by accident.

SCISSORS

The type of scissors you need will depend on the breed or type of dog you own. Straight, curved and thinning scissors are available for different aspects of grooming.

SHAMPOO

There is a large range of dog shampoos to choose from, including flea shampoo and herbal shampoo; dog-coat conditioners are also available. Do not use human products when

bathing your dog, as their pH balance is unsuitable for a dog's skin and coat.

COTTON BALLS OR TISSUES

These are useful for cleaning around the eyes, ears, face and the anal area. Always use a clean tissue or absorbent cotton for each body part so as to prevent the spread of infection.

TOOTHBRUSH

Special dog toothbrushes, which are very soft and are angled for access to the back teeth, are available. "Finger brushes" slide on to the tip of your finger, allowing you to reach more easily around the gums.

TOOTHPASTE

It is essential to use a special dog toothpaste. Most dogs hate the taste of human toothpaste, which has ingredients that may disagree with them. Dog toothpastes come in a range of flavours – natural, chicken, and even liver flavour.

Nail clippers

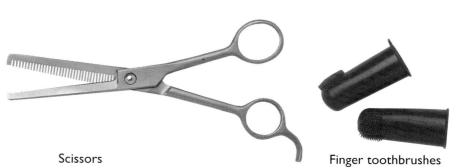

Scissors

Finger toothbrushes

selection of old children's toys, balls or socks tied in knots. Manufactured toys can be fun, but ensure that they are of good quality. Squeaky toys are hugely enjoyable for many dogs but must be sturdily made. Toys that are interactive (for instance, dispensing food during play) keep your dog's mind and body active.

Above: Dog bowls come in a variety of shapes, colors and sizes, from the severely practical to the fashionably patterned.

Below: There is also a variety of collars available to make your dog look really smart.

BEDS

Beds come in a vast array of sizes, designs and price ranges. Bean bags, plastic beds, comforters and even hammocks are available to ensure cozy canine slumber. A warm blanket, however, is probably just as acceptable to many dogs (see page 96).

Above: An activity ball can be filled with tasty treats that fall out when your dog plays.

Left: Dogs of all ages like soft toys.

FOOD AND WATER BOWLS

All dogs need their own food and water bowls. Ceramic, stainless steel and plastic are all practical and easily cleaned.

COLLAR AND NAME TAG

Collars should be lightweight and comfortable, and be made of either leather or nylon webbing. Chain or half-chain collars can become snagged when the dog is running free, so flat-buckle collars are usually best. Attached to the collar should be an identification disc. In most countries it is illegal for a dog not to have some form of owner identification. More permanent means of identification, such as tattooing or microchipping – where a tiny microchip is inserted under the dog's skin – are becoming more popular, and are compulsory in some countries (see page 129).

TOYS

Dogs need toys and objects to play with. Most dogs will be happy with a

CARING FOR DOGS
Essential Equipment

119

LAP OF LUXURY

♦

If you really want to make your pet look and feel special, there are lots of wonderful items to tempt you.

♦ Collars and leads now come in fashionable designs and colors – one for every day of the week.

♦ Flashing collars are also available – you will never lose your dog in the dark again.

♦ Pack up your dog's dinner in a doggie lunch box. A traveling kit, which has a space for both food and water, keeps your pet's essentials cool and fresh.

♦ Hats, clothes and even dog underwear are available. While some of these can be rather frivolous, 'sani-underwear' protects furniture and carpets when a bitch is in season.

They are practical, if not very dignified.

♦ Dog doors, which are essentially larger cat doors, allow dogs to leave and enter the house when they please.

Dogs & Play

Controlled play ✦ Dogs and toys ✦ Fetching and retrieving toys

The adage "those that play together stay together" could have been coined specially for dogs and their owners. Play is at the heart of a good relationship with your dog, and helps to increase understanding, respect and control.

However, it is amazing how few owners ever teach their dogs to play with them properly – having fun, but keeping the dog under control. Some owners think that playing with their dog means getting on the floor for a rough and tumble. This may be enjoyable, but it has little real value.

Dogs use play as a practice for real life. Rolling around on the floor with your dog may be fun when you do it, but it encourages the dog to pounce on humans who are lying down. Think what might happen if your dog sees a toddler fall over in the park. Never encourage any behavior in play that could be misinterpreted in a different context or when you are not there to take control of your dog.

TOYS AND PROBLEMS

Using toys in play is an ideal way to have fun while keeping control of your dog. However, some owners do not find playing with toys easy, usually for one of two very different reasons. Either the dog is not interested in toys and will not play with them at all, or it is obsessed with toys and refuses to bring them back.

Ignoring toys may be breed specific, or it may be a learned behavior. Chihuahuas, for example, seem to lack the instinct to pick objects up and retrieve them. Even a Labrador

Left: Taking time to play with your dog can be rewarding for both of you and can help build a good relationship. Dogs learn through play as much as they do through training.

can be put off playing with toys if the dog has learned to associate them with pain or reprimands.

Being obsessed with toys is much more common. This can occur if the dog discovers that toys are a useful tool in winning a power game. Running after a toy and pouncing on it is fun, but not bringing it back to the owner when called is even better.

Although you may be tempted to accept such behavior, training can improve your relationship with the dog. It is worth persevering so that you and your dog can enjoy hours of healthy play with different toys.

ENCOURAGING PLAY

It is relatively simple to teach your dog to play with toys.
✦ Choose a toy that is dog-friendly, like a soft toy or an old sock.
✦ Place the toy on the floor, or wiggle it around, in front of the dog. Most dogs will go to sniff it straight away.
✦ Click, if you are using a clicker (shown above, and see page 86), or make your approval sound as soon as the dog touches the toy. Give a treat.
✦ Repeat this process until your dog touches the toy with its mouth to get the "signal of reward" and a treat.
✦ Now wait. When your dog discovers that the touching no longer gets the signal and treat, it will probably try something else, such as picking up the toy. Be patient. As soon as the dog picks the toy up, signal and treat.

RETRIEVING

If your dog thinks that chasing a toy and picking it up is fun, but would rather keep it to itself than bring it back, you may need to use the two-toy magic trick. Find a toy that your dog likes and wants to play with, and buy two of them.
✦ Take your two identical toys into the yard, or even the living room. Throw one and allow the dog to play with it for a couple of minutes. Then call it back. If it does not return with the toy, start throwing the other toy up in the air while making lots of noise, but ignoring the dog.
✦ Most dogs will come to see what the fuss is about and drop their toy along the way. As soon as it reaches you, give your signal, "Yes" or click, then throw your toy for it. Pick up the other one, and repeat the procedure. This way, you are always in possession of one of the toys.
✦ Gradually ask more of your dog before you use your signal of reward and throw the second toy. For example, insist that the dog has to bring the first toy right up to you and drop it, or right up to you holding it in its mouth, before you take it and throw the other one.

Before long, your dog will happily retrieve toys, and let go of them.

Above: Many dogs enjoy swimming and it is a good form of exercise. Try to introduce as many forms as play as possible to vary your dog's routine.

Below: Choose imaginative games that allow your dog to let off steam, and also those that exercise its whole body.

Dogs & Exercise

Why dogs need exercise ✦ *On or off the lead* ✦ *Exercise requirements*

Exercise is a fundamental need for all dogs. Although the amount required varies according to breed, age and fitness level, all dogs need to stretch their bodies and minds in the open air in order to achieve optimum health and well-being. Exercise also provides them with the opportunity to play and have fun, which is important for a happy, healthy dog.

PATTERNS OF BEHAVIOR

Dogs in the wild sleep a great deal. However, on waking, most of their energy goes into finding food, hunting it down and eating it. This means that dogs tend to sleep and generally lie around until they are roused to action, when their energy reserves are taxed to the full, by running, jumping, wrestling and playing.

This pattern of behavior suits our human lifestyle and is probably one of the reasons that dogs have remained our close companions. It is convenient to establish a routine of calm, quiet behavior, broken up by spurts of exercise and activity. If you want to get your dog into this sort of predictable routine, establish it from the start. Decide when you are going to give him exercise and when he needs to be calm and quiet. Do not become a slave to your dog's demands, but do recognize that he must have exercise in order to behave well at other times.

WALKING ON OR OFF THE LEAD

Whether you can walk your dog on- or off-lead will depend on a number of factors. The first of these is the area in

Right: Natural retrievers will enjoy a simulated hunt in the woods and, when carefully trained, will normally be willing to fetch anything you request.

which you live. There are restrictions on allowing dogs off-lead in many suburban parks, so check before you unclip. Even if the area allows dogs to be free, check that it is safe and suitable. Is there traffic close by? Are dog waste bins provided? Are children playing nearby? Even if your dog is well trained and friendly, it is polite to keep it on a lead near children's play areas, or where people are riding. Your dog may be obedient and predictable; children or horses may not.

Never risk letting your dog off-lead in an area where livestock are present. A farmer has the right to shoot a dog that is off-lead and causing a nuisance to sheep or cattle.

Whether or not you can let your dog off-lead will depend both on his behavior and on your commitment to training it. If your dog is unsociable towards other dogs or people, do not risk allowing it off-lead until you have sought advice from an expert in animal behavior.

Right: Running with your dog is ideal exercise for both of you, but check that the environment around you is safe and, if you are running in a park, that it is permitted for your dog to be off the lead.

Below: Your dog will enjoy the companionship of other dogs off the lead if it has been well socialized and trained. If your dog is at all aggressive, guidance should be sought and it should be kept on the lead for safety until you feel confident that it can socialize properly.

HOW MUCH EXERCISE?

◆

Just how much exercise a dog needs varies from individual to individual and from breed to breed. It also depends on the age of your dog. Damage can be done to the joints and bone structure, particularly in the case of the large or heavy breeds, through too rigorous exercise when young. A general rule of thumb is that little and often is better for a puppy than a long gruelling hike.

If your puppy starts to look tired, is flagging, or does not want to continue walking, you have definitely done too much. Remember, walking is as much about habituation and socialization at this stage as it is about exercise. This can also apply to an adult re-homed dog that has had little previous exercise. Just like us, dogs need to build fitness levels gradually to avoid straining muscles or harming joints.

Over the age of nine months, all breeds, apart from the largest, can cope with almost any amount of exercise, whether on a hard surface or on grass. However, dogs should not be made to jump until they are over a year old. Any practice for agility competition until this time needs to concentrate on control and confidence rather than on jumping.

Dogs love to run, jump and play games as part of their exercise routine. Interacting with us is more fun than simply walking.

Toys & Games

Walks ◆ Games for the park ◆ Cleaning up

Left: Tug-of-war is an ideal park game, but it is important that you teach your dog to give up the toy willingly when asked.

For most dogs, going for a walk is like an exciting hunt. Sights, sounds and smells stimulate their senses, and they will throw themselves into investigating the environment, hunting for prey, engaging in social encounters or just letting off steam. For many pet dogs their walks are the highlight of the day. Once out of the home, they are not going to let anything stop them enjoying themselves – not even their owners.

Indeed, one of the most common complaints of owners is that their normally quiet and obedient dog becomes impossible to control out of doors. As soon as they are outside, the dog's nose goes down, the brain disengages and it becomes selectively deaf. The answer to this is to make yourself more interesting than squirrels, other dogs and the

wonderful smells in the long grass. This may seem a tall order, but playing games and interacting with your dog when out and about will improve and strengthen your relationship and control enormously.

PARK GAMES

Several toys make ideal accessories for games with your dog in the park.

A ball on a rope is a great toy to for the park, for teaching good retrieves and even for hunting games. The rope attachment means that there is always a part of the toy that you can hold. Some people find that a ball on a rope is easier to throw accurately than an ordinary ball. It can provide hours of fun if you keep it as the dog's "outside only" toy. The novelty value of the toy is retained by never allowing the dog to have it at any other time. Make certain that the ball is large enough not to be swallowed.

It is essential to carry a tasty tidbit with you when you go on a walk with your dog. You never know when you might want to reward a good piece of behavior – such as a super-fast recall or a down stay. In the early stages of recall training, it is essential that you call your dog back to you often, and reward it randomly – sometimes with a food treat, sometimes with a game and sometimes by praise alone. This way your dog will never quite know which reward, if any, it will get. This keeps its motivation to return as high as possible.

Dogs use their noses to sniff the ground and "read" vital information in the scent they find. As humans, we can only guess at the vast amount of information that dogs can pick up from scent. Odors left by other dogs in urine and feces may indicate the dog's sex, hormonal status, and even its

Above: A rubber ball that is large enough to prevent choking is an ideal toy for a growing puppy and will allow it to chew safely. Teach your dog to fetch a toy and bring it back. Most dogs love games and the interaction with their owners that they offer.

health, while scent from other animals may indicate how long ago they were there and what kind of animal it was.

Your dog's natural ability to use its nose can be channeled on walks, and makes you a part of the hunting team, not just a follower. Taking a toy that your dog likes and dropping it in the grass is a good starting point. Send your dog back to find it, giving lots of encouragement and showing excitement when it finds it.

Once mastered, this game can be increased to incorporate basic tracking – where the object may be hidden some time earlier somewhere along the route to be walked. Watching a dog follow an unseen track is a very satisfying sight; even an untrained dog still on its lead can show re- m a r k a b l e tracking ability.

SCOOP THE POOP

◆

There is one piece of equipment that no dog owner should be without when out and about: a poop scoop. It is essential that dog owners clean up after their pets, whether they use a basic plastic bag (without holes in it!), or a commercially made scoop designed for the purpose. Although dogs that are properly wormed and cared for represent very little risk to public health, there is no excuse for leaving dog feces anywhere. It is unpleasant, and may encourage demands that more parks and public areas be made dog-free. Clean up after your dog!

PART 3

YOUR DOG'S HEALTH

Your vet should be your main source of advice on the health of your dog from puppyhood to old age. Ask around to find a practice in your area that has a good reputation among dog owners. Consider the following factors:

◆ Expertise – check for experienced, well-trained staff committed to ongoing professional training.

◆ Staff – look for caring veterinary and lay staff, who will take the time to explain matters to you.

◆ Premises – these should be well equipped and maintained, with a full range of diagnostic, nursing and surgical facilities.

◆ Cost – look for a practice that provides good value for money, but not necessarily the cheapest. Always ask about the cost of any necessary procedures in advance.

◆ Emergency care – find out about the out-of-hours service that the practice provides. If possible, choose one that you can reach fairly easily in an emergency.

Preventative Healthcare

Preventing disease ✦ *Vaccinations* ✦ *Parasites* ✦ *Dental care* ✦
Permanent identification

Most major illnesses can be avoided by implementing a program of preventative healthcare. This involves regular visits to your veterinarian, at-home health checks, vaccinations, a healthy diet (see pages 110–11) and exercise to suit the individual needs of your dog (see pages 122–3).

If you are the owner of a very young puppy, you will want to protect it from picking up infections from other dogs. However, it is important that a puppy meets a number of other dogs at a young age so that problems of inadequate socialization do not develop later in life. The period from 6 to 12 weeks of age is critical for the socialization process. Introduce your puppy to as wide a range of people and healthy dogs as possible. Your vet will be able to advise you on the level of disease risk in your area.

Your puppy or dog should be kept apart from other dogs if it is unlucky enough to become ill, at least until you have identified the problem.

PUPPY VACCINATIONS

The exact timing of the vaccination course will depend upon the disease risks in your particular area and the precise vaccinations used. Normally, it will involve one injection given at between 8 and 10 weeks of age and a second at 12 weeks, although the puppy will not be fully protected by the vaccine until at least a week after the second injection.

Most vets prefer puppies to settle into their new home before starting the vaccination course. However, you should be able to arrange for a veterinary check-over immediately after the puppy is purchased. A vaccination

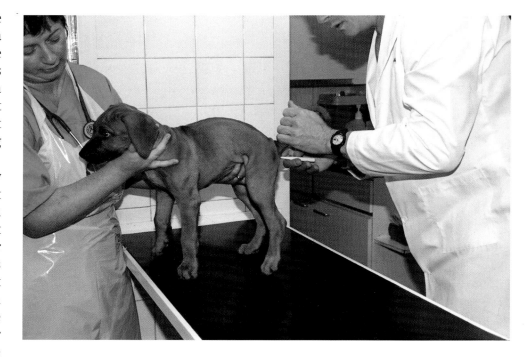

Above: Your dog's temperature may be taken with a rectal thermometer, which should be lightly oiled and then gently inserted into the

anus while the dog is restrained. Most dogs will not object to this procedure, which is painless and usually fairly quick.

Below: Your dog's gums and teeth will be examined for signs of decay or disease, and the teeth may be counted.

Below: The vet will check all parts of your dog carefully for signs of ill-health, in much the same way that you do at home.

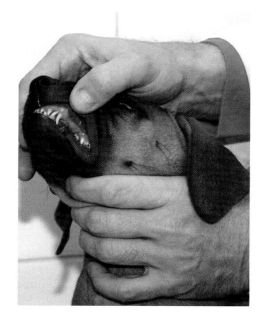

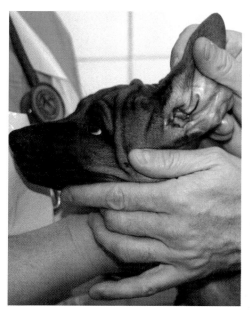

appointment gives the vet a chance to ensure that the puppy is healthy and developing well. It also gives you the chance to ask about puppy care.

DISEASES MOST COMMONLY PREVENTED BY VACCINATION

The following diseases can quite easily be prevented by vaccination.

Distemper: A viral disease that used to be a major killer of dogs, but which is now much less common owing to vaccination. Dogs become ill, with coughing, nasal discharge, diarrhea and sometimes fits. The condition is usually fatal in unvaccinated dogs.

Parvovirus: First appearing in dogs in the late 1970s, when epidemics killed large numbers with severe gastro-enteritis, this disease has now been brought under control by vaccination.

Infectious hepatitis: This is caused by a virus that attacks the lining of the blood cells, especially in the liver.

Leptospirosis: There are two forms of this bacterium: *Leptospira ictero-haemorrhagiae*, which attacks the liver and causes jaundice, and *Leptospira canicola*, which causes kidney problems. Most vaccines provide protection against both forms. Both forms of the bacterium are found in the urine, and can be passed from dog to dog or contracted from rodents' urine. They are both potentially transmissible to

Below: The chest, ribs and abdomen will be examined for signs of distention, obesity, or other problems.

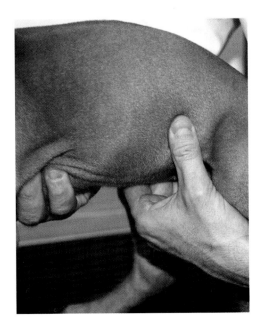

PERMANENT IDENTIFICATION

◆

Once your puppy starts to go outdoors, it is important to ensure that it is properly identified. A collar and tag is compulsory in many areas, but permanent identification can be provided in the form of a tattoo or a tiny injectable microchip, both of which are painless procedures. These give the dog a unique number that can be read with an electronic scanner held at many veterinary hospitals and animal welfare centers.

humans, so regular booster vaccinations are important for both canine and human health.

Rabies: Affecting the central nervous system, the rabies virus is spread by the bite of an infected animal and can be passed on to humans. Symptoms appear anywhere from ten days to six months after infection. Dogs drool from the mouth and their behavior dramatically changes. Some animals become demented and violent, while others seem withdrawn. Death inevitably follows once the infection develops – usually within five to seven days. In the US, rabies vaccination is required. Follow the vaccination proocol specified by your local or state authorities, available through your state health department.

Kennel cough: Far less serious than the other diseases listed, this is a very common, highly contagious disease that causes a dry cough. Although it is called kennel cough, it is actually a number of different diseases with similar symptoms. Most annual booster injections protect against its major viral causes. Other vaccines or nose drops give adequate protection against *Bordetella bronchiseptica*, the most significant bacterial cause.

PARASITE CONTROL

Roundworms are very common in puppies, so it is important that they are wormed regularly from an early age. The exact procedure will depend upon the product used, and you should seek a vet's advice about the most suitable wormer for your dog. Modern veterinary preparations are effective, safe and easy to use.

Fleas are also very common. It is far preferable to take precautions to pre-

vent an infestation, than to wait until a problem develops. Flea control is dealt with in detail on pages 97 and 138. There are several flea preparations that are safe to use on puppies, but always check the directions first.

DENTAL DISEASE

Although dental disease due to the accumulation of mineral deposits on the teeth is not likely to occur until later on in life, it is sensible to get young dogs used to regular tooth brushing. Your vet can show you how to do this, and will also check your puppy's mouth to ensure the teeth are developing properly. Puppies lose their milk teeth at around five months, but sometimes the new tooth grows without the milk tooth being shed. Damage may be caused to the permanent tooth if the temporary one is not removed.

Below: Eyes should be checked regularly for any redness, discharge, sign of pain or sensitivity to light, which may indicate disease.

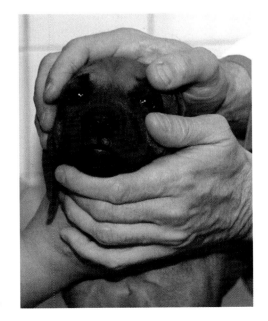

Hereditary Diseases

Common problems ✦ Pedigree puppies ✦ Testing for hereditary diseases

Unless you are planning to breed your dog, you do not need to know a great deal about canine genetics. It is wise, however, to be aware of the types of problem that can occur in your breed, how they are manifested and the possible steps that can be taken to prevent them.

Pedigree dogs are intentionally inbred in order to develop appearance and characteristics thought to be desirable in that breed. There is, however, a risk that this will increase the incidence of unwanted diseases.

Most inherited diseases are carried by recessive genes, which means that both parents have to be carrying the gene for the problem to appear in the offspring. A dog may appear perfectly normal, yet be carrying the gene for a serious disease.

Above: All puppies should be checked from head to tail for health problems. Hereditary disorders may be known to you before you buy your puppy, and certain breeds are prone to certain conditions. Your vet will be able to advise you about special needs after a full examination has been carried out.

Below: Clouding of the eyes or cataracts may occur in younger dogs either as an hereditary condition or due to health problems in the mother during pregnancy.

PEDIGREE PUPPIES

Before choosing your dog, investigate any hereditary disorders common to the breed of dog. Either find a good, reliable book on the subject or speak to your vet. You can then be aware of any potential problems and question the breeder accordingly.

You should also obtain agreement from the breeder that you may return the puppy if any significant health problems become apparent during a veterinary examination. Although some diseases occur only later in life, there are others that can be clearly detected in puppies.

WHEN ARE HEREDITARY DISEASES A PROBLEM?

Some hereditary problems are relatively minor and are only significant if you wish to breed from your dog (only completely healthy animals should be used for breeding stock). These problems include small umbilical hernias and minor misalignments in the teeth. Undescended testicles are another example, but are more serious in that they can cause problems later in life if they are not corrected surgically when the dog is young.

Some diseases are presumed to be hereditary because they tend to be found only in specific breeds, or in specific lines within those breeds. However, it is not always clear exactly how these are inherited. For example, the tendency to develop allergic skin problems, certain types of tumor and some forms of epilepsy appear to follow certain bloodlines, but also occur outside them. Some problems cannot be detected early on in life, so it is only the knowledge and integrity of the breeder that prevents breeding from lines in which these conditions are known to exist.

CONTROL AND TESTING

Special control programs have recently been developed in an effort to help breeders detect and eliminate certain hereditary problems.

The first is for eye diseases, such as cataracts (cloudiness of the lens) and progressive retinal atrophy (see page 134), which is a common cause of blindness in some breeds. This involves an eye examination of the parents by a recognized eye specialist and the issue of a certificate stating that the animal was free from any signs of these conditions at the time at which it was examined.

It is standard procedure in the US to screen dogs, especially breed dogs, for hip dysplasia (see page 140). Almost every type of dog can be affected by hip dysplasia, but it is particularly common in larger breeds. Heredity plays a major role in the development of this deformity.

Control tests involve x-raying the hips of the parents before they are used for breeding, and giving their hips a negative score. Only dogs that have good hips, with scores below average for their breeds, should be used for breeding. A similar testing program is coming into operation for elbow dysplasia, which can cause forelimb lameness (see page 140).

Molecular biology is one of the most rapidly expanding areas of scientific research today. Blood tests have been developed that enable the DNA of animals to be analysed to see if they are carrying defective genes. This could benefit future generations of dogs by taking those that possess defective genes out of the breeding population and eradicating these genes altogether. One day it may even be possible to modify genes artifically to prevent hereditary diseases.

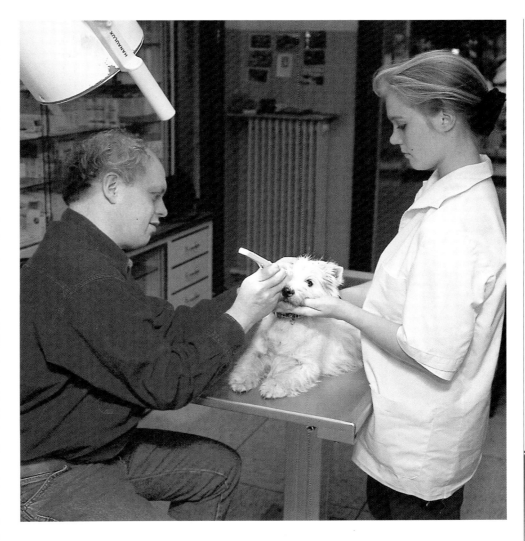

Above: It is important to check for signs of eye disease early so that treatment can be given. Many eye conditions are obvious, but diseases such as progressive retinal atrophy take place within the eye and are not apparent until they are well developed.

Below: Hips will be x-rayed by vets if they suspect hip dysplasia, or other joint, bone or muscle disorders. This healthy hip shows no signs of malformation.

Below: Hip dysplasia occurs when the hip joint is malformed, causing the ball and socket to fit together badly. The problem is most common among large breeds.

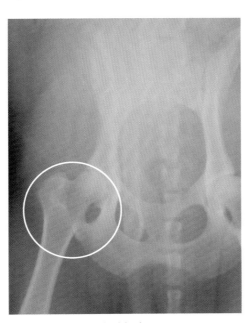

Healthy hip

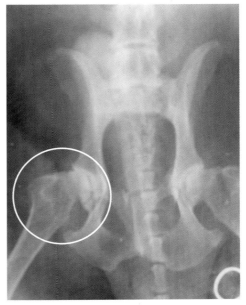

Hip dysplasia

Neutering

When to consider neutering ✦ *Spaying bitches* ✦ *Castrating males*

Dogs are fertile creatures, with a healthy bitch able to produce several litters of perhaps half a dozen puppies each in the course of her lifetime. Since there is not an endless supply of good homes for puppies, it is sensible to restrict the numbers of breeding animals through neutering. Neutering also has more direct advantages for both dog and owner, and it can ease some behavioral problems and diseases.

REASONS FOR SPAYING A BITCH

The neutering of bitches is called spaying, and normally involves the removal of the uterus and both ovaries. Bitches are usually spayed at either five months of age or three months after a season. Bitches that have had pups can be spayed as soon as their milk dries up. Despite the fact that it is a major abdominal operation, the risks of spaying are slight and recovery usually rapid.

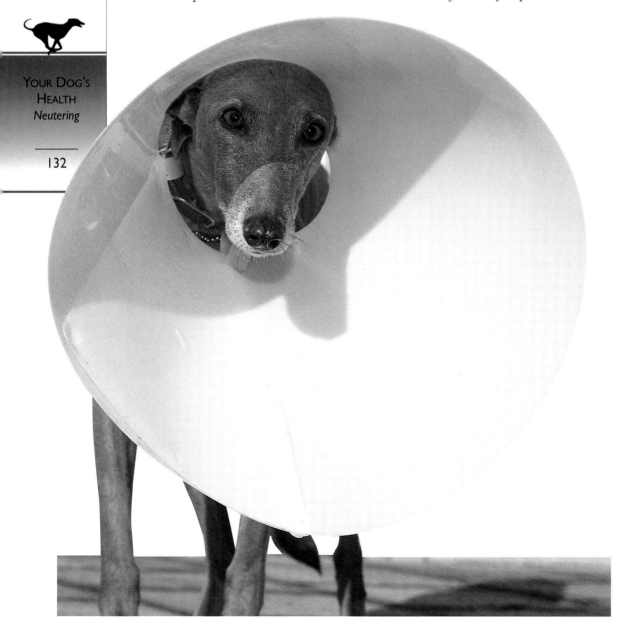

There are several reasons for neutering a bitch if she is not going to breed:

✦ As bitches age, they become prone to uterine infections, particularly if they have not had puppies. They then have to undergo major surgery to remove the infected organ. This can carry a considerable risk, which is more pronounced in older bitches.

✦ Many bitches develop problems with false pregnancies, and spaying prevents these from occurring.

✦ Owners will not find themselves besieged by local male dogs when their pet is on heat, nor will they risk being landed with unwanted puppies.

✦ Spaying is the most effective way of controlling the bitch's seasons. Most of the drugs that are available to do this also increase the risk of uterine infections developing in later life.

✦ Accidental mis-mating may have serious consequences in older bitches.

✦ The risk of mammary cancer is considerably reduced if the bitch is spayed early in life. The possible side-effects of the operation are few. However, some of the following may be expected:

✦ Changes in behavior after spaying may occur, but are very rarely adverse and may even be desirable.

✦ Some spayed bitches have a problem with incontinence as they get older, owing to a weakness of the bladder sphincter muscle, but this incontinence is rare and responds well to drug treatment.

✦ There may be a tendency for your dog to eat more and put on weight

Left: Following an operation, your dog may be provided with an Elizabethan collar, which will help to ensure that he or she does not bite or lick the site of the incision. When it is necessary, the collar will normally be worn until the wound is well healed.

Far left: Neutering can help to prevent or treat excessively aggressive behavior in male dogs, and may also help to prevent roaming.

Left: Castration usually reduces mounting and territorial marking with urine, but there are other benefits as well, even for the dog.

after spaying, but providing that her weight is closely monitored and her diet adjusted, she will not get fat.

CASTRATING MALE DOGS

Behavioral problems in male dogs may be eased by surgical castration. It is sometimes useful to give drugs that have a similar temporary effect first to gauge the effect of surgery, but your vet will advise you. There are many reasons for castrating a dog.

✦ Uncastrated male dogs are often driven to escape and follow the scent of any bitches in season.

✦ Males that are not castrated are more likely to be aggressive and to try to establish themselves as the dominant leader of the family group.

✦ Male dogs that selectively attack other male dogs often become less aggressive once they are neutered.

✦ Many male dogs will mount people's legs, stuffed toys or soft furnishings. This is usually cured, or at least improved, by castration.

✦ Male dogs normally cock their legs and mark their territory with urine, but the frequency of this behavior should be reduced by castration.

✦ Castrated dogs do not suffer from testicular tumors, prostatic disease and certain types of growth that depend upon male hormones for their development.

Possible side effects of castration are similar to those for spaying, such as the dog putting on weight, but these rarely develop into major problems. Although some veterinary surgeons recommend that male dogs are neutered only if they start to develop undesirable behavioral traits, others believe that male puppies should be neutered as a matter of course to prevent possible problems developing.

SURGICAL AFTERCARE

◆

You should be given instructions by your vet for the care of your dog after any surgical procedure, preferably on a written information sheet. Don't hesitate to telephone the clinic when you get home if you find there is something you have not understood.

GENERAL TIPS

✦ Give any prescribed medications as directed, and contact the clinic if you are unable to administer them, or if the dog seems to have any negative reaction to them, such as vomiting.

✦ Do not give food until your dog is fully awake, and then give an easily digestible meal, such as white meat with rice, or as directed by your vet.

✦ Check any dressings or casts regularly to ensure that they are not too tight or causing discomfort. Dressings will probably need to be removed after a few days, or changed regularly. Watch out for any unusual smell or discharge.

✦ If the wound is visible, it may well look slightly inflamed and, at first, may ooze a little blood. Contact your veterinary surgeon if it becomes increasingly reddened, swollen and hot, or if there is any significant amount of discharge or blood.

✦ It is sometimes necessary to fit the dog with an Elizabethan collar around its neck. This prevents the dog from interfering with the wound.

✦ Depending upon the type of operation, your dog may well be off-color while recuperating from the surgery. But after a routine or minor procedure, this should not last for more than a day or two.

✦ Sutures are usually removed about 10 days after the operation, but in some cases may need to be left longer. Absorbable sutures are sometimes used under the skin, and these usually disappear on their own without the need for extraction.

COMPLEMENTARY AFTERCARE

If you wish to use complementary treatments to try to aid your pet's recovery, the following medications may be useful, but always discuss their use with your veterinary surgeon first:

✦ Rescue remedy, a blend of five Bach flower essences, may be given by mouth during the immediate recovery period to help encourage healing and reduce any trauma.

✦ The homeopathic remedies Arnica, Secale and Staphisagria may be used for a few days following surgery. Calendula cream may be applied to wounds.

✦ The herb Comfrey (*Symphytum officinale*) is rich in allantoin and has been used for centuries to help wounds to heal. It can be administered as a cream, but the dog should be prevented from licking it off.

CAUTION

Do not give any home medications without checking with your veterinarian first.

Eye, Ear, Mouth & Tooth Disorders

Problems with the eyes ✦ *Conjunctivitis* ✦ *Corneal damage and Cataracts* ✦ *Ear infections* ✦ *Oral infections*

YOUR DOG'S
HEALTH
*Eye, Ear,
Mouth & Tooth
Disorders*

134

The eyes, ears and mouth are among the most sensitive and critical areas of the dog's body. Any infections or disorders here can lead to great discomfort and potentially serious health problems.

EYE PROBLEMS

Deformation of the eyelids is often hereditary, although problems sometimes develop later in life. Conditions include: entropion – an in-turning of the eyelid; ectropion – where the eyelid turns outwards; and distichiasis – where eyelashes grow inwards and rub on the surface of the eye.

Owing to the way they are bred, some breeds – such as Shar Peis, with their heavy folds of facial skin, and St Bernards, with their droopy lower eyelids – are very prone to eyelid disorders. Eyelid deformities tend to cause irritation of the eye, leading to excessive tear production, and can eventually cause scarring of the cornea so that it loses its normal transparency and vision is impaired. These deformities should be surgically corrected before they cause long-term damage. Affected animals should not be used for breeding.

Conjunctivis

Conjunctivitis is an inflammation of the membrane that covers the eye and the inside of the eyelids. It is the most common eye condition that needs treatment. It can be sparked off by physical irritation, allergic reactions, or by infection – either one that

Above: The painful inflammation caused by conjunctivitis, which may be the result of an infection or the presence of a foreign body.

Below: Excess hair in the ear canal can collect wax, leading to infections, so the hair should be trimmed regularly.

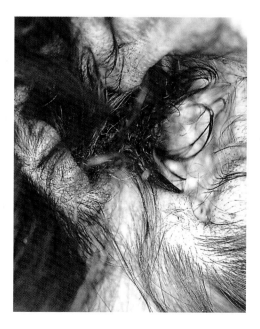

affects the eye alone, or as part of a more generalized condition such as distemper. Conjunctivitis is a painful condition and may cause redness, soreness and a discharge that may be either watery or thick, like pus. The underlying cause must be identified and treated if possible.

Corneal scarring and ulceration

The transparent surface of the eye is called the cornea. Long-term irritation of the eye may cause scarring of the cornea. This is especially the case with a problem called *keratoconjunctivitis sicca*, or "dry eye", which results from insufficient tear production. Fortunately, this can usually be controlled with drug treatment to stimulate the tear glands.

Infection or physical injury may lead to corneal ulceration, a very painful condition that can result in blindness if left untreated. In severe cases, surgical treatment may be required to repair the damage.

Cataracts and retinal damage

Problems further back in the eye can include cataracts, which give the lens a cloudy appearance. Conditions affecting the retina, the light-sensitive area behind the eye, have a variety of causes, but most relate to progressive retinal atrophy – an inherited problem that affects the blood supply. Modern veterinary surgery can now restore vision to dogs with cataracts by removing the opaque lens, but retinal damage cannot be repaired.

EAR CONDITIONS

One of the ear conditions most commonly treated in dogs is *otitis externa*, an infection of the outer ear. This is especially common in breeds with pendulous, hairy ears such as the Cocker Spaniel. Warning signs include irritation, redness, discharge and a smell from one or both ears.

The condition may be caused by a number of factors, such as foreign bodies in the ear, skin problems or ear mites. Usually, however, the problem is caused by a lack of ventilation in the ear canal, which becomes hot and sweaty, an ideal place for micro-organisms such as bacteria, fungi and yeasts to thrive. The underlying cause needs to be identified and corrected, and antibiotic ear drops used to clear any infection. Long-term use of cleaning agents may help to prevent a recurrence, but sometimes an operation is carried out to improve the ventilation to the ear canal.

Otitis media and otitis interna

If infection crosses the ear drum into the middle or inner ear chambers, it causes *otitis media* or *otitis interna* respectively. This affects the dog's

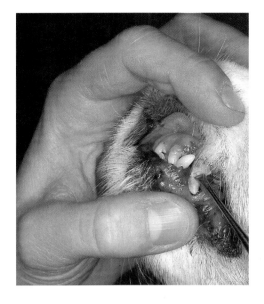

Above: Regular chewing helps reduce tartar, but if it builds up a vet should be asked to arrange removal before gum problems occur.

sense of balance and hearing, and may require a course of surgical and medical treatment to put right.

MOUTH AND TOOTH PROBLEMS

Many health problems can affect the mouth. These may lead to bad breath, drooling, tenderness and an unwillingness to eat. Foreign bodies may become lodged in the mouth and cause infection, while generalized diseases such as kidney failure can cause mouth ulceration.

Dental disease

By far the most common cause of oral discomfort is dental disease, usually a result of the accumulation on the teeth of soft plaque (from undigested food) and hard calculus (from minerals in saliva). These push on the gums and cause gingivitis. The inflamed gums recede, leaving pockets for infection to gain hold, which attacks the membrane that holds the tooth in its socket. If left untreated, abscesses and tooth loss are inevitable.

Regular tooth brushing with dog toothpaste, and a diet that exercises the teeth, will help to delay dental treatment. Once the gums become inflamed, it is necessary for the teeth to be de-scaled under anesthetic. The teeth are then polished, to create a smooth surface. If treatment is not carried out promptly, more radical remedial work, or even dental extractions, may be necessary.

Below: Teeth and gums should be checked regularly for abscesses or inflammation.

YOUR DOG'S HEALTH
Eye, Ear, Mouth & Tooth Disorders

135

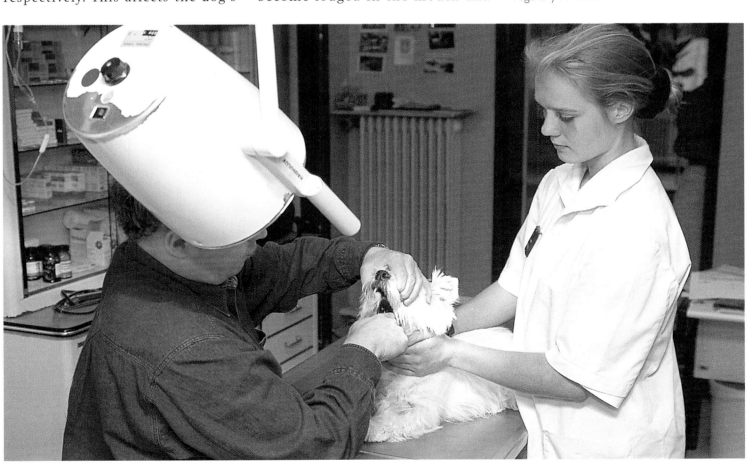

Nervous & Circulatory Disorders

Health and behavior ✦ *Fits* ✦ *Ataxia* ✦ *Spinal cord and nerves* ✦
Blood disorders ✦ *Heart disease*

YOUR DOG'S
HEALTH
*Nervous &
Circulatory
Disorders*

136

Most heart problems in dogs are caused by long-term defects, and the signs of illness usually respond well to drugs. Diseases of the blood or nervous system are more often due to infection or injury and need urgent attention.

NERVOUS PROBLEMS

Some diseases of the nervous system affect the metabolism and can have effects on behavior. However, these should not be confused with nervous behavior, such as fear of doorbells or submissive urination, which are behavioral problems and should be treated as such.

Fits

Fits in dogs have a range of causes, including brain tumors, poisoning and infections that affect the brain – such as distemper and meningitis. Epileptic fits may be caused by an injury to the brain, but may also be hereditary, especially in certain breeds such as the Golden Retriever. In addition to any treatment to help the underlying cause, dogs that have regular fits are likely to be given anticonvulsant drugs such as phenobarbitone, to suppress the seizures.

Ataxia

This loss of balance and coordination may be due to a problem within the middle ear (see page 136). However, it may also be caused by a cerebrovascular accident, similar to a human stroke, when the blood supply to a part of the brain is cut off. This results in loss of balance, a head tilt and uncoordinated body movements. Like those of a human stroke, the symptoms tend to improve over time.

Spinal cord

Nervous problems can also affect the spinal cord, or the major nerves that meet it. A spinal condition that is very common in long-backed breeds such as the Dachshund, is a prolapsed intervertebral disc. Normally, the vertebrae are separated and cushioned by a soft cartilage disc, held in position by an encircling ligament. If this ligament weakens, the disc is able to squeeze out of place and push on the

Below: Vets regularly check heart action using stethoscopes. But drugs can alleviate symptoms for problems that are identified early enough.

spinal column. This causes back pain and paralysis of the hind legs, although it can affect all four legs if it occurs in the neck. Mild spinal disc problems will often respond to anti-inflammatory drugs and strict rest, but severely affected dogs may require prompt surgery to avoid paralysis.

BLOOD CONDITIONS

Blood problems in dogs are generally of two major types, as follows.

Anemia

A fall in the number of red blood cells, known as anemia, is not one disease, but a symptom of many underlying problems. It can be caused by internal bleeding, the breakdown of red blood cells by blood parasites, or a fall in the production of red blood cells.

Heartworms

Tiny parasites known as heartworms can live in the veins and arteries, sapping the

dog's vitality. Dead heartworms caught in the bloodstream may cause internal blood clotting or thrombosis.

HEART PROBLEMS

Dogs do not have heart attacks as a result of coronary thrombosis (blocking of the arteries with fatty deposits), but they can suffer from other heart problems. Chest radiographs and electrocardiographs (ECGs) can diagnose heart disease and drugs can help to control the condition, but it is not usually possible to cure the problem.

Heart murmur

Some small breeds of dog are prone to endocardiosis, a thickening of the

Above left: An ECG test is used to confirm a heart murmur in a King Charles Spaniel.

Above: An emergency heart massage on a border collie.

heart valves that reduces their efficiency. In its early stages this is audible through a stethoscope as a swooshing noise, known as a heart murmur. As this condition progresses, the heart begins to fail and the dog develops symptoms such as coughing, reduced ability to exercise, or fluids in the abdomen.

Cardiomyopathy

Giant breeds of dog are susceptible to cardiomyopathy, a degeneration of the heart muscles. This problem may cause fainting or even sudden death, if the dog's heartbeat goes into an abnormal rhythm.

Left: Doberman Pinschers may suffer from an hereditary blood-clotting disorder similar to hemophilia in humans.

YOUR DOG'S
HEALTH
*Nervous &
Circulatory
Disorders*

———

137

Skin Disorders

Parasites ♦ Dermatitis ♦ Skin tumors ♦ Hormonal disorders ♦ Impacted glands ♦ Flea control

Right: Pyoderma in puppies can be caused by a reaction to bacterial infection. Urgent treatment will prevent permanent scarring.

Skin problems are common in dogs and many owners have to become accustomed to dealing with them. A good quality diet and regular flea control will inhibit skin problems. The more common causes of skin disease are outlined here, but it is wise to consult your veterinarian about any persistent problems.

PARASITIC SKIN PROBLEMS
A great many skin problems are caused by parasites. Fortunately, most of these can be controlledonce they have been identified.

Fleas
These blood-sucking insects are the number-one canine parasite. They cause many skin problems, frequently triggering allergic dermatitis.

Sarcoptic mange mites
These animals are related to spiders and burrow into the skin to lay eggs. They cause intense irritation, known as scabies, especially on the ear flaps and elbows. Sarcoptic mites can be contracted from foxes, then passed to other dogs, and even to humans. Prescription shampoos clear up the problem.

Demodectic mange mites
Most dogs are host to small numbers of these creatures, which rarely cause problems. They are long and thin, and live in the hair follicles. Occasionally they will multiply and cause bald

Below: All dogs scratch themselves from time to time. However, constant scratching may indicate the presence of a skin parasite.

patches, especially around the head. This is not usually an itchy condition, unless secondary bacterial infection gains hold. Antibiotics to clear any infection and a well-balanced diet will usually clear the problem, but parasiticidal washes may be necessary.

Cheyletiella mites
Short-haired dogs are particularly susceptible to these animals, which are related to spiders. They live on the surface of the skin, causing irritation and scurfiness. They are treated with a special parasiticidal shampoo.

Ticks
These wingless, blood-sucking creatures feed only once a year, filling up their sac-like bodies with blood and then dropping off to breed on the ground. Dogs often pick up ticks when they brush through long grass, since the ticks climb up the grass and grab on to any likely meal that passes. In some areas, ticks transmit potentially fatal diseases. It is important that ticks are not just pulled off, because their mouthparts may remain embedded in the skin and lead to infection. They should be removed after treatment with an insecticidal product from your vet.

Lice
These common wingless insects live on hairs, on which they stick their eggs, called nits. They can

be seen with the naked eye and cause intense irritation. They should be treated with a parasiticidal shampoo.

Ringworm
This fungal infection causes patches of scaliness and hair loss, especially around the head and forelimbs. It is easily passed on to other animals, and to humans. Ringworm is treated in dogs with a drug called griseofulvin.

ALLERGIC DERMATITIS
This common cause of itchiness may affect any dog, but some breeds, the West Highland White Terrier and Labrador Retriever for example, seem to have a tendency to inherit it. The incessant itching can lead to constant scratching, creating infected skin and causing severe self-trauma.

In dogs, the most common allergic reaction is to flea saliva, but other factors can trigger the problem, so time and patience are needed to identify the cause. It is sometimes possible to give desensitization injections, and anti-inflammatory drugs are often used to control the itching.

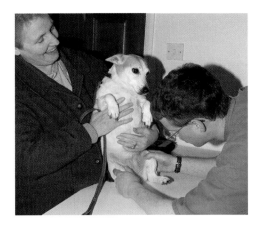

Above: Areas that appear inflamed or bald should be checked by a veterinary surgeon.

SKIN TUMORS
Skin tumors are often harmless, but any abnormal lumps should always be checked over by a veterinarian. If there is any doubt, they should be removed, and a specimen sent off to a laboratory for analysis by a pathologist to see if their cause may lead to any further problems.

HORMONAL IMBALANCES
Hormonal imbalances can cause skin problems, which are usually not itchy, but do involve hair loss and result in poor coat quality. The most common hormonal skin disorders are caused by an underactive thyroid gland (hypothyroidism) or by an overactive adrenal gland (Cushing's disease, or hyperadrenocorticalism). Blood tests are necessary to pinpoint the precise cause of hormonal imbalances.

ANAL SACCULITIS
Dogs have two anal sacs situated under the skin on either side of the anus. These secrete a strong-smelling scent that is squeezed out on to the feces to act as a territory marker.

In some dogs, the duct occasionally becomes blocked and the sacs impacted, causing severe irritation around the anal region. The dog often rubs its bottom along the ground to try to clear the blockage, or may repeatedly lick the area. The sacs can be emptied manually (see page 115), though sometimes drug treatment is needed in severe cases. If the condition recurs frequently, your vet may recommend that the sacs be removed surgically to prevent the problem.

CONTROLLING FLEAS

Fleas are the most common skin parasite of dogs in the US. They are wingless insects, generally brown in color, with deep, narrow bodies, and powerful legs that enable them to jump considerable distances. Fleas thrive in the warm, humid environment found in most modern homes. Since fleas may cause irritation to owners as well as their pets, a major industry has grown up around controlling the problem.

LIFE CYCLE OF A FLEA
◆ Adult fleas live on the host, where they suck blood, mate and die. A female will lay about 200 eggs during an adult lifetime of about two weeks.
◆ The eggs fall to the ground, where they hatch into larvae that crawl downwards into bedding or carpets. There they feed upon dead skin cells from their host and feces of the adult flea, 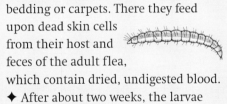 which contain dried, undigested blood.
◆ After about two weeks, the larvae form pupae in a protective cocoon, which can lie dormant for months or years if undisturbed.
◆ The immature flea emerges from the pupa in response to vibrations and carbon dioxide, which may indicate that a host is near. Once hatched, it can wait for up to eight weeks for a host to walk past.

FLEA INHIBITORS AND INSECTICIDES
◆ Environmental preparations should be used to reduce the numbers of fleas around the living area of your dog.

These cannot affect the pupae, but can kill off the eggs, larvae or young adults. Some preparations used on the dog can help to control fleas in the environment if they contaminate the dead skin cells that are eaten by the larvae.
◆ Insect development inhibitors can be given to the dog orally once a month. They are taken up by the adult flea when it feeds, and ensure that any young do not grow beyond the pupa.
◆ Insecticides come in many different formulations and are designed to kill the adult fleas on your dog. The older organophosphate insecticides have largely been replaced by more modern alternatives, which should be available from your vet. Topically applied formulations, a few drops of which are placed on the back of the neck once a month, are particularly popular, replacing the traditional sprays.

Bone, Muscle & Joint Disorders

Musculoskeletal problems ✦ *Hereditary diseases* ✦ *Arthritis and damaged cartilage* ✦ *Tumors* ✦ *Injuries*

YOUR DOG'S
HEALTH
*Bone, Muscle
& Joint
Disorders*

140

Musculoskeletal problems are particularly common in large breeds of dog, partly owing to hereditary factors but also because of excessively rapid growth. Recent research has suggested that puppies of large breeds should be fed on a diet with a lower energy and calcium level in relation to body weight than should smaller breeds, which is contrary to what was previously thought.

The most obvious symptom of joint or muscle disorders is lameness. It is essential to see a vet at once if this occurs, since the type of treatment given will depend on the cause. X-rays help to diagnose the cause of lameness in dogs, but usually require a general anesthetic, or at least deep sedation, to restrain the animal.

HEREDITARY CONDITIONS

Hereditary joint disease is very common and can take several forms. Hip dysplasia (see also page 130) is a deformation of the hip joint that is known to be largely hereditary, but diet and other environmental factors also play a significant role.

Hip dysplasia

This usually starts to cause problems in adolescent dogs, but can lead to severe osteoarthritis later on in life. Mild cases may respond to conservative treatment that involves restricted exercise and the use of anti-inflammatory drugs. More severe cases may benefit from surgery, and in some cases, even total hip replacement.

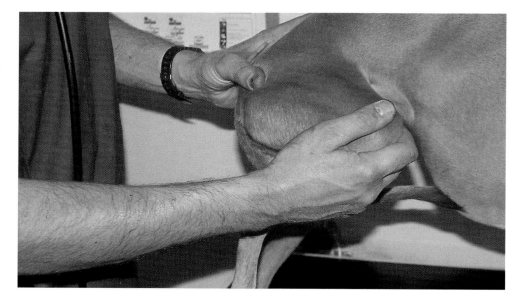

Above: Hips are manipulated for signs of hip dysplasia, a condition that can sometimes be eased by anti-inflammatory drugs.

Below: Some bone injuries require surgical repair. This Border Collie's fractured femur has been fitted with a steel pin (bottom).

Elbow dysplasia is not dissimilar, with growth abnormalities in the elbow joint generally showing up at around five or six months of age and causing lameness in one or both forelimbs.

Patella (kneecap) luxation

Smaller dogs are most commonly affected by this deformity in the shape of the knee joint. The patella slips out of the groove on the end of the femur (thigh bone) in which it normally sits. The most usual symptom is a sudden, but temporary, lameness in one hindleg as the patella jumps out of place, then slips back of its own accord. An operation is usually required to deepen the shallow patellar groove and stabilize the

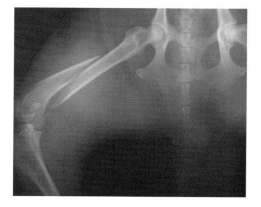

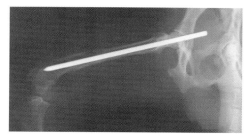

ligaments that hold the patella in place. Such problems may also be caused by injury.

Perthe's disease

This is more correctly called avascular necrosis of the femoral head, and is caused by a problem with the blood supply to the head of the femur, resulting in hip pain. It occurs mainly in small terriers and often requires an operation to remove the head of the femur to allow a new joint to form.

ARTHRITIS

Arthritis is an inflammation of one or more joints, and it usually develops secondarily to some other condition that affects the normal structure and functioning of the joint, such as an injury, or a congenital abnormality. Degenerative osteoarthritis is extremely common in old age among larger breeds of dog and is exacerbated if the dog is overweight. There is a wide range of treatments for arthritis, which have been used with varying degrees of success. These include both conventional and complementary forms of medicine, some of which are listed below.

Non-steroidal anti-inflammatory drugs (NSAIDs): These drugs help to reduce the pain and inflammation in the joints, but can cause side effects, particularly digestive upsets.

Corticosteroids: As very strong anti-inflammatory drugs, these are reserved for the most severe cases.

Copper collars: In a similar way to copper bracelets given to humans with arthritic joints, copper collars have also been produced for dogs.

Acupuncture: This practice is known to have an analgesic effect and can be very helpful in controlling the pain of chronic arthritis.

Massage and physiotherapy: Along with hydrotherapy in water, massage and physiotherapy are now used to help keep damaged joints mobile.

Complementary remedies: A wide variety of complementary remedies is now being used, including the homeopathic remedies *Rhus tox.* and Bryonia, and the herbs Angelica and Devil's Claw (see pages 146–7).

Above and top: Arthritis is common in older dogs. An early sign of the problem is your dog being unusually stiff after rest.

DAMAGED CARTILAGE

Cartilage that has been damaged through injury can be healed using conventional medicine given as injections, or using complementary products that are usually given orally. Complementary remedies include products containing sharks' cartilage, cod liver oil or evening primrose oil.

TUMORS

Other conditions that can affect the musculoskeletal system include a wide variety of tumors, which can be cancerous or benign. Osteomyelitis, which is an infection within the bone, can be quite difficult to differentiate from bone cancer on x-rays, and requires a long course of antibiotics.

INJURIES

Injuries to the bones, ligaments and joints are very common. As with humans, fractured bones are likely to require either placing in a cast or surgical repair, with stainless steel implants or external braces. In most cases, surgery is preferred for canine injuries, since it allows a more rapid return to normal use of the limb. Most dogs do not take well to casts and have been known to try to gnaw them off. The cruciate ligament is commonly torn in larger dogs, and in most cases, surgical repair of the ligament is required.

YOUR DOG'S
HEALTH
*Bone, Muscle
& Joint
Disorders*

141

Below: The bark of the White Willow has long been used to treat arthritis, and is now known to contain aspirin-like chemicals.

Digestive & Respiratory Ailments

Upper and lower respiratory disease ◆ Digestive problems ◆ Internal parasites

YOUR DOG'S
HEALTH
*Digestive &
Respiratory
Ailments*

142

Easily irritated or upset, the dog's respiratory and digestive tracts may fall victim to congenital problems, infection or simple irritation. As they include organs that are delicate, both systems need careful treatment.

UPPER RESPIRATORY DISEASES
The upper respiratory tract comprises the nose, the throat and the major airways leading down into the lungs. Various

Below: Kennel cough, a highly contagious disease of the upper respiratory tract, can be guarded against with a vaccine, administered as drops into the nose.

medical conditions can affect this area of the dog's body.

Kennel cough
Kennel cough is a dry, hacking cough and although cases can be mild, most require antibiotics. Sufferers should be isolated because the condition is highly contagious (see page 128).

Foreign body
Owners often suspect that dogs with a cough may have a foreign body lodged in their throat. If a foreign body is present, however, the dog is usually extremely distressed. He will gag, drool saliva, retch and be unable to swallow anything. It is usually necessary to give the dog an anesthetic to look for and remove any foreign bodies that may have got stuck.

Nasal problems
Several different problems can cause sneezing or a discharge from one or both nostrils. These include allergies, foreign bodies in the nose, tumors and viral, bacterial or fungal infections. Nasal tumors are quite common in older dogs, and may well be malignant. Further tests may be necessary as a precaution against cancer.

Laryngeal paralysis
This condition results from damage to the nerves that pull the vocal cords open when the

Above: Overweight dogs are unfit and incapable of leading an active life. In some breeds, such as the Labrador, excess weight may also lead to respiratory problems.

dog breathes in. It is sometimes seen in older dogs, especially overweight Labradors. The affected dog suffers from coughing, noisy breathing, difficulty in barking and may even collapse if it gets excited and is unable to breathe properly. Weight reduction may help, but often the dog needs to have an operation to tie the vocal cords out of the way.

Elongated soft palate

The larynx can get blocked by an elongated soft palate. This is quite common in breeds with shortened noses, such as the Pug and the Bulldog. The soft tissues at the back of the throat are pushed into a much smaller space than normal, and the soft palate gets sucked into the larynx. In severe cases, the palate may need to be shortened surgically.

LOWER RESPIRATORY DISEASES

These diseases affect the smaller air passages and the lung tissue itself, causing a cough, reduced ability to exercise and difficulty in breathing. Before the appropriate treatment can be determined, a chest x-ray under sedation is usually needed to pinpoint the cause of the problem.

Pneumonia and pleurisy

These are serious diseases that need intensive antibiotic or anti-inflammatory treatment. Pneumonia is an infection of the lungs, while pleurisy affects the membranes surrounding them. Inhaled fluids can also cause

pneumonia to develop, so care must be taken when force-feeding liquids to ensure that they are swallowed and not inhaled.

Pulmonary edema

Heart disease usually causes this build-up of water on the lungs, which must be treated with diuretic drugs.

Lung cancer

This often fatal condition is quite common in dogs, and can be due to secondary tumors that spread from other parts of the body, or to primary ones that develop in the lung tissue.

PROBLEMS WITH DIGESTION

Dogs tend to be greedy, and can easily become ill from eating indigestible or putrid material. Sudden changes of diet can also cause problems.

Gastro-enteritis

Hard objects such as bones can become stuck in the esophagus, the stomach or lower in the digestive tract, and need surgical removal. Dogs that vomit repeatedly can become weak and dehydrated. They may need blood tests and gastroscopy (looking into the stomach via a tube fitted with a fiber-optic light) to find the cause, and fluids to rehydrate them.

Diarrhea

Dehydration because of an attack of diarrhea will not occur rapidly as long as the dog is drinking normally. Mild cases will often return to normal if the dog is fed on a bland diet, such

Below: A barium meal fed to a dog will show up in an x-ray, helping veterinarians to locate problems in the digestive system.

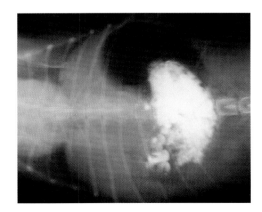

as chicken and white rice, for a few days, and then gradually returned to a normal diet. Special oral rehydration fluids are available to help prevent dehydration. However, in puppies or in adults showing severe diarrhea with blood loss, the condition can become life-threatening.

Colitis

This inflammation of the large (lower) bowel tends to cause soft feces, blood streaking and mucus, with the dog straining to pass motions. Some cases are due to a food allergy, but others need long-term control with drugs.

INTERNAL PARASITES

◆

The most common worms found in the intestinal tract of dogs are the following three types.

Roundworms: These creatures are like thin, pale earthworms, and can reach up to 4 in (10cm) long. Their eggs are passed in dog feces and become infective after lying on the ground for a few weeks. There is a slight risk to the eyesight of children who ingest the eggs accidentally, so all dogs should be wormed twice a year, and puppies and pregnant bitches more often.

Tapeworms: These parasites of the intestine are long and flat. Segments break off from the end of the adult tapeworm and may be seen around the hairs of the anus or in the feces. Tapeworms can be contracted from fleas, or by eating infected animal tissue. Many all-in-one wormers available from your veterinarian will kill tapeworm as well as roundworm.

Whipworms and hookworms: These bloodsuckers are common in warm climates. Both can cause great loss of blood.

If there is any question that your dog may be harboring intestinal parasites, your veterinarian may request a fecal sample to send to the laboratory for examination.

Reproductive & Urinary Disorders

False pregnancies ✦ *Uterine problems* ✦ *Breast problems* ✦ *Testicular and prostate problems* ✦ *Diseases of the bladder and kidneys* ✦ *Incontinence*

YOUR DOG'S
HEALTH
*Reproductive
& Urinary
Disorders*

144

Detailed information on dog breeding is not within the scope of this book. The average pet owner is more likely to be concerned with preventing a bitch from breeding than with controlling how she does so (see neutering, page 132). If your bitch does become pregnant, you should contact your veterinarian for advice.

However, even if you decide not to breed from your pet, you should know a little about the reproductive system of the dog. Various problems can arise within the reproductive system and these should always be dealt with promptly.

FALSE PREGNANCY

Bitches go through many of the hormonal changes of pregnancy whether they are mated or not. Some non-pregnant bitches behave as if they are pregnant, even to the point of treating toys and shoes as if they were puppies and producing large amounts of milk. This can be distressing for the bitch and may require medical treatment, although the problem should improve with the passage of time. Spaying will prevent this condition.

PYOMETRA

Pyometra is a condition in which the uterus fills up with a pus-like fluid, which may discharge from the vagina

Below: Relatively large-headed breeds, such as the Chihuahua, may have birth problems.

or accumulate internally. It is more common in older bitches, and almost always requires an emergency hysterectomy, since poisons from the infection released into the bloodstream can quickly cause damage to internal organs. Any unneutered bitch that goes off color and starts drinking more than normal, with or without vaginal discharge, should be suspected of suffering from this dangerous condition and taken to a veterinarian immediately.

MAMMARY NEOPLASIA
Breast cancer is more common in bitches than in women. Any abnormal mammary swellings or lumps should be checked over by a veterinarian. If there is any doubt about them, they should be removed and sent off for analysis. Quite often, a more radical mastectomy is carried out, and a whole length of mammary tissue is removed. This is another problem that can be largely prevented by spaying, since the tumors seem to need female hormones in order to grow.

TESTICLE AND PROSTATE PROBLEMS
There are several problems that are found mostly in older, unneutered male dogs. These include testicular tumors, prostatic disease and certain types of growth that depend upon male hormones for their development. Castration will often form all or part of the treatment.

Enlargement of the prostate is common in male dogs, causing abdominal discomfort, straining to

Below: The testicles of a puppy should be checked to ensure that they have descended.

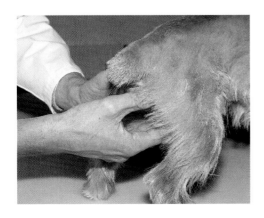

Above: Incontinence may occur with old age, or may be a symptom of kidney disease.

pass a motion and sometimes bleeding from the prepuce. It only very rarely causes a urinary obstruction, as it tends to do in men.

A yellowish discharge from the prepuce is found in all male dogs from time to time. The bacteria that cause this may multiply abnormally and the discharge become a nuisance that requires treatment with antibiotics.

KIDNEY AND BLADDER DISEASE
There are many diseases that can cause renal (kidney) damage in dogs. These include infection of the kidney, kidney stones, tumors, physical injury, poisoning and auto-immune disease (attack by the body's own immune system).

However, the main cause of kidney problems is simply wear and tear over the years. This is known as chronic interstitial nephritis.

The first sign of kidney problems is an increase in thirst, followed by lack of appetite, weight loss and bad breath. If left untreated, vomiting, and severe dehydration will occur and, in extreme cases, the dog may die. Dogs with kidney problems suffer from an internal build-up of phosphorus and other waste products, such as urea, which are produced when protein is broken down within the body. These go on to cause further damage to the kidneys.

Blood and urine tests will help to detect kidney problems at an early

stage, when treatment is most likely to be effective. A diet that is low in phosphorus and has restricted levels of good-quality protein may help greatly to slow down the progression of the disease.

Bladder disease may cause incontinence or straining to urinate, often with blood in the urine. This can be due to cystitis, an infection to which bitches are especially prone. Cases that do not respond to antibiotic treatment need to be x-rayed to check for other causes, such as bladder stones or growths.

DEALING WITH INCONTINENCE
There are many possible causes of incontinence in dogs and bitches, including prostatic and bladder disease. However, it is a problem most often found in older dogs, in which it may simply be caused by a weakness of the bladder sphincter muscles or cognitive disorder (dementia).

A weak bladder sphincter is very common in spayed bitches and often responds well to treatment. Senility is a problem that may affect any dog as it grows older. There are several drugs that have at least some beneficial effect in older dogs suffering from the senile dementia, but severe cases that fail to respond to treatment may require ongoing care.

YOUR DOG'S
HEALTH
*Reproductive
& Urinary
Disorders*

145

Natural Medicine

Complementary medicine ✦ *Herbal remedies* ✦ *Acupuncture* ✦
Manipulative therapies ✦ *Homeopathy* ✦ *Flower remedies*

There is an increasing trend towards using complementary medicine for both humans and animals, as more and more people believe that conventional treatment may not always offer the best cure. Complementary treatment aims to take a broader view of the well-being of the patient, rather than treating one specific illness in isolation.

Complementary medicine is often thought of as "natural" and therefore safer and relatively free of side effects. Certain forms of complementary treatment have proved to be most effective, but it must be remembered that others are more controversial and it is always best to check with your vet before using any complementary treatment.

Many pet owners buy complementary remedies because they

Right: Natural remedies aim to treat the whole animal – mind, body and spirit – and not simply deal with the particular symptoms of one problem.

are available without prescription. This may be appropriate for minor ailments, but it is always wise to seek the advice of a veterinarian, who will carry out a proper examination of the dog to ensure that there is not a more serious underlying problem.

It is easy to cause considerable pain and suffering to your dog, as well as extra cost to yourself in the long run, through trying out complementary remedies instead of consulting a veterinary surgeon. Many vets now practice complementary therapies

alongside conventional medicine. If they do not, they should be able to recommend a local practitioner of complementary medicine.

HERBAL REMEDIES

Herbal remedies are a powerful form of healing, and they should therefore be used with as much caution as we use with orthodox drugs.

Herbal remedies have been used for thousands of years, and many of our modern drugs are based upon compounds that have been isolated from plant extracts. Conventional medicine holds that it is best to use highly purified compounds that can be administered in precisely controlled quantities. However, herbalists feel that because they use the whole plant (as opposed to the active ingredient alone), there are fewer side-effects, and that the dog's body will be encouraged to heal itself. Always consult a qualified herbalist before giving your dog any herbal remedies.

ACUPUNCTURE

Acupuncture involves stimulating certain points on the body that lie along the so-called energy channels or "meridians". Acupuncturists believe that illness is largely caused by the stagnation of energy, which can become blocked in parts of the body. They use fine needles to stimulate the flow of energy to the appropriate parts. They may also use finger pressure (acupressure) or burn herbs (moxibustion) to the same effect.

Acupuncture certainly has measurable effects. Operations on animals, as well as humans, have been carried out solely under acupuncture and without other anesthetics. Scientific researchers believe that it works by stimulating the production of chemicals called endorphins that act as natural painkillers. Acupuncture is particularly useful for conditions involving chronic pain, such as advanced arthritis. The symptoms of many long-term illnesses may also respond to this treatment.

MANIPULATION

Physiotherapy, and other forms of manipulation such as osteopathy and chiropractic, have a clearly identified role in human conditions such as back pain. Although manipulation is more difficult to use in animals, it can be beneficial.

HOMEOPATHY

Many dog owners have reported good results after using homeopathic treatments. Homeopathic remedies are sometimes confused with herbal ones, as the base ingredients used are often similar, but the principles of treatment are very different. Herbal remedies are chosen to counteract specific conditions and are used in clearly measurable doses. Homeopathy works on the principle of "like cures like". This means that a tiny dosage of a substance that would cause a symptom in a healthy individual may help to alleviate it in one that is unhealthy. Homeopathy is said to work by encouraging the body to heal itself, but it can only be effective if the "correct" remedy is chosen. You should always consult a qualified veterinary homeopath for advice.

FLOWER REMEDIES

Flower remedies are based on the work of Dr Edward Bach. Flowers are "energized" by floating in water while exposed to sunlight. The water is then preserved with brandy. If your dog suffers from emotional or behavioral problems, various flower essences are recommended to treat "negative emotions". Flower essences are available from many chemists, but should only be used on the advice of a suitably specialized expert or veterinarian.

NATURAL REMEDIES

◆

HOMEOPATHIC REMEDIES

Arnica: Derived from the plant *Arnica montana*, this is probably the best known of all homeopathic remedies. It is used to counteract the effects of injury, reducing swelling and bruising, and to help promote rapid healing. It is available in tablet and ointment form.

Sulphur: Sulphur is commonly used to help animals with skin problems, particularly if the skin is red and inflamed. The typical patient will have a dry, smelly coat and often be overweight.

Rhus toxidodendron: This is another homeopathic remedy of plant origin, used in cases where there has been damage to muscle tissue. It is said to be particularly effective for animals that exhibit signs of stiffness after rest.

Evening primrose

HERBAL REMEDIES

Calendula, or pot marigold: This has an antiseptic action; it can be applied externally to help soothe wounds and certain skin problems.

Peppermint: This (or the milder spearmint) may be used as an infusion to relax the digestive tract of animals that are suffering from stomach upsets.

Dandelion: This plant has a diuretic action and the leaves are rich in potassium, which helps to relieve the side-effects of potassium loss. Potassium can be lost through the use of synthetic diuretics to remove excess fluid from the body.

Garlic: Known to have several actions on the body, garlic acts as an antiseptic within the bowel, inhibits blood clotting, and discourages parasites such as worms and fleas. Purists prefer the use of fresh cloves.

Evening primrose: Oil from this source has been used for many years, and has been scientifically proven to help animals suffering from some allergic skin disorders. This is due to a substance called gamma

Calendula

linolenic acid, which is found in the plant in large amounts.

Nettle leaves: These common leaves contain iron, so are a good tonic for animals suffering from anemia, as well as helping to ease arthritis. Boil the leaves first to neutralize the stings. The stings contain histamine, so it is useful that dock leaves, which have an anti-histaminic effect, usually grow close by. These have their own therapeutic uses.

BACH FLOWER REMEDIES

Rescue Remedy: This contains a mixture of five flower essences, and is particularly useful in emergency situations to counteract the effects of shock, collapse and trauma.

Mimulus: This can be helpful to treat fear of noises or of being left alone, as well as shyness and timidity.

Impatiens: Dogs exhibiting signs of irritability and impatience may benefit from this remedy.

Impatiens

Nursing & First Aid

Administering food and medication ✦
Post-operative care ✦ *Treatment for*
cancer ✦ *First aid* ✦ *Euthanasia*

Owners become very attuned to the normal behavior patterns of their dogs and can often sense if something is amiss before any obvious signs of illness become apparent. It is always better to obtain veterinary advice at that stage, rather than wait until a relatively minor problem becomes more serious.

FEEDING A SICK DOG

Dogs are often very fussy about what they eat, especially when they are unwell. A wide range of prescription diets are now available to help treat many conditions. High-energy liquid food also exists, specifically to tempt the dog that is unwilling to eat. The following tips may help:

✦ Feed fresh food. Opening a new can excites many dogs and often tempts them to eat more than an opened can taken from the fridge.

✦ Try different formulations and brands. Most prescription diets are available in either canned or dry form, and some in different varieties.

Your vet could supply you with a different brand if your dog refuses to eat the first it is offered.

✦ Change over gradually. If your dog is happily eating its existing diet, you may be able to fool it into accepting the new diet by gradually adding a steadily increasing proportion to its normal food. You should aim to feed your dog only the prescribed food in the long run.

✦ Hand feeding may entice your dog to eat. Liquid foods are easier to use because they can be given by syringe.

Below: If your dog requires surgery, it may be necessary for it to be on a drip at the vet's surgery for a short time after the operation.

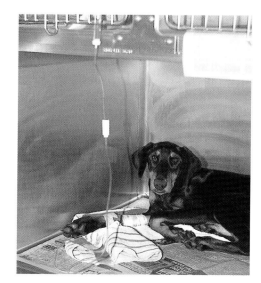

ADMINISTERING MEDICATION

Medication comes in many different forms, and it is important that you know how to administer them to your dog. The following tips may help you:

Tablets: If tablets can be given with food, crush them in a small amount of strong-smelling food and offer it to the dog when it is hungry. Alternatively, you could hide a tablet in a small piece of your dog's favorite food. If you have to give the tablet whole, you should lubricate it with butter, and push it right to the back of the dog's throat. Hold the dog's head up high, with its mouth closed, and dribble in a little water after the pill, if necessary, until you are sure that the dog has swallowed the tablet.

Liquids: Bend the dog's head back as above, and dribble drops of the liquid into the side of the mouth. Allow the dog to swallow, or the medicine may be accidentally inhaled.

Eye ointment: Before applying eye medicine, you may need to clean the eye area using moistened cotton. Pull down the lower eyelid with one finger and drop the ointment into the space between the lid and the eye. Avoid touching the end of the dropper itself, or letting the surface of the dropper touch the eye. Discard eye medicines a maximum of six weeks after opening the pack.

Ear drops: Ask someone to hold the dog's head and muzzle. Hold the ear flap between the finger and thumb of one hand, and use your other hand to administer the drops so that they drip well down into the ear canal. Keep hold of the ear flap until you have inserted all the drops. Then massage the side of the ear canal to encourage the drops to run well down into the ear. Let go of the ear flap, and wipe away any excess drops around the top of the ear canal.

CARE AFTER AN OPERATION

Pay close attention to the instructions you are given when you collect your dog. If there is any instruction you do

Below: Only ear medicines prescribed by a vet should be applied. Inappropriate substances can lead to blocked ears.

not understand, or any stage in his recovery that does not proceed as expected, contact the vet's clinic immediately. General tips include:

✦ Follow all instructions carefully when giving the prescribed medication; ask the vet for help if the dog rejects the medication or shows any unexpected reaction or side effect.

✦ Do not feed the dog until it is fully awake, and then give it a small, easily digestible meal, such as white meat with rice, or any specific food recommended by your vet.

✦ Check regularly to see that dressings or casts are not too tight or uncomfortable. Most dressings should be removed altogether after a few days, or changed regularly. Contact

the vet if you detect any unusual smell or discharge from the wound.

✦ Seek your vet's advice if the wound becomes reddened, swollen and hot, or if there is a significant discharge or bleeding. A dog will nearly always lick a wound in an effort to heal it, and this is not necessarily harmful – but excessive licking may make it sore; it may even pull out the stitches. If necessary, an Elizabethan collar can sometimes be fitted around its neck to prevent this.

✦ Stitches are usually removed seven to ten days after the operation, but in some cases they may need to be left longer. Absorbable stitches are sometimes used under the skin and do not need to be taken out.

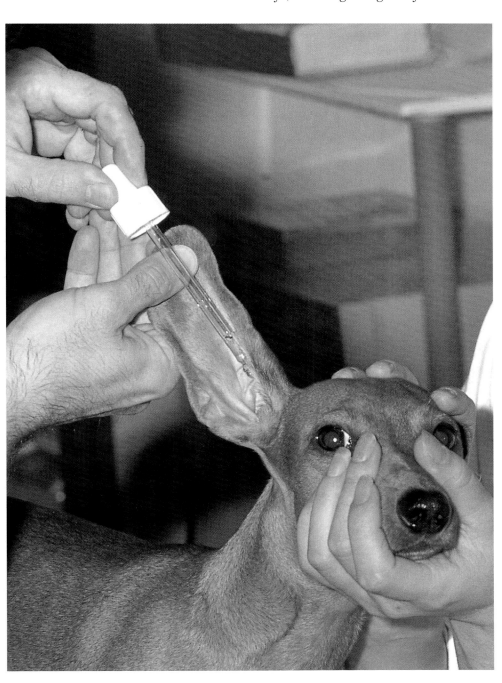

*C A R I N G   F O R
A   D O G   W I T H
C A N C E R*

✦

✦ The diagnosis of a malignant (cancerous) tumor is not necessarily a death sentence. There are different types of treatment that can be used with the various types of cancer, to provide a cure in some cases, or at least to give a worthwhile extra lease of life.

✦ Surgical removal of the malignant tumor may be followed up by other forms of treatment if the problem has spread, or may result in a complete cure if all the affected tissue is removed.

✦ Chemotherapy involves the use of drugs to control cancer. This is particularly effective in cases of lymphosarcoma, a cancer of the white blood cells. A combination of drugs is used to inhibit the effectiveness of the cancer cells, hopefully with few side effects.

✦ Radiotherapy can only be used at specialized centers, but can be very successful for tumors in certain types of skin cancer.

✦ You may also consider applying some forms of complementary healthcare, which can improve the quality of your dog's life.

Nursing & first aid

CANINE FIRST AID

There are three steps that should be followed in an emergency:
✦ Remove the dog from danger, but do not put yourself at risk.
✦ Take any immediate first aid steps necessary to preserve life.
✦ Contact a veterinary surgeon for further advice and assistance.

THE ABC OF FIRST AID

There are three important things you need to remember for applying basic first aid. These are as follows:
✦ Ensure that the **Airways** are clear, especially if the dog is unconscious. To do this, clear any fluid or debris from the mouth and pull the tongue forward to keep the throat clear.
✦ If the dog is not **Breathing**, you can attempt artificial respiration by compressing the chest with your hand once every couple of seconds to force air out of the lungs.
✦ Try to maintain the **Circulation**. Try to stop serious bleeding by applying firm pressure with a bandage over the wound.

MUZZLING

— ✦ —

Injured dogs may try to bite, so fit a temporary muzzle, except to short-nosed breeds. Remove the muzzle if the dog has trouble breathing.

✦ Tie a bandage or necktie loosely, then slip it over the nose and pull tight.

✦ Cross the two ends under the jaw, then tie them at the back of the head in a loose double bow.

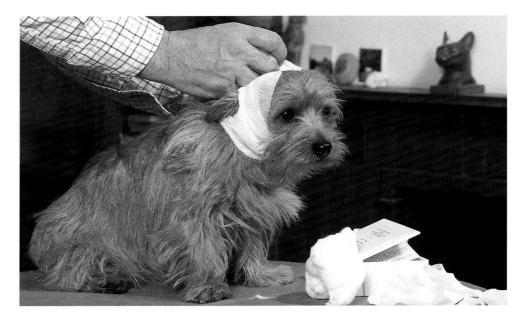

Above: Straightforward cuts and abrasions can be treated at home by bathing in salt water and binding securely with sterile gauze and bandages.

The following conditions need immediate veterinary attention, but the first aid tips given below may improve your dog's chances of survival.

Bleeding: It may be possible to staunch the flow of blood by applying a pressure bandage to the affected area. Ideally, you should apply a swab of sterile gauze, or some similar material, and then firmly apply a bandage over that. Do not make the bandage too tight, since it will need to be removed as soon as you arrive at the vet's surgery.

Burns: These can result from heat, electricity or contact with corrosive chemicals. Turn off the electric current at the mains before attending to an electrocuted dog. Flush any type of burn liberally under cold running water, which will cool down the damaged tissues and wash off any chemicals. When the burns are chemical, prevent the dog from licking the contaminated area.

Choking: If the dog is unconscious, you may be able to pull his tongue forward out of the mouth and grasp any visible foreign body. In a conscious dog, you can try sharply compressing the chest between your hands in the hope that the rapid exhalation of air will force the offending item out of the throat. Alternatively, reach into the mouth using tweezers.

Drowning: If the dog is unconscious and small enough, hanging him upside down and gently swinging him back and forth may be help water to drain out of the lungs. Even if the dog recovers from the original incident, there is still a chance of pneumonia developing from the water that has

Left: A dog should be allowed to rest quietly after a fit until it is fully recovered.

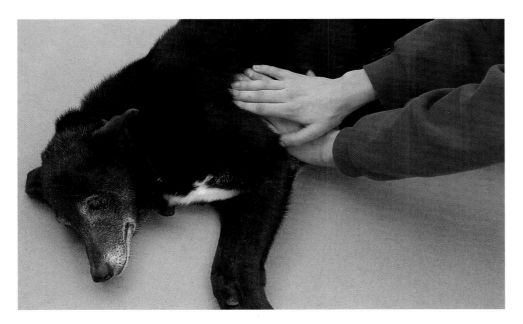

Above: Use basic first aid to keep a collapsed dog alive until you can get it to a vet.

been inhaled into the lungs. Always seek advice from your vet.

Fits: Do not to disturb a dog suffering from a fit, but make sure that it is safe, preferably in a dark and quiet room. Be cautious after the fit as many dogs are disorientated and may be temporarily aggressive. If the fit lasts for more than about five minutes, or if fits recur in quick succession, you must seek urgent veterinary attention.

Fractures, dislocations and sprains: Do not struggle to apply a splint or bandage to your dog, since you may well end up causing more severe injury. Keep the dog confined and do not give him any painkillers except under veterinary advice. A sprained joint may benefit from cold compresses being held on it.

Injuries: Minor wounds can be bathed in one pint of warm water in which one teaspoonful of salt has been dissolved. Seek veterinary attention if the wound is gaping open or if it has penetrated a critical area such as the chest or abdomen.

You should also seek help from a veterinarian if the wound becomes inflamed or smelly, or begins to discharge, and if your dog appears generally unwell or refuses food.

Poisoning: Unless the substance is caustic, you can try to make the dog vomit during the half hour while it is still in the stomach. Give your dog a strong solution of salt water. Keep any information about the nature of the poison, such as the packet, and contact your veterinarian without delay.

If your dog has contaminated its coat with a harmful substance, prevent it from grooming itself until it has been thoroughly cleaned.

Left: Keep a collapsed dog warm using an emergency or ordinary blanket.

If your dog is diagnosed as suffering from an incurable condition, you may have to face the difficult decision of if, and when, to have him put to sleep. Factors such as the cost of ongoing treatment and coping with problems such as incontinence need to be taken into account, but for most owners the most important consideration is whether their dog is enjoying a reasonable quality of life.

If your dog is eating and responding to attention, and is not suffering from any specific effects of the illness, such as repeated vomiting, then it is likely that it is still enjoying life. But if your dog is not enjoying such quality of life and no further improvement can be expected, euthanasia may be the kindest option. Seek advice from your vet before you decide.

Euthanasia is carried out by the intravenous injection of a concentrated barbiturate solution. The dog literally "goes to sleep" within seconds, after which the heart stops beating and breathing ceases. Vets usually allow owners to stay with their dogs to help their dog relax, and to reassure them that it is a peaceful process.

Some bereaved owners find it helpful to get a new dog quickly, while others prefer to wait. Either way, it is normal to feel a sense of bereavement after the loss of a pet. Your vet may be able to recommend a pet bereavement counsellor to help you if required.

Having Puppies

General guidelines ✦ Practicalities of raising a litter

Allowing your bitch to have puppies can provide a wonderful and exciting event. It can help to teach children about the process of reproduction and to understand the burden of responsibility that comes with creating new life.

Watching the birth and development of puppies over those first weeks is rewarding, but very hard work too. You may need to be up in the night, not only for the birth, but also to keep an eye on the mother and puppies during the first few weeks. An enormous amount of cleaning up is necessary, particularly with large litters. You may also have to spend a considerable amount of time and money ensuring that mother and pups have the best possible care. There are far too many unwanted dogs in the world, so you should consider carefully the work involved before letting your bitch have pups.

Before embarking on a breeding program, or a one-off litter, there are several major issues to consider:
✦ Your bitch must be healthy and ready for the rigors of pregnancy, birth and the care of her litter. It is

Right: Before breeding your dog, it is essential to investigate any hereditary disorders common to the breed. The Japanese Akita is a robust breed, rarely affected by such illnesses.

advisable to take your bitch for a veterinary check prior to mating. Your vet can also advise you on the optimum time for mating in your dog's cycle, and where to find a suitable mate.
✦ Your bitch must be of flawless temperament. Nervousness, aggression or other behavioral problems can be passed on to the puppies, either genetically or by example.
✦ Not all bitches need to have a litter, and allowing your bitch one will not cure an existing behavioral problem.

✦ Bitches should be mature, but not too old to have a litter. You should never breed from a bitch in her first season, and the UK Kennel Club, for example, will not accept registrations for pups born to bitches over eight years of age.
✦ Breeding puppies should not be undertaken for financial gain. Well-bred and well-reared puppies do not make much profit for the breeder. Stud fees, appropriate food for both bitch and puppies, registration, innoculations and other veterinary costs all add up.

Whoever said you can't buy happiness, forgot little puppies.
GENE HILL, "HE'S JUST MY DOG", TEARS & LAUGHTER, 1997

- ✦ Homes must already have been secured for puppies before breeding.
- ✦ Most people who breed dogs are involved in showing, trials or obedience, and have a litter when they want to continue a particular breeding "line" by keeping a puppy themselves. The bitch must already be registered with the Kennel Club if you want to register the puppies before selling them.
- ✦ Puppies from pet bitches can make wonderful companions, because they have often been raised in the home environment. Registration is generally not required for these puppies.
- ✦ The choice of stud dog should be governed by temperament and soundness. Many breeds with hereditary health problems now have scoring systems to protect the future of the breed. Ensure that both the dog and bitch have been tested and that you understand the result. See the chart below for guidance.
- ✦ It is not a good idea to use a male pet dog as stud, unless you want him to pursue it as a career. Once males realize what they have been missing, their behavior can change as they become obsessed with finding bitches and begin to behave aggressively to other interested male dogs.

RAISING A LITTER

Consider the practicalities of raising a litter. Where are the puppies going to be born and raised? Your home will usually be ideal, since puppies benefit from the stimulation provided by a domestic environment from as early an age as possible. Do you have time to devote to raising a litter? Sometimes a mother will need help rearing her puppies, and hand feeding may be required every few hours. Even assuming that everything goes according to plan, puppies need to be introduced to solid food at about four or five weeks, and this process can be time-consuming, messy and costly.

Above: No matter how beautiful the dog, temperament comes first. Never breed from a dog or bitch that shows signs of aggression or nervousness.

HEREDITARY DISEASES

◆

Many pedigree breeds suffer from hereditary diseases. Screening for most of these anomalies is now possible, so it is vitally important that both the stud dog and brood bitch are tested and found to be clear, before mating.

PROBLEM	BREEDS MOST AFFECTED	TESTING SYSTEM
Hip dysplasia	Golden Retriever, German Shepherd Cocker Spaniel and Labrador Retriever	X-rays are taken of each hip, which is then scored. The lower the scores, the better.
Eye defects, including PRA (progressive retinal atrophy), entropion, ectropion, cataracts and glaucoma.	German Shepherd, Border Collie, Shar Pei, Cocker Spaniel, Cavalier King Charles Spaniel	Each breed society has its own testing system. Eyes should always be scored clear of any defect.
Heart defects	Cavalier King Charles Spaniel, Boxer	Always make sure that any parents and grandparents have been long-lived, with no history of heart problems. Both dog and bitch should be clear of heart murmurs, which can be detected by a vet.

Selecting a Mate

Choosing a mate ✦ Stud dogs and bitches

*I*n the wild, wolves, jackals and coyotes select a mate carefully and often remain loyal to this one individual, forsaking all others while he or she is still able to breed. Domestic dogs are not as fussy, so it is normally the owner that chooses a suitable mate and engineers their meeting. This way, the puppies will arise from known parents.

Selecting a mate for your dog will depend on a number of factors. The first of these is breed. It is usual for pedigree dogs to be mated only to others of the same breed, normally in an attempt to create the perfect show specimen or working dog. A good breeder will select behavioral and physical characteristics in the male that complement or balance those of the female. "Line breeding", that is, breeding from dogs with at least one common ancestor, usually in the first

Above: The Basenji is one of the very few examples of domestic bitches that normally comes into season only once a year, rather than twice.

few generations of the pedigree, is used by those who are striving to achieve a certain look in their kennel.

Many experienced breeders will trace back generations of dogs in order to select the ideal mate. If you are new to the world of breeding dogs, it is highly advisable to seek help and advice from those who are knowledgeable in the breed. Stud dogs should always belong to a reputable and responsible breeder, never to a puppy farm or dealer. It is usual to pay a stud fee to the owner of the dog. This varies, but it is often the equivalent of the price of a puppy.

A suitable mate also needs to be judged on its temperament and on its physical soundness. A stud dog may look beautiful, but if he suffers from a behavioral problem, or a hereditary disorder, he is unsuitable as a mate.

YOUR DOG'S CYCLE

Most domestic bitches come into season twice a year. (Basenjis are the exception to this rule, and have only one season a year.) The first season,

---

CROSSBREEDING

✦

Deliberate matings between dogs of two different breeds can often result in the most wonderful crosses, combining the best aspects of each breed in one dog. The Labradoodle, as it has become known, is a first cross between the Labrador and the Standard Poodle. This cross combines the intelligence and stamina of both breeds with the added advantage of minimum hair loss, since Poodles do not shed hair. This crossbreed has been created in an attempt to provide guide dogs for blind people with dog-hair allergies. However, it is possible that other, unwanted characteristics could be "doubled" by mating rather incompatible breeds. The Choweiler – a first cross between the Rottweiler and the Chow Chow – potentially combines the determination of the Chow with the fearlessness of the Rottweiler, making this a dog only for the truly experienced owner.

Left: Most domestic bitches, like this Retriever, come into season twice a year. This is a major difference between domestic dogs and wolves, which have only one season.

MATING RITUALS

Most bitches are quite clear about whether or not they are ready to mate and it is always best to allow nature to take its course. Forcing a bitch to be mated is cruel and often results in a problematic pregnancy. Many rituals surround courtship and mating. Contrary to popular belief, dogs do not always know what to do the first time, and it helps to ensure that one of the pair has had previous experience.

Most stud dog owners will require that the bitch is brought to the dog. On first meeting, much sniffing and licking takes place. The stud dog will show obvious interest in the bitch, and they may play. Although he may try to mount her, it is always the bitch who decides when she is ready to mate, by standing still and putting her tail to one side. She will then allow the male to mount. He clasps her with his forelegs around her middle. Ejaculation usually occurs within one minute, but the mating is far from over. Now, a bulbous area at the base of the dog's penis, the bulbourethral gland, swells with blood and becomes so enlarged that it is impossible to separate the male and female for 5 to 30 minutes. Helping them to maneuver so that they stand back to back ensures that they suffer no discomfort or injury. Separation occurs naturally and both dogs usually then settle down to wash themselves.

which indicates the onset of sexual maturity, can be any time between 6 and 18 months old, but between 8 and 13 months is most common.

In some bitches, early indications of coming into season are hard to detect. Most owners notice that the bitch's vulva is slightly swollen, and then bleeding starts. Bleeding may last from four days to two weeks. During this time, her scent is highly attractive to males, but she will not let them mount her. Indeed, during this time she may snap at males and become generally irritable. It is only after the bleeding finishes that the bitch is fertile. This stage lasts between 5 and 12 days. Mating is most successful if the bitch is mated at the beginning of this time, and again two days later.

Right: After mating, the dog and bitch stand tail to tail, with the dog's penis still inside the bitch. The "tie" can last for 30 minutes and stops another male from mating the bitch.

The Pregnancy

Stages of pregnancy ✦ *Fetus development* ✦ *Preparing for birth*

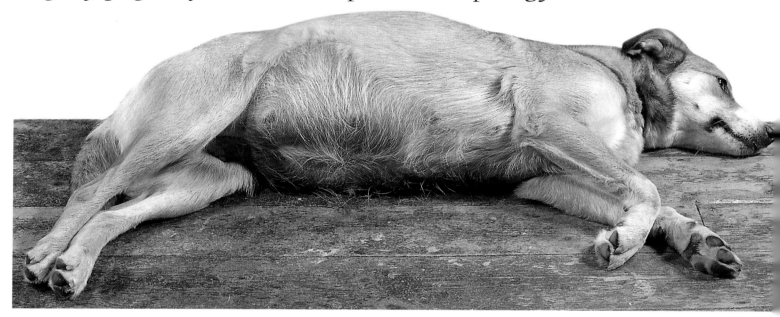

The average length of a bitch's pregnancy is 63 days. Very few changes occur until the fifth week of pregnancy and, even then, it can be hard to determine whether or not the bitch really is pregnant. It is also virtually impossible to tell how many puppies she is carrying, although scanning is now available for those who cannot wait to know.

From the fifth week of pregnancy, the teats and mammary glands swell and darken in color, in readiness for feeding the puppies later on. Your bitch may be a little quieter than usual, but apart from this no other

Above: In the final days before giving birth, a pregnant bitch needs to spend as much time as possible resting in a comfortable place.

physical changes take place until the sixth or seventh week, when the bitch's shape may look different, as her abdomen becomes thickened with the growth of the pups. Around this time your bitch may need to relieve herself more than usual.

At about eight weeks into the pregnancy, your bitch's mammary glands may secrete fluid, and they will have enlarged considerably. There may be a slight, clear discharge from her

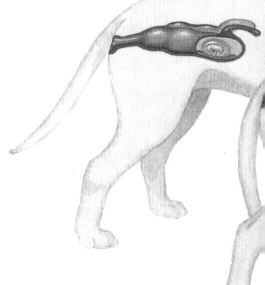

28–33 days: At 28 days, the fetus is gaining nourishment from the placenta, rather than the original yolk sac. The eyes, limbs and head are developing. At 33 days: Internal organs are forming and the fetus is growing steadily. Hormonal changes may now influence the mother, but the puppies are still too small to alter her shape.

THREE'S A CROWD!

✦

It is possible for more than one dog to be the father of a litter of puppies. This is because the bitch may accept more than one mate during her fertile season, and she may conceive on any of these occasions. Even if you have taken your bitch to a stud dog, and she has mated successfully, it is necessary to keep her away from other male dogs until the risk of further mating is over. This fact may account for the amazing diversity seen in litters of puppies that can be born to stray bitches. Half the litter may look like their mother and one father, while the other half resemble her and another father.

vulva, but this is quite normal unless it becomes discolored.

As long as your bitch has been fed a high-quality diet prior to the mating, she should not require any additional food, or any changes to her diet, until she reaches the last few weeks of her pregnancy. At that time, her appetite is likely to increase noticeably, so be sure to feed her little and often, on quality food, high in protein. She will not need large amounts of extra carbohydrate or fats, since these will simply cause her to put on weight, rather than give her what she needs to nourish the pups.

BE PREPARED

At least two weeks before the bitch is due to whelp, decide on where the pups are to be born and make sure that you have all the necessary equipment (see page 158). Although it is unusual for puppies to be born more than one or two days either side of the 63 days, there are sometimes exceptions to the rule. Pups can be born up to a week early, in the middle of the night, or in all sorts of places.

FALSE PREGNANCY

It is common for bitches that have not been mated during their season to have a false, or "phantom" pregnancy, eight or nine weeks after the end of the season. This occurs when the body has prepared itself to give birth, despite a lack of conception. Bitches may dig holes, build nest sites and even hoard soft toys or other objects and defend them as if they were puppies. Some bitches also produce milk.

Although false or phantom pregnancies cause no physical harm, and usually only last a fortnight or so, they can be distressing for the bitch and may be repeated at each season. Ask your vet for advice on managing or preventing a recurrence.

Development of the fetus

A true pregnancy lasts for 63 days, or about two months, during which time, the fetuses develop in the womb. During the first half of this period, the bitch shows little sign of being pregnant.

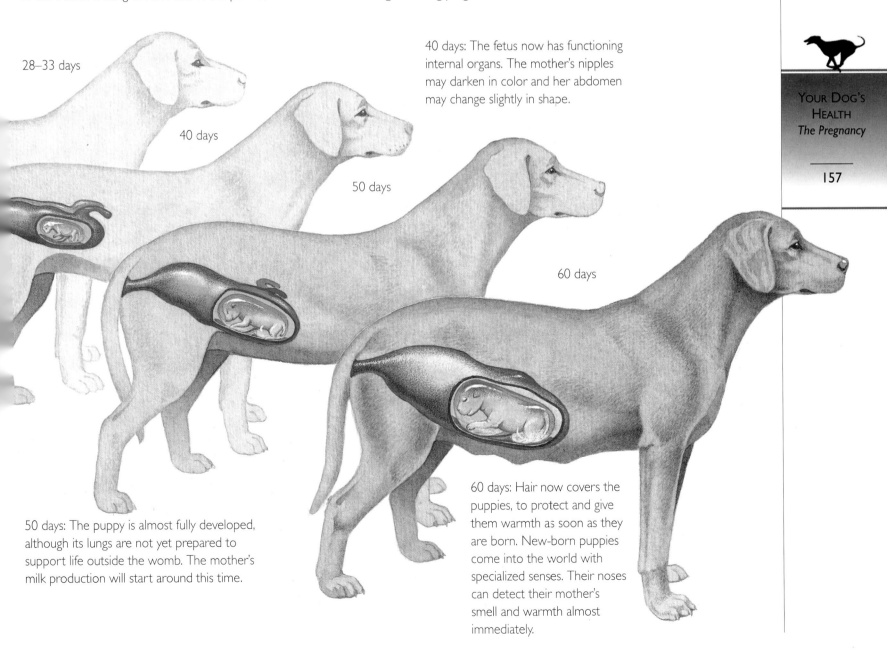

28–33 days

40 days

50 days

40 days: The fetus now has functioning internal organs. The mother's nipples may darken in color and her abdomen may change slightly in shape.

50 days

60 days

50 days: The puppy is almost fully developed, although its lungs are not yet prepared to support life outside the womb. The mother's milk production will start around this time.

60 days: Hair now covers the puppies, to protect and give them warmth as soon as they are born. New-born puppies come into the world with specialized senses. Their noses can detect their mother's smell and warmth almost immediately.

The Birth

Prenatal care ✦ Normal and problem births

The birth of puppies requires a great deal of preparation in advance, even in cases where you intend to call upon the services of a veterinarian for the event itself.

BASIC EQUIPMENT

A whelping box is traditionally a wooden or plastic box that is large enough for the bitch to stretch out in. The sides can be about 18in (45cm) high on three sides, with the fourth left open, and only a low ridge to keep out drafts. Inside the box, a narrow guard-rail can be fixed about 4in (10cm) above the base. This allows the puppies space when the mother climbs in and settles down, and prevents them from being inadvertently squashed against the sides of the box. If this happens, most puppies squeal and the mother moves, but some breeds are quicker at moving than others, so it is a good safety feature.

The whelping box needs to be placed in a part of the house that is quiet but allows easy access. Your bitch may need to go outside quite frequently to relieve herself. Let the bitch become familiar with the whelping box at least two weeks before the puppies are due. Otherwise,

she may decide that behind the sofa will do just as well.

It may be useful to have the following equipment to hand for the birth:
✦ A pair of sharp, sterilized, blunt-ended scissors, in case you need to cut the umbilical cords.
✦ White thread for tying the cords before cutting them.
✦ Towels, for drying the puppies.
✦ A water dish, kept close to the bitch.
✦ A watch or clock to time the intervals between births.
✦ Some breeders use an overhead infrared lamp to keep the puppies warm once they are born. This may be needed if ambient temperatures are extremely low, but in a warm room it should not be necessary.

THE BIRTH

About 12 hours before a bitch is due to whelp her temperature will drop to below 100.4°F (38°C). If you do not feel confident about taking her temperature, watch for behavioral changes to predict the timing.

Normally, a bitch will go off her food the day before whelping. She may seem restless, and possibly even nauseous. Nesting, preferably in the whelping box, will be energetic. The

bitch may lick herself repeatedly in order to clean a clear, white discharge from her vulva. This often indicates that her waters have broken and the puppies are on their way. She will start to pant and labor will begin in earnest. Make a note of the time that this happens. Some bitches want to move around as the contractions grow stronger and the first puppy is on its way. This should be allowed, and gentle reassurance given.

Puppies are usually born covered in a strong membrane. Ideally, the bitch should start to lick this away from the puppy's face, and then chew through the umbilical cord. If she does not, you need to act quickly, breaking the membrane with your fingers, so the puppy can breathe. The umbilical cord needs to be tied close to the puppy's abdomen and cut with scissors about 1in (2.5cm) away, between the thread and the placenta.

Each puppy should be born either with a placenta around it, or the placenta should follow shortly after. It is normal for bitches to eat the afterbirths. However, they have a laxative effect, so try to limit consumption.

Puppies may be born every few minutes, or up to two hours apart.

Below: After the birth of each puppy, the mother cleans away the membrane of the water sac and chews the umbilical cord.

Below: In cleaning and drying the newborn puppy, the mother's vigorous licking also stimulates the puppy to take its first breaths.

Below: If a bitch is having a large litter, she may need help cleaning the puppies; rubbing gently with a clean towel helps to dry them.

Above: After birth, a puppy will normally find its way to the mother's nipples to suck.

Each puppy should be licked by the mother or dried with a towel, then encouraged to suckle as soon as possible, even while the mother is giving birth to the next puppy. The sucking may even help to stimulate the next contractions. Once labor is over, your bitch will appreciate being taken into the yard to relieve herself. She will also need to have a drink. Most mothers will check over their new brood, and then sleep.

Occasionally, health problems in the mother can occur after a litter has been born. Any unusual discharge, signs of a raised temperature, distress, or convulsions in the bitch should be investigated by a vet immediately.

WHEN TO CALL AN EXPERT

Most bitches, even inexperienced ones, manage to give birth relatively easily over a period of about six hours, for an average-sized litter. (It depends on the breed, but, on average, a bitch will produce between five and eight puppies in a litter.) However, if it takes your bitch more than two hours to deliver one puppy, or she is straining afterwards, with no production of either another puppy or the after-births, contact your vet. Only intervene in an emergency.

Occasionally, a Cesarean section may be required, in which the vet surgically removes the puppies through the stomach wall. Most bitches and puppies come through well.

Most bitches do not need help in giving birth, but keep the telephone number of your local vet to hand, and don't be afraid to call for help.

Above: A whelping box provides a secure area for a mother and her newborn pups.

Below: When all the puppies are born, the the litter will feed while their mother dozes.

The New Arrival

Postnatal and early care

Though they are born blind and deaf, new-born puppies have a well-developed sense of smell and can locate the bitch's teats in order to feed. Pups need to gain the important antibodies contained in the mother's colostrum, which she produces in her milk for the first 24 to 48 hours after whelping. Once attached to a teat, they may knead their mother's belly with their front paws to stimulate the milk flow. New-born puppies can also cry out, and this helps the mother to find one if it accidentally loses contact with her.

The bitch takes full responsibility for the helpless pups, even stimulating them to urinate and defecate by licking them. Although it may seem distasteful to us, she consumes the puppies' waste, keeping the nest site scrupulously clean. This is a survival strategy left over from the dog's wild origins, which helps to minimize the scent signals that could otherwise be given off to predators.

Handling the puppies properly from day one is vitally important. Newborn pups should not be removed from the nest unless absolutely necessary, since this will distress the mother. However, gentle handling to place them to suckle and to check each one over is essential. This helps to accustom them to the smell and touch of human beings, and encourages the mother to be confident about having people around her pups.

PUPPY PROBLEMS

Occasionally, one puppy may cry and yowl and appear less than contented in the litter. This may be because it is not feeding properly, and it is essential that this is addressed quickly. The greatest danger to young puppies is dehydration. To test this, gently pull up the loose skin on the back of the neck and then let it fall again. The skin should return quickly to the neck, not sink slowly. If you are in any doubt, call your vet for advice.

BEGINNING SOCIALIZATION

During the next few weeks, puppies grow and develop at an incredible pace. Their eyes open and their hearing gradually improves, so that by four weeks they are quite agile and mobile, playing with each other and showing an interest in everything around them. From this stage, the puppies' psychological development is of paramount importance. They need stimulation and to learn about life. Exposing puppies to various floor surfaces and noises, such as the washing machine, helps to prepare them mentally and to socialize them. It will also teach them strategies to cope with the challenges of life ahead. Some experts recommend trips outdoors, but it is important that the puppies don't come into contact with disease. Ask your vet for advice.

FOSTERING A PUPPY

◆

Occasionally, for any one of a number of reasons, a bitch may not be able to feed her own puppies. This leaves two options: hand-rearing or fostering. If another lactating bitch can be found, fostering is nearly always the better option, for both medical and behavioral reasons. Rubbing the mother with your hands, then immediately rubbing the puppy, will help to create an artificial "scent-exchange" between the puppy and foster mother, which may help her to accept it as her own.

Hand-rearing is a difficult and time-consuming process. Puppies need to be bottle-fed on a specially prepared milk substitute, in the correct amounts, and at two-to-three hour intervals, including during the night. They also need to be stimulated to relieve themselves after every feed, since newborn puppies cannot do so themselves. Apart from the practical difficulties of hand-rearing puppies, there are other considerations. Expert advice on the puppies' behavioral development should be sought. Puppies that do not experience the mother's early discipline through weaning can become highly excitable, undisciplined dogs, difficult to train and with poor social skills around other dogs.

WEANING: LIFE'S FIRST LESSON

By about four weeks, the novelty of motherhood has worn off, and most mothers will be glad to get away from their puppies for short periods of time. The behavioral importance of weaning now takes over.

Weaning is a natural process. The mother cannot afford to feed the pups forever, at the expense of her own health. Puppies become more demanding as they get older, so that on the mother's return to the nest, she can almost be "mugged" for milk.

Most bitches start the weaning process by standing while the puppies suckle for a short period, then simply walking off when she has had enough. This is the first experience the pups have of being thwarted in their attempts to get what they want, and is a very important lesson.

The bitch will deny the puppies access to her teats more and more frequently, which creates frustration for them. As the puppies try harder to get to her, she will need to redirect their demands for food to another source. In the wild, the new source of food would be regurgitated, semi-digested food from the mother's mouth, but in our domestic situation this will come from a bowl of suitable weaning food provided by the owner.

Good mother dogs make their displeasure at their puppies' repeated attempts to feed known in firm, but gentle, ways. A hard stare is the pups' first warning. A growl may follow. Very persistent puppies may then be pushed firmly away with a nose-butt, or even an inhibited snap, where the bitch snaps her jaws close to the puppy without making contact. This discipline is essential, for it teaches the puppy to resolve the conflict between its feelings and other dogs, and forces it to find an alternative source of food. Resolving this conflict is life's most important lesson, and it explains why hand-reared puppies and those separated too early from their mothers may always have difficulties coping with the many challenges that life later presents.

WEANING PUPPIES

◆

◆ Different breeders have their own timetable, but weaning usually starts at around three to four weeks.

◆ Good-quality complete puppy food is widely available and is easily digested. It contains the highly concentrated calories that puppies need at this important growth stage. Complete puppy food contains all nutritional requirements, and supplementation is unnecessary.

◆ To use a complete puppy food, soak it in warm water and mix it to a smooth gruel that is the right consistency for lapping. You may need to encourage the puppies to eat by placing food on the end of your finger and allowing them to lick or suck.

Leave the food down for 15 minutes at each feed, then remove any leftovers.

◆ Once the puppies are established on the food, gradually start to reduce the amount of water added.

◆ As the puppies grow, leave a small bowl of dry food down in addition to normal feeds.

◆ The amount of puppy food required will vary according to the size of the litter and the breed. Use the suggested feeding quantities of bought puppy food only as a guideline.

◆ Puppies do not need additional milk in their diets. Its consumption can cause digestive problems such as diarrhea, because shortly after weaning puppies lose their ability to digest milk sugar.

Dogs in Action

Dogs come in a seemingly limitless variety of shapes and sizes, with physiques defined and senses heightened to produce astonishing skills, and a host of breathtaking feats. From the discipline of the working dog, the playful antics of a puppy and the determination of the hunters to the graceful speed of the

greyhound and the capricious intelligence of the poodle, dogs exhibit a stunning array of talents, demeanors and abilities. Whether leaping for a ball at play, negotiating an agility course, employing skill at work or simply running free in a field, a dog in action embodies a particular type of genius.

I am called a dog because I fawn on those who give me anything, I yelp at those who refuse, and I set my teeth in rascals.

DIOGENES (C.400 – C.325 BC)

It was inevitable that the clash for leadership should come ... it was his nature, because he had been gripped tight by that nameless, incomprehensible pride of the trail and trace — that pride that holds dogs together in the toil to the last gasp, which lures them to die joyfully in the harness, and breaks their hearts if they are cut out ...

JACK LONDON, THE CALL OF THE WILD, 1903

The months went by, binding stronger and stronger the
covenant between dog and man. This was the ancient
covenant that the first wolf that came in from the
Wild entered into with man. And, like all succeeding
wolves and wild dogs that had done likewise,
White Fang worked the covenant out for himself.
The terms were simple. For the possession of a
flesh-and-blood god, he exchanged his own liberty …
his allegiance to man seemed somehow a law of his being
greater than the love of liberty, of kind and kin.

JACK LONDON, WHITE FANG, 1906

Here lies one, who never drew
Blood himself, yet many slew…
Stout he was, and large of limb,
Scores fled at sight of him;
And to all this fame he rose
Only following his nose.

WILLIAM COWPER, "AN EPITAPH", 1779

Who finds me out,
both far and near,
Tracing my footsteps
everywhere,
And when I whistle's
sure to hear?
My Rover.

JOHN CLARE, "MY ROVER", 1809

If you pick up a starving dog and make him prosperous, he will not bite you. This is the principal difference between a dog and a man.

MARK TWAIN, PUDD'NHEAD WILSON, *1894*

PART 4

DOG BREEDS

B reeds of dog are grouped according to their characteristics, and are divided into different categories in different kennel clubs. The groups listed here are Hounds, Terriers, Utility Dogs, Toy Dogs, Working Dogs and Gundogs. Each breed's characteristics and needs are assessed, and its exercise and grooming requirements are graded. Exercise is graded as: minimum, meaning a short walk or two each day; moderate, for dogs requiring more than a short walk; plenty, for dogs needing exercise for long periods each day; and a few miles daily, for breeds that require a great deal of regular exercise. Grooming is classified as: low maintenance, for dogs needing only a regular brush and wash; moderate, for breeds needing more than a monthly polish; considerable, for dogs that need regular attention; and high maintenance, for breeds requiring regular professional grooming or a great deal of care by an enthusiastic amateur.

Hounds

History ◆ Types of hounds ◆ Keeping hounds as pets

Hounds are among the most ancient breeds of dog, and have changed little over the centuries. Greyhounds, for example, are the first hunting dogs for which there are historical records.

HOUND HISTORY

Early hunting hounds lived with the Celts, and moved across Europe wherever they settled. Many hound breeds were destroyed as their Celtic owners were conquered by invaders, but where the Celts survived – in Ireland, Brittany and Britain – their hounds continued to thrive. When conquered Celts were absorbed by other cultures across Europe, their dogs bred with other native canine populations.

One of the forefathers of many modern hound breeds was the 6th-century St Hubert Hound. This breed was developed by a group of Belgian monks at a temple named after their patron, Hubert, who converted to Christianity after seeing a vision of a stag with a cross between his antlers. The Bloodhound is directly related to the ancient St Hubert Hound.

Below: The Finnish Spitz, still used as a hunting companion in its native Finland, is a popular pet and an excellent watchdog.

Above: The Hamiltonstövare tends to hunt alone, rather than in a pack.

Left: Unlike many other hounds, the Pharaoh Hound hunts by sight, sound and smell.

Over the centuries most countries and regions developed their own types of hound, but France excelled at it, creating more breeds than any other nation. The hounds of many other countries, such as the Devon Staghound and the Welsh Hound, are now extinct, and France has retained the honor of being the original home of the hound.

Hunting was the chief recreation of the nobility in France and dogs were carefully bred to attend to their needs. In the 13th century, Louis IX planned his wars for the autumn and summer so that he would be free to hunt in the winter and spring. Many breeds became extinct with the fall of the nobility in the French Revolution. Other breeds, like the Basset Griffon Vendéen, came close to extinction, but in more recent times have been re-established, and are now thriving once again.

GROUP DISTINCTIONS

Hounds are distinguished from one another by the way in which they locate their prey, and are roughly broken down into two types: scenthounds and sighthounds (also known as gazehounds). Most sighthounds are renowned for speed, while some scenthounds are not particularly fast, cornering prey instead of catching it.

Scenthounds

Scenthounds were bred to sniff out and chase game. Unlike some other hunting dogs, they would kill their prey, and wait for the hunter to come and collect it. Originally bred to hunt prey such as wolves and boar, scenthounds were large and bulky, and had tremendous stamina. Later, breeds required for hunting foxes and stags needed to be quicker, so smaller hounds, sometimes crossed with sighthounds, were favored. Short-legged Bassets, for example, were developed to work in heavy cover. This meant that hunters on foot could keep up with the dog and, with its nose close to the ground, the dog could follow a scent more keenly.

Sighthounds

Persian and Assyrian pottery dating from around 6000 BC clearly depict athletic sighthounds, suggesting that sighthounds date back considerably further than their scenthound cousins. As their name suggests, they relied on their eyes, rather than their noses, to find and hunt prey.

These dogs originated in some areas of the southern hemisphere where trees were scarce and the next meal was easy to spot. Scent was, therefore, not as vital a sense as sight. As hunting evolved, sighthounds were selected and bred for their speed so that they could run down fast prey, such as gazelle and antelope. Unlike the scenthounds, which gradually exhausted their prey through a long, steady chase, sighthounds had to run down their prey quickly. Long legs, muscular loins and a sleek body soon became the sighthound trademark. A deep chest for maximum lung capacity was also important. The popularity of sighthounds increased with the growth of the ancient sport of dog racing, in which sighthounds excelled. Although the sport is now dominated by Greyhounds, other hounds like Irish Wolfhounds, Deerhounds and Afghan Hounds were all successful in chasing artificial hares.

HOUNDS AS PETS

Because they were bred to hunt in packs, most scenthounds should get along with other dogs, although they need to develop a strong social order if they find themselves in a large group. When hounds find a scent in a park, they will follow it with determination, making early recall training (see page 86) essential. They can also be vocal, a legacy of the days when they summoned hunters with a call.

Sighthounds are often quieter dogs. Used to hunting alone, rather than in packs, the sighthound has an independent spirit. They can be equally single-minded when chasing what they consider to be prey, so early recall training (see page 86) is crucial.

Afghan Hound

The elegant but hardy Afghan Hound has been used for centuries in Afghanistan for hunting, where its long hair was evolved to cope with the cold climate. This ancient breed probably originated in the Middle East.

Characteristics
The Afghan Hound has a stunning, long, silky coat, which makes him a popular show dog. Despite an aloof air, he is affectionate and sensitive. This dog demands considerable care and attention from its owners. Afghans are large, intelligent dogs that are not easy to train, but they respond well to modern motivational training techniques.

Appearance
The Afghan Hound's long, smooth-flowing coat requires daily brushing and expert grooming. Although white markings are undesirable, any color of coat is acceptable to the Kennel Clubs. The almond-shaped eyes give an Eastern expression. The long, silky ears are set low, almost blending with the coat. The tail should be long and slender, ending in a curl. The front feet are large and covered with long hair. The elegant neck, which gives the breed a regal aspect, curves to a muscular body. The back should stand level all the way to the powerful hind legs.

Breed Assessment
LIFE EXPECTANCY 11–12 years
EXERCISE A few miles daily
GROOMING High maintenance
NOISE Talkative
HEALTH PROBLEMS None known
SIZE 25–30in (63–74cm)
BREED RECOGNIZED BY AKC, CKC, FCI, KC

Breed Assessment
LIFE EXPECTANCY 10 years
EXERCISE Moderate
GROOMING Moderate
NOISE Fairly quiet
HEALTH PROBLEMS None known
SIZE 27–30in (68–74cm)
BREED RECOGNIZED BY AKC, CKC, FCI, KC

Borzoi

Once the wolf hunter of Russian noblemen, the tall, slender Borzoi has retained its regal elegance and looks. The breed was popularized in Britain when given as a present to Queen Alexandra by the Tsar of Russia.

Characteristics
A graceful hound, with a sleek, proudly held head and long nose, this breed is known for its speed and agility. Borzois need space and plenty of exercise, and will not tolerate being cooped up. Reserved and gentle in nature, the Borzoi is affectionate with its owners and enjoys attention. Like most breeds, the Borzoi responds best to children who are not too rough or boisterous.

Appearance
The Borzoi's sleek, wavy coat needs regular grooming. The color of the coat can be mixed, but white with darker markings is most common. The curly frill on the neck gives the lean body a fuller look. Borzois have dark, slightly triangular eyes that give an intelligent expression. Small ears are carried high and well back. The tail is graceful and feathered, while the feet are long and arched, like those of a hare. The back is slightly arched and bony. Toes should be well arched and body length should come from the rib cage, rather than the loin.

Greyhound & Saluki

Both of these breeds are Middle Eastern in origin. Built for speed, they are capable of reaching 40 miles (64km) per hour. Egyptian wall paintings of what could be either breed suggest they are very ancient dogs.

Saluki

Characteristics
Light and effortless in full flight, these breeds are admired for their speed, rather than their endearing qualities. Greyhounds make wonderful family companions, being both gentle and faithful, and the Saluki, in particular, has an extremely loyal character. Both breeds can be aloof with strangers, but the Greyhound is especially sensitive and loving. They are generally quiet, unexcitable dogs, but they need ample opportunity to run freely on open ground.

Appearance
Their colors vary greatly. The Greyhound's fine, short coat is very easy to groom. The Saluki is also easy to groom but needs gentle combing to avoid breaking the delicate feathered hair. The ears differ widely: the Greyhound has very small ears, while those of the Saluki are long and silky. Tails are long with a natural curve, but are longer haired on the Saluki. Both breeds are large chested with long, powerful necks and hindquarters.

Breed Assessment
LIFE EXPECTANCY *Saluki* 12 years; *Greyhound* 10 years
EXERCISE *Saluki* A few miles daily; *Greyhound* Moderate
GROOMING *Saluki* Moderate; *Greyhound* Low maintenance
NOISE *Both* Fairly quiet
HEALTH PROBLEMS *Both* None known
SIZE (AVERAGE) *Saluki* 25in (63cm); *Greyhound* 29in (72cm)
BREEDS RECOGNIZED BY AKC, CKC, FCI, KC

Breed Assessment
LIFE EXPECTANCY 14 years
EXERCISE Moderate
GROOMING Low maintenance
NOISE Fairly quiet
HEALTH PROBLEMS None known
SIZE 18–23in (44–57cm)
BREED RECOGNIZED BY AKC, CKC, FCI, KC

Whippet

A descendant of the Greyhound with some Terrier blood, the Whippet was originally used for racing and hunting rabbits in northern England.

Characteristics
The Whippet's lean and delicate appearance is deceptive. For a small dog, this breed has rapid acceleration and is almost as fast as the Greyhound. Clean and well behaved, he makes an excellent family pet and may even tolerate the family cat, although few others. Courageous and energetic on the hunting field, the Whippet needs plenty of exercise, but is also quite happy with home life. Although Whippets can be nervous around lively children, they generally welcome the attention of both family and strangers.

Appearance
The very short, fine coat is easy and quick to brush clean and can be any color or mixture of colors: fawn, brindle, blue or black, normally with white. The tail is long and tapers slightly into a gentle curve. The feet are very neat with thick pads. The oval eyes are dark, and the small, rose-shaped ears are held back. This is an exceptionally lean breed with a deep chest giving plenty of heart room.

Pharaoh & Ibizan Hounds

The Pharaoh Hound is descended from the dogs depicted on ancient Egyptian tombs. The Ibizan Hound bears a great resemblance to the Pharaoh Hound. Brought from Egypt thousands of years ago to the Mediterranean island after which he is named, the Ibizan Hound was used as a hunting dog.

Characteristics
Both breeds are agile and alert and have retained strong hunting instincts. The Pharaoh Hound is friendly and affectionate and enjoys vigorous and stimulating playtime. The Ibizan Hound can be reserved around strangers, but is loyal and not normally aggressive.

Appearance
The Pharaoh's coat is short, silky and smooth but the Ibizan's can be smooth or rough. Both breeds have oval-shaped eyes and large distinctive ears that are carried erect when alert. The Pharaoh's tail should be fine, but thick at the base, and should not be tucked between the legs. The feet should be round and compact. The Ibizan's tail should be long and set low. It may be carried high, but should never be curled. The feet should have thick pads and well-arched toes. Both breeds have lithe bodies with an almost straight topline.

Pharaoh Hound

Breed Assessment
LIFE EXPECTANCY 15 years
EXERCISE Plenty
GROOMING Low maintenance
NOISE Fairly quiet
HEALTH PROBLEMS None known
SIZE *Pharaoh* 21–25in (53–63cm); *Ibizan* 22–30in (56–74cm)
BREEDS RECOGNIZED BY AKC, CKC, FCI, KC

Breed Assessment
LIFE EXPECTANCY 11 years
EXERCISE Plenty
GROOMING *Smooth and Wire-haired* Low maintenance;
Long-haired Considerable
NOISE Very talkative
HEALTH PROBLEMS Back problems. Miniature Long-haired should be eye-tested
SIZE *Miniature* 7in (18cm); *Standard* 10in (23cm)
BREED RECOGNIZED BY AKC, CKC, FCI, KC

Dachshund

The Dachshund is better known as the "sausage dog". *Dachs* means badger in German, and this dog was used for flushing badgers out of their setts. There are six types: standard and miniature with short, long or wire hair.

Characteristics
All varieties are intelligent and lively, with strong personalities. The Dachshund's long back can lead to back problems, so limit activities such as climbing stairs. Weight gain also puts strain on the back, so watch out for overeating. This bold and courageous breed makes a great family dog. Long-haired Dachshunds tend to be independent, but both the Wire- and Smooth-haired types are affectionate.

Appearance
Coats vary according to type. The Smooth-haired's coat is dense, short and smooth, while the Long-haired's is soft and straight, or slightly wavy. The Wire-haired's coat is short, straight and harsh, with a dense undercoat. Eyes should be medium sized and almond shaped. Ears should be set high, but not too far forward. Hind feet should be smaller and narrower than the front feet. The tail should be carried low or level with the back. The body is long and muscular, with the back lying straight.

Irish Wolfhound

The Irish Wolfhound was much favored by the nobility in Ireland for hunting wolves. It was popular until well into the 17th century, but numbers dwindled as a result of famine in Ireland and excessive exportation. The breed was revived by the late 19th century for rescue work.

Characteristics

Gentle and good natured, Irish Wolfhounds are wonderful with children. They are quite easy to train and, despite their giant stature, they require little more exercise than smaller breeds, but they do need plenty of living space. Although the Irish Wolfhound can be fairly easily domesticated, he retains much of its hunting instinct. You cannot force this breed to do anything it does not want to do, so be kind and understanding during training and it will obey you because it wants to.

Appearance

The harsh, rough coat is long over the jaw and over the dark, oval eyes, which have black lids. The ears are small and velvety in texture and do not hang very close to the face. The tail should be long, slightly curved and carried low. The feet are straight with well-arched, closed toes. The body length should come from the rib cage, rather than the loin.

Breed Assessment

LIFE EXPECTANCY 7 years
EXERCISE Moderate
GROOMING Moderate
NOISE Fairly quiet
HEALTH PROBLEMS Prone to liver disease, heart problems and bone cancer
SIZE 28–32in (71–79cm)
BREED RECOGNIZED BY AKC, CKC, FCI, KC

Breed Assessment

LIFE EXPECTANCY 12 years
EXERCISE Moderate
GROOMING Moderate
NOISE Fairly quiet
HEALTH PROBLEMS None known
SIZE 28–30in (71–76cm)
BREED RECOGNIZED BY AKC, CKC, FCI, KC

Deerhound

The Deerhound is a working dog with a long history. Traditionally it was used for hunting in the Scottish Highlands, and many paintings depict this handsome breed sleeping at the feet of noble masters. The introduction of the rifle for hunting quickly led to a decline in numbers of the deerhound, but thanks to the enthusiasm of breeders, this canine aristocrat still exists.

Characteristics

The Deerhound is strong enough to bring down a deer, but gentle enough to make a perfect pet. Plenty of exercise is essential, as is supervision around livestock. Gentle, loving, affectionate and devoted, this dog has few character flaws.

Appearance

The coat should be slightly shaggy and harsh to the touch. Eyes should be dark with black rims. Ears should be set high and folded, whether resting or aroused, and unlike the rest of the coat, they should be soft and glossy. The chest should be deep and the loin well arched, drooping to the tail, which should be long and tapered, reaching to just over 1in (2.5cm) from the ground; it should be carried in a curve when the dog is moving. Feet should be compact and well knuckled.

Basset Hound & Petit Basset Griffon Vendéen (PBGV)

Originating in medieval France, the Basset Hound was transformed by the British, who bred it with short legs so that hunters on foot could keep up while tracking hare. Some experts believe that the Basset may have been crossbred in the Middle Ages with a now-extinct Beaver Hound to produce the Petit Basset Griffon Vendéen.

Characteristics

Despite a lugubrious appearance, the Basset is happy and outgoing and makes a great companion. Moderate exercise is necessary because he has a tendency to put on weight. A well-fenced yard is a good idea, since the Basset loves to investigate interesting smells.

Appearance

The Basset has a short, smooth coat that is usually black, white and tan, or lemon and white. The PBGV's rough coat is white with lemon, orange, tricolor or grizzled markings. The Basset's lower eyelids reveal some red, and the ears are long and velvety. The PBGV has large, dark eyes and the ears should reach to the end of the nose. The Basset's long tail lifts high and the feet are big and well knuckled. The PBGV's saber-like tail is of medium length. The Basset has a long body and a broad back, while the PBGV has a deep chest and a medium-length back.

Basset Hound

Breed Assessment

LIFE EXPECTANCY *Basset* 12 years; *PBGV* 15 years
EXERCISE *Basset* Moderate; *PBGV* Plenty
GROOMING Moderate
NOISE *Basset* Talkative; *PBGV* Fairly quiet
HEALTH PROBLEMS *Basset* Eye problems; *PBGV* Skin diseases
SIZE 13–15in (33–38cm)
BREED RECOGNIZED BY AKC, CKC, FCI, KC *(Basset);* FCI, KC *(PBGV)*

Breed Assessment

LIFE EXPECTANCY 14 years
EXERCISE Moderate
GROOMING Low maintenance
NOISE Talkative
HEALTH PROBLEMS Some eye problems
SIZE Divided in to two sizes in America: up to 13in (33cm) and 13–16in (33–40cm); 13–16in (33–40cm) in UK,
BREED RECOGNIZED BY AKC, CKC, FCI, KC

Beagle

The Beagle is the smallest of the hounds. The first reference to the breed appears in the 14th century. Today, it is larger than its ancestors, which were sometimes carried by hunters on foot in pockets or saddlebags.

Characteristics

Energetic and enthusiastic, the Beagle is a sturdy, bold dog that will enjoy boisterous games. Placid and tolerant when faced with noisy children, it will adapt to most households. This dog will accept any amount of exercise, but training it to come when called should begin early to control its strong, deep-seated instinct to hunt. Although not noisy, the Beagle produces a distinctive baying sound when it is aroused.

Appearance

The short, dense, weatherproof coat is easy to keep clean and comes in all hound colors. The eyes are dark brown and should be set well apart. The long ears should be able to reach the tip of the nose. Feet should be tight, firm and well padded. The dog has a sturdy tail which should be carried up, but never over the back. The well-muscled, compact body should be well balanced and lithe, and should give the impression of power and suppleness.

American & English Foxhound & Harrier

The American Foxhound has European influences and is rangier than the Harrier which is a scaled-down version. The English Foxhound dates from perhaps as early as the 13th century, when fox-hunting first became an organized pastime. All share the same hunting ability and have the essential baying call.

Characteristics

These independent breeds make excellent family pets when raised in the home. Single-minded, but rarely aggressive, they need training and will want to feel that their human family is their pack. All are friendly dogs, although sometimes obstinate. Hounds of each breed have distinctive voices that can be recognized by their owners.

Appearance

Tricolor hound coats are common with these breeds, with white prevailing. The coat is short, dense and hardy. The medium-sized brown or hazel eyes are keen. A working English hound's ears sometimes have 1in (2.5cm) cropped from the tips to make tears less likely in pack activity. The tail is long and the feet are hard, round and cat-like. The American Foxhound is longer in the leg and finer boned; the English is broad chested, with a balanced, symmetrical look.

English Foxhound

Breed Assessment

LIFE EXPECTANCY 12 years
EXERCISE A few miles daily
GROOMING Low maintenance
NOISE Very talkative
HEALTH PROBLEMS None known
SIZE Average *American Foxhound* 25in (63cm); *English Foxhound* 24in (61cm); *Harrier* 20in (49cm)
BREEDS RECOGNIZED BY AKC, CKC, FCI *(American Foxhound)*; AKC, CKC, FCI, KC *(English Foxhound)*; AKC, CKC, FCI *(Harrier)*

Bloodhound

Breed Assessment

LIFE EXPECTANCY 10 years
EXERCISE A few miles daily
GROOMING Low maintenance
NOISE Talkative
HEALTH PROBLEMS *Bloodhound* Some eye defects; *Coonhound* None known
SIZE *Bloodhound* 24–26in (61–66cm); *Coonhound* 21–27in (52.5–67.5cm)
BREEDS RECOGNIZED BY AKC, CKC, FCI, KC *(Bloodhound)*; AKC, CKC *(Coonhound)*

Bloodhound & Coonhound

The Bloodhound, which originated in Belgium, is one of the oldest hound breeds. This breed is famous for amazing scenting skills. The Coonhound was bred in North America to hunt raccoons and bears by chasing them up trees, then baying to alert the hunter.

Characteristics

Extremely gentle and affectionate, the Bloodhound depends on human company. Both breeds need plenty of exercise and are not suited to town life. They are generally obedient, but once they are on the trail of a scent, it will be difficult to call them back. Most Coonhounds are even tempered, but the English and Wainer Coonhounds can be highly strung.

Appearance

Both breeds have short, dense coats. The Bloodhound's eyes should be dark and medium sized; the Coonhound's range from hazel to dark. The long, pendulous ears should be set low. The Bloodhound's tail should be long and thick, and the feet strong and well knuckled. The Coonhound's tail should be set just below the level of the topline, and the feet compact. Both breeds have strong, muscular bodies with well-sprung ribs. The Bloodhound's chest should be set well down between the forelegs.

Basenji

This breed originated in Africa, where the dog is still used for hunting and flushing game. It is sometimes known as the African Barkless dog because, instead of barking, it has a unique kind of yodel.

Characteristics

The Basenji is not very dog-like: it cleans itself by licking, like a cat, it is odorless, and the female generally comes into heat only once a year. This is a muscular, agile dog with a playful sense of humor. The Basenji makes an excellent household companion if kept occupied. If bored or unhappy, it can be destructive, so needs regular, vigorous exercise and stimulation.

Appearance

The Basenji has a short, sleek coat that comes in black, tan and red, all with white markings, which should be on the feet, chest and tail tip. It has dark, almond-shaped eyes, and when its ears are pricked its brow is wrinkled, giving it a perplexed expression. The ears are very pointed and upright, and are set far forward. The breed's distinctive tail is set high and curls tightly, close to the spine. The back is short and level and there is quite a defined waist. The dog carries its head high and moves with a swinging stride on small, compact feet.

Breed Assessment
LIFE EXPECTANCY 15 years
EXERCISE Plenty
GROOMING Low maintenance
NOISE Fairly quiet
HEALTH PROBLEMS Puppies and parents should be eye-tested
SIZE 16–17in (40–43cm)
BREED RECOGNIZED BY AKC, CKC, FCI, KC

Breed Assessment
LIFE EXPECTANCY 10–11 years
EXERCISE A few miles daily
GROOMING Considerable
NOISE Very talkative
HEALTH PROBLEMS Hip-testing recommended
SIZE 24–27in (60–67cm)
BREED RECOGNIZED BY AKC, CKC, FCI, KC

Otterhound

One of the earliest recorded English breeds, the water-loving Otterhound was bred to follow the drag and wash of otters as a pack dog.

Characteristics

A rough, shaggy, lovable hound, this dog has a mind of its own and its boisterous nature needs to be controlled with a firm hand. Although adequate exercise should keep it calm in the home, it is perhaps not the best pet for the house-proud. This dog is also noisy and has a loud baying call. Mild and gentler than most hounds, even with small children, the Otterhound is tolerant of other dogs, and friendly with people in general.

Appearance

The Otterhound has a waterproof undercoat and a long, rough topcoat, which can be any of the noted hound colors: whole colored, wheaten, sandy, red, grizzled or blue. The bright, deep-set eyes vary in color according to his coat, and the long, draping ears have an inward fold close to the cheek. It has a large, heavily boned body, with a broad back and deep chest and should carry its thick tail up when moving, never over the back. Its large, round feet are slightly webbed, which facilitates its work in the water.

Rhodesian Ridgeback

A South African dog, the Rhodesian Ridgeback gets its name from the unusual ridge of hair that runs up the spine. Now a good guard dog, it was bred for hunting game and even to hunt lions.

Characteristics
This breed is large and strong, but not usually as fearsome as its association with lion hunting would suggest. The distinctive ridge on its back is formed by a patch of hair that grows in the opposite direction to the rest of the coat. An excellent family dog, it is quite placid and confident at home, but is unlikely to be friendly with strangers and can be a tenacious fighter when aroused. The Ridgeback requires careful training from a young age.

Appearance
The Ridgeback's short coat is quite easy to care for and ranges in color from light red to wheaten. The ridge on the back has two crowns at the top and tapers off evenly. Its lively, intelligent eyes are set fairly far apart. The ears are soft, rounded and often darker in color. The strong, long tail has a slight upward curve. The feet are round and tough padded for hard ground. The Ridgeback's very deep chest and powerful back give it a muscular, balanced look.

Breed Assessment
LIFE EXPECTANCY 12 years
EXERCISE Plenty
GROOMING Low maintenance
NOISE Fairly quiet
HEALTH PROBLEMS Dermoid sinus skin disease
SIZE 24–27in (61–67cm)
BREED RECOGNIZED BY AKC, CKC, FCI, KC

Breed Assessment
LIFE EXPECTANCY 12 years
EXERCISE Moderate
GROOMING Moderate
NOISE Talkative
HEALTH PROBLEMS Parents should be eye-tested
SIZE 20–21in (49–52cm)
BREED RECOGNIZED BY AKC, CKC, FCI, KC

Elkhound

The Elkhound has ancient Norwegian ancestry. Watchdog and elk hunter for the Vikings, its loud voice still makes it a good guard dog.

Characteristics
An independent, courageous dog, this strong hound needed all its weight to hunt its much larger traditional prey, the elk. Today, it retains its hunting instinct and will be happiest with an energetic family who can provide plenty of vigorous exercise. It is alert and very trainable, a high achiever in obedience and agility competition. As a family dog, the Elkhound is usually affectionate and good natured.

Appearance
The Elkhound has a thick coat but it is not difficult to keep it presentable. The undercoat is woolly, dense and weather resistant, with a straight outer coat, and there are distinct harness marks, created by longer, darker hairs from the shoulder to the elbow. Its ears are small, sharp and pricked; when it is aroused, the outer edges of the ears should be vertical. Its thick tail curls strongly over the middle of his back. It has good, straight legs and small feet, designed for neat, fast trotting. Its body is compact, with a powerful, straight and level back.

Gundogs

Types of gundog ✦ *Changes in the group* ✦ *Keeping gundogs*

Gundogs – known as sporting dogs in the United States – were bred to work from the hunter's gun. The name "gundog" is fairly recent, as these breeds assisted hunters long before the advent of gunpowder. Prior to this, when falcons, nets and bows were used in the hunt, they were known as "bird dogs".

GROUP DISTINCTIONS

Despite a variety of backgrounds and appearances, gundogs are grouped because of their shared hunting skills.

Traditionally, each group of gundogs has had a specific task, although there has been some overlap between their functions. It was mainly in England that dogs were developed for specific purposes. In continental Europe, many of the dogs in the group were multiskilled and were used for a variety of tasks on the hunt, from pointing, setting and flushing on land and water through to retrieving. The Italian Spinone and Weimaraner are good examples of such versatile gundog breeds.

Several types of gundogs are recognized today: retrievers, water dogs, spaniels, pointers and setters.

Pointers

Pointers were developed from hounds that showed a tendency to pause before concealed game rather than flushing and chasing it. The dogs were bred to sniff out game birds and,

Below: The Auvergne Pointer, little known outside France, probably descends from the Old Pyrenean Braque and the Gascony Pointer.

Left: This Gordon Setter puppy's slender frame belies the fact that Gordon Setters are the heaviest and strongest of all the setters.

With the decline of field sports in Germany after the 1848 revolutions, German pointing and setting dogs virtually disappeared. Around 1890, however, German hunters turned their attentions to these old breeds and developed pointers in three coat variations: the Weimaraner, Munsterlander and Czesky Fousek.

GUNDOGS AS PETS

Generally, gundog breeds make excellent companions. Labradors and Golden Retrievers, for example, are hugely popular as pets throughout the world. The nature of the group's heritage, however, means that gundog breeds are country dogs, with boundless energy and a desire to work for their owners. They need lots of exercise to channel their energy and enthusiasm, and their minds also need to be kept occupied.

A gundog's hunting instincts are so strong, that they may be difficult to harness. Once a pointer or setter catches an interesting scent in the park, your pleas will fall on deaf ears. Early recall training (see page 86) is essential for all gundog breeds.

once located, to point towards them with an upraised leg. Pointers worked some distance from the hunter.

Setters

Setters are larger and longer-legged than spaniels. Like pointers, setters were bred to freeze when they spotted game. They would then "set", or drop to the ground, and wait until the hunter gave his instruction.

Spaniels

Spaniels are the largest subgroup of gundogs, and were used to spring game from its cover once it had been found. The dogs would crouch down and slowly creep towards the game to allow the hunter time to approach, his nets or gun at the ready. It has long been believed that spaniels originate from Spain – *espaignol* being the old French word for "Spanish (dog)". However, the French word *espanir* means "to crouch or flatten", which has led some experts to believe that France may, in fact, be the spaniel's country of origin.

Retrievers

Retrievers, thought to have been of mastiff origin, worked with spaniels, which would spring the game. The

retriever remained fairly close to the hunter and waited to be instructed to fetch the shot bird.

Water dogs

Water dogs became prominent around the Mediterranean and Europe about 2000 years ago, when they were bred to flush and retrieve game from the shore and the water. Their traditional curly or corded coats became very heavy when waterlogged, and it was customary to trim them so that only the coat around the ribs and legs was long. This enabled them to be buoyant. The Poodle and Portuguese Water Dog retain this traditional trim to this day.

GROUP CHANGES

Some of the original gundogs have moved on to other breed groups. The British miniaturized some spaniels, such as the King Charles Spaniel and the Papillon, which are now grouped with the toy dogs.

Right: The thick, waterproof coat of the Pudel Pointer makes this breed ideal for all-weather tracking and retrieving. This breed is rare, even in its native Germany.

English Setter

Originally bred by the British nobility to hunt game, this is one of the oldest gundog breeds, dating back to the 14th century. Now the Setter is a popular pet that has not forgotten its roots and loves the outdoors.

Characteristics
Elegant, active and fun-loving, the English Setter retains many puppy-like qualities well into adulthood. The need for daily maintenance of the coat and plenty of exercise mean it can be a time-consuming pet. This breed also hates to be alone and thrives on companionship. But this breed is affectionate, gentle and devoted to family life.

Appearance
The English Setter's long, slightly wavy and silky coat comes in a variety of colors, in both solid and flecked (belton) forms: black and white, orange and white, lemon and white, liver and white and tricolor (blue belton and tan, or liver belton and tan). The eyes range from hazel to dark brown in color. The velvety tipped, low-set ears should hang by the cheeks. The tail should be slightly curved without turning upwards. The feet should be well padded and the toes arched. The back is short and level. This breed should be "well ribbed" – that is, have a round ribcage that is set deep in the back ribs.

Breed Assessment
LIFE EXPECTANCY 12 years
EXERCISE Plenty
GROOMING Considerable
NOISE Talkative
HEALTH PROBLEMS Hip dysplasia; some skin disorders
SIZE 24–27in (61–68cm)
BREED RECOGNIZED BY AKC, CKC, FCI, KC

Breed Assessment
LIFE EXPECTANCY 13 years
EXERCISE A few miles daily
GROOMING Considerable
NOISE Talkative
HEALTH PROBLEMS Hip dysplasia
SIZE 23–27in (57–68cm)
BREED RECOGNIZED BY AKC, CKC, FCI, KC

Gordon Setter

This hardy Scottish breed is believed to have originated from the Duke of Gordon's estates in the late 18th century. Bred to work in the field, the Gordon Setter was highly prized for its stamina and scenting abilities.

Characteristics
The stylish Gordon Setter is a real gundog at heart. It has boundless energy and loves being outdoors. It is devoted to its owners and very protective, so it can be wary of strangers. This intelligent and strong-willed breed needs consistent and sensitive handling during training. Outgoing and bold, it has a gentle, even disposition and makes a wonderfully loyal companion.

Appearance
The moderate-length coat should be flat and curl-free, apart from on the head, front of the legs and tips of the ears. This dog is black and tan in color, with mahogany markings over the eyes, on the muzzle, chest, feet, inside the hind legs and under the tail. The bright, dark brown eyes have a keen, intelligent expression. The ears are thin, low set and lie close to the head. The tail can be straight or slightly curved, and can be carried either horizontally or below the level of the back. The body is moderate in length, with a deep brisket and back ribs.

Irish Setter

The Irish Setter, also known as the Red Setter, was originally bred to scent out game, which would then be retrieved by smaller spaniels. Gradually, dual-purpose dogs became more popular and the Irish Setter was used less. The breed is now more favored as a pet.

Characteristics
Handsome and athletic, this dog has irrepressible energy, coupled with an innate need to follow a scent; as a result, walks can be adventurous. Affectionate and anxious to please, the Irish Setter makes a good family dog, but it can be a handful to train, not because of its ill-deserved reputation for being stupid, but because its instincts are difficult to overcome.

Appearance
The Irish Setter has a rich chestnut coat; some white markings are not unusual. The head, front of the legs and tips of the ears are short and fine. The rest of the coat is longer and straight, with some feathering and fringing. Eye color ranges from hazel to dark brown, and the ears are set low and well back. The tail is carried just below or level with the back. The small feet have strong toes that are close together and arched. The chest is deep but narrow, with well-sprung ribs.

Breed Assessment
LIFE EXPECTANCY 12 years
EXERCISE A few miles daily
GROOMING Considerable
NOISE Talkative
HEALTH PROBLEMS Hip dysplasia and eye problems
SIZE Up to 27in (68.5cm)
BREED RECOGNIZED BY AKC, CKC, FCI, KC

Irish Red & White Setter

The breed dates back to at least the mid-17th century and is thought to have preceded its close relation, the Irish Setter. The rise in popularity of the Irish Setter around the end of the 19th century almost brought about the extinction of the Red and White, although it is now an established breed that is on the increase.

Characteristics
Energetic, powerful and athletic, this breed adores the countryside and needs lots of exercise. The Irish Red and White Setter is a happy dog that is affectionate, good natured and obedient. This dog fits well into family life as long as it is given enough exercise to quench its thirst for being outdoors.

Appearance
The coat has some feathering and can be slightly wavy. The pearly white base brings out the solid red patches beautifully. Some mottling is also present, particularly around the face, which gives an impression of freckles. The hazel or dark brown eyes are round. The ears are set well back and level with the eyes and lie close to the head. The tail is amply feathered and carried level with the back or below it. This dog has a strong, muscular build with a deep chest, well-sprung ribs and sinewy limbs.

Breed Assessment
LIFE EXPECTANCY 13 years
EXERCISE Plenty
GROOMING Moderate
NOISE Talkative
HEALTH PROBLEMS Eye problems
SIZE Up to 27in (68.5cm)
BREED RECOGNIZED BY FCI, KC

Golden Retriever

The Golden Retriever was probably first bred in Scotland to retrieve game in the shooting field. Its natural working ability, intelligence and good looks have made it one of the world's most well-loved breeds. Still used for working, it is equally popular as a family pet.

Characteristics
This is an elegant, yet sturdy, dog that is friendly, obedient and even tempered. The instinct to retrieve remains, and it will often bring its owner unexpected gifts. The ease with which it can be trained has led it often to be employed as a guide dog. If deprived of the company of its family for too long, it can be destructive, but virtually nothing will ruffle its composure.

Appearance
The Golden Retriever's coat can be flat or wavy with good feathering and a dense, water-resistant undercoat. Any shade of cream or gold is acceptable to Kennel Clubs. The eyes are big and dark, with dark rims, and set well apart. Ears are of moderate size, set on a level with the eyes. The tail is level with the back and curled at the tip. The feet are round and cat-like. The body is well balanced and powerful, without being heavy. The neck should fit well into the shoulders and the ribs be deep in the body.

Breed Assessment
LIFE EXPECTANCY 13 years
EXERCISE Plenty
GROOMING Considerable
NOISE Talkative
HEALTH PROBLEMS Eye- and hip-testing recommended
SIZE 20–24in (51–61cm)
BREED RECOGNIZED BY AKC, CKC, FCI, KC

Breed Assessment
LIFE EXPECTANCY 11 years
EXERCISE A few miles daily
GROOMING Moderate
NOISE Fairly quiet
HEALTH PROBLEMS None known
SIZE 25–27in (62.5–67.5cm)
BREED RECOGNIZED BY AKC, CKC, FCI, KC

Curly-coated Retriever

Bred as a multipurpose hunting retriever, the Curly-coated Retriever was popular in the 19th century with English gamekeepers. Famed for its field ability, it is now more popular in the USA than in Britain.

Characteristics
Loyal, affectionate and intelligent, this Retriever makes an excellent guard dog, and will probably bark only when there is trouble. Bold, friendly and supremely confident, it is primarily a working dog. It may appear aloof, but this dog loves its family. It will work and play enthusiastically and, provided it gets sufficient exercise, will be content and happy to relax when at home. Training needs to be consistent and stimulating to keep this dog's interest.

Appearance
The waterproof coat is a dense mass of tight curls that should run from the occiput bone on the head to the tip of the tail. Elsewhere the coat should be short and without curls. The coat should be brushed as little as possible to avoid altering its curliness. The eyes should be large, but not prominent, and brown or dark brown in color. The ears should be quite small and set just above the level of the head. The body is deep chested and oval in cross section, with a slight tuck up to the flank.

Flat-coated Retriever & Chesapeake Bay Retriever

The Flat-coated Retriever developed in Britain and gained popularity through its good temperament and working ability. The Chesapeake Bay Retriever evolved in America as a working dog and this remains its principal role.

Characteristics
Both breeds are friendly, intelligent and energetic. They love to retrieve and swim, and are best-suited to the country. The Flat-coated Retriever is easy-going and will adapt to most situations. The Chesapeake Bay Retriever is trickier to train but responds well to kind handling.

Appearance
The Flat-coated Retriever's black or brown coat has moderate feathering. The medium-sized eyes should be dark brown or hazel. Small ears should be set close to the side of the head. The tail should be short and straight and the feet round with arched toes. The body should be well arched in the center, with flat ribs. The Chesapeake Bay Retriever's coat should be thick and slightly wavy with a woolly undercoat, and dark brown or yellow-brown in color. The yellow eyes should be set wide apart. Small ears should hang loose on the head. Feathering on the tail is not acceptable. The feet should be webbed, and the chest strong and deep.

Flat-coated Retriever

Breed Assessment
LIFE EXPECTANCY *Flat-coated* 14 years; *Chesapeake Bay* 12 years
EXERCISE *Both* A few miles daily
GROOMING *Flat-coated* Considerable;
Chesapeake Bay Moderate
NOISE *Both* Fairly quiet
HEALTH PROBLEMS *Both* Eye-testing recommended
SIZE *Flat-coated* 23–26in (56.5–65cm);
Chesapeake Bay 21–26in (53.5–66cm)
BREEDS RECOGNIZED BY AKC, CKC, FCI, KC

Breed Assessment
LIFE EXPECTANCY 15 years
EXERCISE Plenty
GROOMING Low maintenance
NOISE Fairly quiet
SIZE 21–23in (54–57cm)
HEALTH PROBLEMS Elbow disease; eye- and hip-testing essential
BREED RECOGNIZED BY AKC, CKC, FCI, KC

Labrador Retriever

Native to Newfoundland and later moved to Labrador, this Retriever was originally used to retrieve fishing nets, but its skills as a gundog were soon recognized. Initially black, its coat can now also be yellow or chocolate.

Characteristics
Great intelligence and a natural working instinct make the Labrador an almost perfect gundog. Although boisterous as a puppy, it is usually quickly trained. It forms close relations with its owners, loves to play and is a reliable companion for children. It is greatly sought after as a pet, and is commonly used as a guide and therapy dog. Happy, it needs to be active or it may become bored. A huge appetite can lead to weight problems if its diet is not carefully managed.

Appearance
The Labrador's outercoat is short and dense, without wave or feathering. A soft undercoat provides all-weather protection. The brown or hazel eyes are medium sized. Ears are set slightly back, and do not hang very close to the head. The tail is thick at the base and tapers gradually, with no feathering. The feet are round and compact, with well-developed pads. The chest is wide and deep with well-sprung ribs. The back has a level topline.

Cocker Spaniel

The most popular member of the spaniel family, this dog was originally known as the Cocking Spaniel because it was used to flush woodcock. Spaniels were not classified separately until dog shows were established, so although the Cocker has existed for some time, it was only recognized in the late 19th century.

Characteristics
Its working instinct means that it enjoys games of fetch. This breed should always be kept physically and mentally stimulated, although it will adapt to town or country living. The show Cocker is less sturdy than its working relation. Affectionate, gentle and eager to please, it is a playful companion but can be strong-willed. Some experts believe that animals with solid-color coats can suffer from "rage syndrome", and suggest that those that display unacceptable aggression should not breed.

Appearance
The coat is flat and silky, never wavy or wiry. Forelegs, body and hind legs above the hocks are well feathered. The the lobular ears are set level with the full, brown eyes. The tail is set slightly lower than the line of the back, and must be carried level. Ribs are well sprung, and the topline is level. Feet are firm and thickly padded.

Breed Assessment
LIFE EXPECTANCY 12 years
EXERCISE Plenty
GROOMING High maintenance
NOISE Talkative
HEALTH PROBLEMS Eye test recommended; ear and kidney problems
SIZE 15–16in (38–41cm)
CUSTOMARILY DOCKED Yes
BREED RECOGNIZED BY AKC, CKC, FCI, KC

Breed Assessment
LIFE EXPECTANCY 12 years
EXERCISE Plenty
GROOMING High maintenance
NOISE Talkative
HEALTH PROBLEMS Eye-testing recommended; ear problems
SIZE 13.5–15.5in (33.75–38.75cm)
CUSTOMARILY DOCKED Yes
BREED RECOGNIZED BY AKC, CKC, FCI, KC

American Cocker Spaniel

Although derived from English Cocker Spaniels introduced into America in the 1880s, this dog is now easily distinguished. The American Cocker Spaniel's head is rounder and narrower, its muzzle shorter, and its coat more profuse. The breed was first recognized as a separate breed in the 1930s.

Characteristics
Good with humans, the American Cocker makes an excellent family dog. To keep its coat in shape, grooming must be part of a daily routine; if it is allowed to matt or knot, it can suffer much discomfort. Keen to work, with a trusting and gentle character, it is a rewarding companion. As long as it gets adequate exercise, it should adapt to life in the city. This is a gentle and playful dog that is both intelligent and obedient.

Appearance
Its flat or slightly wavy silky coat is short and fine on the head, medium length on the body, and well feathered on ears, chest, abdomen and legs. Eyes are large, round and full. Ears are long and low set. The tail is carried level with or just above the strong back, which slopes from withers to set of tail. The chest is deep, the hips wide. Feet are compact, round and firm, with hair between the toes.

Clumber & Field Spaniel

The heaviest of the spaniel family, the Clumber originated in France. It was developed by the Duc de Noailles, who worked the dog in the field as a beater and retriever. The duke took the breed to Clumber Park, near Newcastle, England, after which it is named. All sporting spaniels were once known as Field Spaniels, but when this group was divided, the larger spaniels kept the name.

Characteristics

The Clumber is an excellent retriever with tremendous scenting ability. Deliberate efforts should be made to keep it active, since it can become lazy. It is not an ideal dog in a small house, but makes a good pet. The Field Spaniel is a devoted family member that may be reserved with strangers. It is very docile and friendly, but introduce other animals early to avoid problems later.

Appearance

The Clumber's coat is abundant, straight, thick and silky, and the legs and chest well feathered. Dark amber eyes are slightly sunk, ears large and neatly shaped. Its back is straight and long, with a low-set, well-feathered tail. Feet are large and round. The Field Spaniel has a long, flat, glossy coat, with waves. The dark hazel eyes are almond shaped. Both ears and tail are set low. The chest is deep.

Clumber Spaniel

Breed Assessment

LIFE EXPECTANCY *Clumber* 10 years; *Field* 13 years
EXERCISE *Both* Plenty
GROOMING *Both* Considerable
NOISE *Clumber* Very talkative. *Field* Fairly quiet
HEALTH PROBLEMS *Both* Hip and ear problems
SIZE *Clumber* 19in (47cm); *Field* 18in (45.7cm)
CUSTOMARILY DOCKED *Both* Yes
BREED RECOGNIZED BY *Both* AKC, CKC, FCI, KC

chest, and the back ribs must also be deep.

Breed Assessment

LIFE EXPECTANCY 12 years
EXERCISE Plenty
GROOMING Considerable
NOISE Fairly quiet
HEALTH PROBLEMS Hip-scoring; some eye and ear problems; prone to eye and lip infections
SIZE 15–16in (38–41cm)

Sussex Spaniel

The Sussex Spaniel originates from the English county of the same name, where it was used to work through dense undergrowth. It faced extinction in the early part of the 20th century but now enjoys increased popularity.

Characteristics

This spaniel's appearance tends to belie its energetic disposition. It is affectionate, with a placid outlook, but, like all spaniels, needs plenty of exercise. It is both lovable and cunning, and likes to bark. The Sussex Spaniel is sociable and usually gets on with children, cats and other dogs. A devoted pet, this breed generally favours one person. Its long, rich coat makes it an unsuitable breed for hot or humid conditions unless its coat is kept clipped.

Appearance

The coat is abundant and flat, with an ample undercoat, and is a characteristic rich, dark liver color. The hazel eyes are fairly large, and the ears are large and lobular. The tail should never be carried above the level of the back. The feet are round and well feathered between the toes. The dog should have a deep

English Springer Spaniel

One of the oldest British spaniels, this breed was separated from the Welsh Springers in 1902. It was once known as the Norfolk Spaniel, after one of the Dukes of Norfolk who kept the strain. The breed got its "springer" title because of its ability to "spring", or startle, game. Show dogs are often smaller than the working strain.

Characteristics
This dog has a cheerful, extrovert nature, which makes it a good companion. It is faithful, intelligent and devoted to its family. Although gentle and amenable, this is a hardy dog that will walk or work tirelessly all day. It loves to retrieve and to swim, and will need long, regular walks, with a chance to play off lead. Bred as a working dog, it is nevertheless a popular, sociable pet.

Appearance
The straight, weatherproof coat should never be coarse. Colors are liver and white, black and white, or either of these colors with tan markings. The kind, alert eyes are dark and of medium size. The fairly long ears sit close to the head and are nicely feathered. The dog has a lively tail, always carried low. Compact, rounded feet have strong pads. Built for endurance and activity, it should have a strong muscular body.

Breed Assessment
LIFE EXPECTANCY 13 years
EXERCISE A few miles daily
GROOMING Considerable
NOISE Talkative
HEALTH PROBLEMS Eye test strongly recommended; ear problems
SIZE 20in (51cm)
CUSTOMARILY DOCKED Yes
BREED RECOGNIZED BY AKC, CKC, FCI, KC

Breed Assessment
LIFE EXPECTANCY 14 years
EXERCISE Plenty
GROOMING Moderate
NOISE Talkative
HEALTH PROBLEMS Hip and eye test recommended; ear problems
SIZE 18–19in (46–48cm)
CUSTOMARILY DOCKED Yes
BREED RECOGNIZED BY AKC, CKC, FCI, KC

Welsh Springer Spaniel

Wales's distinctive red and white spaniel was identified in the medieval Laws of Wales, although it was not recognized until about 1900. Known as the "starter" in Wales, its purpose was to "spring" game.

Characteristics
Loyal and hard working, this spaniel combines the role of family pet and sportsman's companion well. The active tail emphasizes its merry nature, and it is a tough, faithful, willing worker. Its strong nose and sporting instincts are strong and can become a problem if it is not trained from an early age. It can be boisterous, but most Welsh Springers are not naturally aggressive or nervous. It is usually very friendly to people, loves company and does not like to be left on its own. This breed will happily live in a town as long as it receives adequate exercise.

Appearance
The thick, flat, silky coat has a unique keep-clean quality, and is always rich red and pearly white in color. The medium-sized eyes are hazel or dark, and the small ears are set low and hang close to the cheeks; they should narrow towards the tip. The tail should never be carried above the level of the back. The firm, round, cat-like feet have hard pads. The body is strong and muscular.

Irish Water Spaniel

The survivor of two varieties of water spaniel found in Ireland, and once known as the Southern Irish Water Spaniel, this is the tallest of the spaniels and, as its name suggests, its expertise lies in retrieving downed fowl shot over water.

Characteristics

The Irish Water Spaniel's topknot gives this breed a quizzical expression, which adds to its appealing appearance. It is a sporting and companionable dog that enjoys affection and fun. Like all sporting dogs, it thrives on exercise and likes to be kept occupied. A good family dog, it can be headstrong if not trained from an early age.

Appearance

Long, loose curls on the head form a topknot; the muzzle has smooth, short hair. The coat, which has an oily quality and is a rich dark liver color, sometimes with a purplish tint known as puce-liver, should be free from woolliness and there should be crisp tight ringlets. The small eyes are almond shaped and the long, oval ears hang close to the cheeks. The short tail tapers to a fine point and acts as a good rudder in the water. The large, round feet are well covered with hair. A square body with barrel ribs gives the dog his unique rolling gait.

Breed Assessment

LIFE EXPECTANCY 12 years
EXERCISE Plenty
GROOMING Considerable
NOISE Talkative
HEALTH PROBLEMS Hip-testing recommended
SIZE 20–23in (51–58cm)
BREED RECOGNIZED BY AKC, CKC, FCI, KC

Breed Assessment

LIFE EXPECTANCY 12 years
EXERCISE Plenty
GROOMING Considerable
NOISE Very talkative
HEALTH PROBLEMS None known
SIZE 15–18in (38–45cm)
BREED RECOGNIZED BY AKC, CKC, FCI

American Water Spaniel

A relatively modern American breed with little history, this dog is thought to have descended from other spaniels, including the Irish Water Spaniel. Originally bred for its size, color and ability to retrieve ducks and geese in water, it will also retrieve on land.

Characteristics

True spaniel traits make this an easy dog to handle. Hunting is its natural instinct and it likes to be kept occupied all the time. This spaniel therefore enjoys all types of training and is never happier than when in water. Affectionate and charming, it is also hardy and intelligent and an ideal pet that will play well with all members of the family. It needs companionship and regular exercise. Although a good pet, this breed can be boisterous with other animals.

Appearance

It has a closely curled, or marcelled, coat with short hair on the face and tail. It is always dark brown in color, but a small amount of white on the chest and toes is allowed. The eyes tone with the color of its coat and the ears are typically spaniel-like and covered in curls. The tail is moderately long. Large, round spread feet have hair over them and between the toes. It is sturdy and muscular.

Pointer

The Pointer was bred for the speed and alertness necessary for gun sports. Developed from the Spanish Pointer, the English Pointer, now known simply as the Pointer, has been exported all over the world.

Characteristics

This is a straight, no-nonsense breed of dog, perfectly developed for the job that it does so well: rigidly pointing to the whereabouts of scented game with its muzzle, often with a foreleg raised. Obedient and good natured, it can be suspicious of strangers. Its need for exercise is great, and it will be happiest living in the country. The Pointer is good with children, but will take hunting responsibilities seriously when tested.

Appearance

The short, smooth coat is easy to look after. The most common colors are lemon, orange, liver and black, all with white; tricolors and self-colors are rarer. The Pointer's head, with a slightly concave muzzle, is its most important feature. Acute hearing is essential for hunting prowess, and its ears lie close to its head. The shoulders slope and the long neck is slightly arched. The medium-length tail tapers to a point and is carried level with the back, and the well-knit feet have arched toes.

Breed Assessment
LIFE EXPECTANCY 14 years
EXERCISE A few miles daily
GROOMING Low maintenance
NOISE Fairly quiet
HEALTH PROBLEMS None known
SIZE 24–28in (61–69cm)
BREED RECOGNIZED BY AKC, CKC, FCI, KC

German Wirehaired Pointer

Breed Assessment
LIFE EXPECTANCY 13 years
EXERCISE A few miles daily
GROOMING *Wirehaired* Moderate; *Shorthaired* Low maintenance
NOISE Talkative
HEALTH PROBLEMS *Wirehaired* Some entropion and skin problems;
Shorthaired None known
SIZE *Wirehaired* 22–27in (56–67cm);
Shorthaired 21–26in (53–64cm)
CUSTOMARILY DOCKED Yes
BREED RECOGNIZED BY AKC, CKC, FCI, KC

German Wirehaired & Shorthaired Pointer

A cross between the Spanish Pointer and the Bloodhound, the original German Pointer was too heavy and slow to match the performance of other pointers. But careful breeding in the 19th century meant that the Wirehaired Pointer and its cousin, the Shorthaired, now have the strength, speed and stamina to be versatile hunting dogs.

Characteristics

These fearless pointers will work hard in all conditions, on land or water. Behind the slightly austere expression lurk affectionate and loyal dogs. With too little exercise they can become boisterous, but their cheerfulness makes them good family dogs.

Appearance

The coats of both breeds are variations on liver and liver and white, although the Wirehaired can also be black and white. The Shorthaired Pointer has a coarse, tough coat; the Wirehaired a thicker, harsher outercoat and a dense undercoat. It has bushy eyebrows and a small beard. Both breeds have brown, intelligent eyes and their ears are set high, reaching the lips when brought forward. They have compact feet and sturdy nails.

Hungarian Vizsla

The word *vizsla* means "alert and responsive" in Hungarian, and this pointer is a master at tracking. His working history can be traced back to the 10th century. The breed nearly died out during the Second World War, but has since spread to other parts of the world. Today, the unusual color of the Hungarian Vizsla makes the breed a popular pet and show dog.

Characteristics
Attractive copper red coloring gives a shine and elegance to the Hungarian Vizsla's coat. A bold hunter, relatively easy to train, the Hungarian Vizsla is a good swimmer and retriever. Easy to please, it does not like to be left out. It is sociable with people and dogs, and is happier in the country than in the town. Affectionate, this dog will be protective towards its family.

Appearance
The Vizsla's short, close coat is easily managed. The dark copper color gives a reddish reflection. Spotted coats or white feet are seen as faults in the show ring. Soulful brown eyes, normally a shade darker than its coat, are its hallmark. Its ears are quite long and heavy. Its low-set tail is carried horizontally. Its feet are cat-like and neat. It has a short, muscular, arched back with a long chest.

Breed Assessment
LIFE EXPECTANCY 14 years
EXERCISE A few miles daily
GROOMING Low maintenance
NOISE Talkative
HEALTH PROBLEMS Possible eye problems; hip-testing recommended
SIZE 21–26in (53–64cm)
CUSTOMARILY DOCKED Yes
BREED RECOGNIZED BY AKC, CKC, FCI, KC

Weimaraner

The Weimaraner is named after the German city of Weimar. Famed for its silver coat, its ghostly appearance has won it many admirers. It is a master at pointing and retrieving.

Characteristics
Weimaraner puppies are oddly striped at birth. An intelligent, hard-working breed, it thrives in the house and needs a warm, draft-free environment. Energetic and independent, it is a delight when given proper social training; untrained it can be impossible. A friendly dog, it can be good with children and other animals.

Appearance
An almost metallic sheen is given off by the silver-grey short coat; shades of mouse, roe-grey or iron-grey also occur. Ideally, the Weimaraner's coat will not shed too much, making this an ideal dog for house-proud owners. The round, surprisingly pale, amber or blue-grey eyes tone with its coat, and it has a keen, intelligent expression. Long, folded ears should miss the nose by 1in (2.5cm) if pulled forwards. The firm, thickly padded feet have amber or grey claws. It has a long, sleek, aristocratic look, and its body length should equal its height.

Breed Assessment
LIFE EXPECTANCY 11 years
EXERCISE A few miles daily
GROOMING Low maintenance
NOISE Talkative
HEALTH PROBLEMS None known
SIZE 22–28in (56–69cm)
CUSTOMARILY DOCKED Yes
BREED RECOGNIZED BY AKC, CKC, FCI, KC

Italian Spinone

Traditionally a hunter, pointer and retriever, the Italian Spinone may be descended from the Griffon, Barbet and other hounds, or it may have some of the Segugio in its blood. Either way, it is an ancient breed dating back to the Middle Ages and was known in its present form in the 13th century.

Characteristics
An easy-going and calm breed, with a good sense of fun and a playful nature, the Spinone also enjoys working. At its best it is faithful, quick to learn, amiable and loving. It can take a long time to tire this breed out, and it will do its best to come back wet wherever you take it.

Appearance
Thick and wiry without an undercoat, the Spinone's coat is somewhat scruffy looking, and some hand-stripping will be required. The color can be white, or white with orange or brown. The dog's large, wide-open, placid-looking eyes are either deep yellow or ochre in color. Its long ears are set level with its eyes and hang heavily in a triangular shape. Its feet are heavily padded with strong nails; the front feet are round and back feet oval, and they are pigmented to match its coat. It has a slightly concave, sloping back and strong shoulders.

Breed Assessment
LIFE EXPECTANCY 10/11 years
EXERCISE Plenty
GROOMING Considerable
NOISE Talkative
HEALTH PROBLEMS Hip-testing recommended, some elbow problems
SIZE 24–28in (59–70cm)
CUSTOMARILY DOCKED Yes
BREED RECOGNIZED BY FCI, KC

Breed Assessment
LIFE EXPECTANCY 12 years
EXERCISE A few miles daily
GROOMING Moderate
NOISE Talkative
HEALTH PROBLEMS Hip-testing recommended
SIZE Average 19in (48.5cm)
CUSTOMARILY DOCKED Yes
BREED RECOGNIZED BY AKC, CKC, FCI, KC

Brittany

The Brittany is a tireless French Spaniel that works in a hunting, pointing and retrieving style more like that of a Pointer or Setter than a spaniel. This popular dog is bred to be an all-rounder.

Characteristics
Its Gallic ancestry goes back to a tail-less Brittany, which sometimes results in tail-less puppies today. It has a light build, but is still capable of carrying hare and pheasant. This breed is quick-witted, intelligent, affectionate and endlessly playful. Birds are a primary interest, but in their absence it will expect to be kept busy with other forms of work or play. Regular, long walks are essential, and the Brittany will be happiest if it is allowed to work.

Appearance
The pretty, slightly wavy coat is either orange, liver or black (all with white), tricolor or roan. It features longer hair on the back of the hocks and feet, but does not require excessive attention. Eyes are amber to dark brown and do not protrude. The floppy, lightly fringed ears are set high. The tail is either naturally short or docked and should be no more than 4in (10cm) in length. Somewhat squarer looking than other spaniels, it has a short, straight back that slopes slightly downward.

Wirehaired Pointing Griffon

A mix of Barbet and French Braque has provided this rugged-looking Griffon with the ability to work in water and on dry land. Not particularly fast, it is nonetheless a versatile worker. This breed is also called the Korthals Griffon, after Edward Korthals, who developed the breed in the Netherlands and Germany in the 19th century.

Characteristics
Although this Griffon is happy to live in the city for short periods – when given enough exercise – it is very much an outdoor dog, and favors country life. An excellent family pet, it can provide great entertainment.

Appearance
Characteristically shaggy, it has tufty, individual facial hair, with a comical moustache and bushy eyebrows. The long, wiry topcoat is hardy in rough weather and can be either part white and part tan or steel grey. It should never feel woolly. The undercoat is soft. It has bright, intelligent eyes shaded by large eyebrows. Its ears are floppy, fairly long and expressive. A thick, strong tail is docked by some breeders and it has tough, rounded feet which carry it with an efficient movement. The body is fairly long and low to the ground. The shoulders have a smooth slope, giving the breed an elegant stance.

Breed Assessment
LIFE EXPECTANCY 10/11 years
EXERCISE Plenty
GROOMING Moderate
NOISE Talkative
HEALTH PROBLEMS Some entropion and ectropion, keep an eye out for skin allergies
SIZE 20–24in (51–60cm)
CUSTOMARILY DOCKED Yes
RECOGNIZED BY AKC, CKC, FCI

Breed Assessment
LIFE EXPECTANCY 13 years
EXERCISE A few miles daily
GROOMING Moderate
NOISE Talkative
HEALTH PROBLEMS None known
SIZE 24–26in (60–66cm)
BREED RECOGNIZED BY FCI

German Longhaired Pointer

This breed is not the longhaired brother to the German Shorthaired Pointer, but was developed from the Epagneul Français, and other longhaired bird dogs. A speedier gundog than the other Pointers of its time, this Pointer owes something of its existence to the Gordon Setter and is almost spaniel-like in physique.

Characteristics
This is probably the least known of the German gundogs, and deserves to be more widely appreciated. This breed has a passion for adventure, and though not the most aristocratic of Pointers, it is patient and sensible. It has a good scenting nose, and is a reliable working dog. If it is kept sufficiently active and gets enough exercise, it will be a good family pet. It likes to learn and is easy to train, which may appeal to a first-time owner.

Appearance
It has a thick undercoat, and a wavy, rough-textured topcoat. The color is normally either liver-brown or liver-roan, with or without markings. Bright eyes and long, drooping ears give the dog an enquiring look. Its full tail provides balance to its muscular frame and is left long. Its feet are neat and firmly padded. Rectangular and muscular, it resembles a large spaniel.

Terriers

History ✦ Types of terrier ✦ Keeping terriers

Terriers have been developed, mainly in the British Isles, over the past few hundred years, although there are records of small hunting dogs from earlier times. Invading Romans named them *terrarii* from the Latin *terra,* meaning "earth". Originally bred to hunt vermin, they were developed to chase out quarry that had gone to ground, often by actually digging it out of burrows.

TERRIER HISTORY

Terriers have always enjoyed a close relationship with farmers, for whom they have worked tirelessly, killing rats and other vermin.

Unlike gundogs or hounds, which were mainly used to find and chase quarry, terriers were usually expected to kill their prey. Their strong, locking jaws and sharp teeth were powerful weapons against animals fighting for their lives. Function therefore ruled the terrier's development. Terriers are normally small, for example, because they had to get into the smallest of bolt holes. Some notable exceptions include the Kerry Blue Terrier and the Soft Coated Wheaten Terrier. These

Below: The Border Terrier is thought to have originated in the border region between England and Scotland.

dogs were developed in their native Ireland to herd, guard and hunt. Irish law forbade peasants from owning hunting dogs, and they adapted their terriers to perform various tasks that were normally the responsibility of other breeds of dog.

The terrier coat was developed for easy maintenance, often needing only a quick brush and a hand-strip once or twice a year: most farmers had neither the time nor the inclination to spend hours on grooming. The short terrier coat is either wire-haired, to protect against harsh weather conditions and brambles, or smooth-haired if a less strenuous task was required from the dog. Even so, most smooth-haired terriers, such as the Smooth Hair Fox Terrier, boast a much coarser, more protective coat than smooth-haired breeds from other groups.

Those terriers that worked underground had short legs to enable them to get into tunnels after prey, and their eyes were usually deep-set in their sockets, which protected them during an attack. The terrier tail is usually carried up and is often docked to about half or less – a legacy of the time when the owner needed to grab a short, firm tail in order to retrieve the dog from its work underground.

Today's terriers have lost none of their ancestors' feisty spirit. Although they do not usually initiate a fight, they are unlikely to lose one.

GROUP DISTINCTIONS

Most regions of the British Isles produced terrier breeds of their own. Many, such as the Devon and Cheshire Terriers, are now extinct, but several, such as the Manchester, Kerry Blue and Airedale Terrier, are still thriving. Each region had particular qualities it needed and these were reflected in its dogs. Cairn Terriers, for example, had to have a thick, almost shaggy coat to deal with the extreme weather conditions in their native Scotland.

Around the world, terriers have been used for a variety of different functions, and countries outside the UK have grouped them according to their main use. In America, for instance, the Boston terrier is considered to be a "non-sporting" dog. On the European continent, the word "Pinscher" is German for "terrier", yet this breed is categorized in the working group. German Pinschers are

Right: Although primarily a pet and no longer a working dog, the athletic Smooth Fox Terrier enjoys regular exercise.

larger than most English terriers and were unable to work underground, but like most terriers they make excellent watchdogs and vermin hunters. The Schnauzer also has many terrier traits, but its lack of defining characteristics make it more suitable for the utility group (see page 206).

Equally, there are many terriers that could be at home in other groups. The Staffordshire Bull Terrier, the American Staffordshire Bull Terrier, the Bull Terrier and the Boston Terrier all originated from the Mastiff, a large working dog, and the Tibetan Terrier comes from the Spitz family. Others – like the Yorkshire Terrier and the English Toy Terrier – started out as working terriers and were miniaturized into toy dogs (see page 230).

TERRIERS AS PETS

Terriers are very popular pets, and many people are attracted to their roguish, plucky, exuberant characters. Their size makes them ideal for most households, and they are loyal and rewarding pets. They can be a handful, but they respond well to training, and generally make affectionate and playful companions.

Airedale Terrier

The Airedale Terrier dates back to around the middle of the 19th century, when it was used by miners and mill-workers to hunt otters along the Aire and Wharfe rivers in Yorkshire in northern England. It is also said to have hunted bears in the Rockies. The largest of all the terrier group, it is known as the King of the Terriers.

Characteristics
The noble title and demeanor of the Airedale belie its willingness to work, although it can be stubborn. It is known for its versatility and during the First World War even worked on the front line, where it acted as a messenger and located injured soldiers. This is a very friendly, confident and outgoing dog, which is normally good with children and can be protective of its family.

Appearance
The wiry and stiff outercoat is slightly wavy, and it has a short, softer undercoat. The body is saddle black or grizzled (as is the neck and top surface of the tail), and all other parts of the coat are tan. The eyes are small and dark. The V-shaped ears fold over slightly above the level of the skull. The feet are small and round, with well-cushioned pads. The Airedale is a muscular-looking dog, with a short, strong and level back.

Breed Assessment
LIFE EXPECTANCY 12 years
EXERCISE A few miles daily
GROOMING Considerable
NOISE Talkative
HEALTH PROBLEMS Hip dysplasia
SIZE 22–24in (56–61cm)
CUSTOMARILY DOCKED Yes
BREED RECOGNIZED BY AKC, CKC, FCI, KC

Breed Assessment
LIFE EXPECTANCY 14 years
EXERCISE Moderate
GROOMING Considerable
NOISE Talkative
HEALTH PROBLEMS Some eye problems
SIZE 16in (39cm) maximum
CUSTOMARILY DOCKED Yes
BREED RECOGNIZED BY AKC, CKC, FCI, KC

Welsh Terrier

The Welsh Terrier bears a close resemblance to the Lakeland Terrier, with which it may have shared ancestors. The breed originated in North Wales during the 18th century, and is probably directly descended from the now extinct black-and-tan terrier. The Wire Fox Terrier may have also contributed to its appearance.

Characteristics
Bold and energetic, the Welsh Terrier is a cheerful, uncomplicated dog which is affectionate and intelligent. This breed is fearless and has a competitive nature. Less noisy than many other terriers, it is not quite as hot-headed. Loyal, obedient and easy to train, it gets along well with people and makes a good pet. It tends to bond closely with its family, but can be reserved with strangers. The coat will need to be plucked two or three times a year, or even more often depending on its condition.

Appearance
The abundant, hard and wiry coat is black and tan, or grizzled black and tan. The small, dark eyes are very expressive, and the small, V-shaped ears are carried forward, close to the cheek. The tail is well set, but is not carried too gaily. The feet are small, round and cat-like. The back is short and the loins strong.

Irish Terrier

Something of a Celtic enigma, the Irish Terrier is believed to be one of the oldest Irish breeds, but very little of its history is documented. It is an excellent water dog and vermin hunter and was used as a messenger dog during the First World War.

Characteristics
A courageous and feisty little dog, the Irish Terrier has earned its nickname "The Daredevil". It can be eager to fight when challenged by other dogs, so must be carefully trained to prevent this behavior. It loves to please and responds well to training. Affectionate with people – particularly children – it is known for its loyalty and sense of fun. This terrier requires regular, long walks, and must be hand plucked at least twice a year.

Appearance
This dog has a harsh, wiry coat and a softer undercoat; the most preferred "whole color" coats are red, red/wheaten or yellow/red. The hair on its small, V-shaped ears is darker than on the rest of the body, and they drop forward close to the cheek. Its eyes are small and dark. The tail, which is covered with rough hair, is set high, and its feet are small, round and strong. It has a graceful outline, a deep, muscular chest and a fairly long body.

Breed Assessment
LIFE EXPECTANCY 14 years
EXERCISE Plenty
GROOMING Considerable
NOISE Fairly quiet
HEALTH PROBLEMS None known
SIZE 18-19in (46-48cm)
CUSTOMARILY DOCKED Yes
BREED RECOGNIZED BY AKC, CKC, FCI, KC

Breed Assessment
LIFE EXPECTANCY 14 years
EXERCISE Moderate
GROOMING High maintenance
NOISE Talkative
HEALTH PROBLEMS None known
SIZE 15in (37cm) maximum
CUSTOMARILY DOCKED Yes
BREED RECOGNIZED BY AKC, CKC, FCI, KC

Lakeland Terrier

The Lakeland Terrier derived its name from the Lake District in northern England, where it was used to chase out foxes and badgers when they went to ground. Breeds such as the Border Terrier, Bedlington Terrier and Fox Terrier probably contributed to its make-up. A breed club was formed in 1912, and it was first recognized in 1921.

Characteristics
A small but hardy little dog, the Lakeland is described as being "workmanlike". It comes into its own in the countryside. Like most terriers, it has a tough and competitive nature. It has a friendly and compliant personality and can get along with children as well as other dogs. This is a sporty dog that learns easily and likes to be regularly challenged. It will need regular, intensive grooming.

Appearance
This terrier's undercoat is protected by a harsh, dense weather-resistant topcoat. Colors include black and tan, blue and tan, red, wheaten, red grizzle, liver, blue or black. The eyes are dark or hazel. The fairly small, V-shaped ears are carried alertly. The tail is held high, but should not be curled or carried over the back. Its chest is quite narrow and it has a short but strong back.

Wire Fox & Smooth Fox Terrier

There is little to distinguish these two old British breeds, apart from their coats. Bred to drive foxes out of holes, they have kept their name, despite the fact that other terriers do the same work. They probably descended from dogs used in fox hunting in the early 19th century.

Wire Fox Terrier

Characteristics
The Wire's beard accentuates the square muzzle that has become its distinguishing feature. Its tufty eyebrows give it a sharper look than its Smooth cousin. The Smooth is an unpretentious, solid breed; the Wire may need a tight rein in the country, where it will find every hedgerow movement exciting. The Smooth is generally less vivacious, but both are robust dogs that enjoy lots of exercise. Properly socialized, they make good family pets.

Appearance
The Wire has a rough outercoat and a softer undercoat. The Smooth has a soft, straight coat. The clipping of a Wire for the showring is complicated. Its small, penetrating eyes are small, dark and set fairly close. Ears are V-shaped and neatly folded forward so that the tips hang close to the cheeks. Occasionally docked, its tail is held high. Its feet pads are thick. Its frame is solid and muscular with rounded ribs and a short, level back.

Breed Assessment
LIFE EXPECTANCY 10 years
EXERCISE Plenty
GROOMING *Wire* Moderate; *Smooth* Low maintenance
NOISE Very talkative
HEALTH PROBLEMS Eye-testing necessary
SIZE Should not exceed 16in (39cm)
CUSTOMARILY DOCKED Yes
BREED RECOGNIZED BY AKC, CKC, FCI, KC

Breed Assessment
LIFE EXPECTANCY 13 years
EXERCISE Plenty
GROOMING Low maintenance
NOISE Very talkative
HEALTH PROBLEMS Von Willebrand's disease
SIZE 15–16in (38–41cm)
BREED RECOGNIZED BY AKC, CKC, FCI, KC

Manchester Terrier

A supreme ratter, this breed was developed in Manchester in the 18th century. Used to living in the home, it is happy in the town as well as in the country.

Characteristics
The Manchester Terrier probably inherits its leanness from the Whippet, but in other respects it is a true terrier, with a sharp face, high, folded ears and an inquisitive nature. It is likely to listen solely to its owner. Quick and lively, it can be slow to make friends, but once it has accepted someone, they will be showered with loyal affection. Its tendency to express itself noisily should be discouraged early in life with modern motivational training methods. It demands plenty of exercise and enjoys running fast, particularly off the lead.

Appearance
This breed has a single coat, which should be glossy and smooth and is easy to care for. Its dark black-and-tan coat has specific markings and the colors are clearly defined. Typical bright terrier eyes are almond-shaped and lively. Its up-standing ears are folded, with the V-shaped point hanging close to its head. Its tail, which is carried low, tapers to a point. The strong feet are hare-like. It has a narrow, deep chest and a fairly short body.

American Staffordshire Terrier & Staffordshire Bull Terrier

The American Staffordshire Terrier is larger and taller than the British version. A cross between a Bulldog and a terrier, the Staffordshire has suffered through being confused with Pit Bull-type dogs. Its courage and amiability have made it a popular pet, despite the fact it was bred to be a fighting dog.

Characteristics
Staffordshire Bull Terriers make excellent guard dogs. They are "people dogs" and are generally not keen on other dogs, so must be trained to curb their fighting instincts. Although capable of fierceness, these dogs have a happy disposition. They can be loving with children and will make good pets in a family that is consistent and able to cope with a boisterous dog.

Appearance
They have short, glossy coats that need little grooming and come in almost any color combination except nearly all white. Their eyes are dark and dark rimmed. Ears are cropped to reduce the chances of their being ripped during dog fights. They have strong, medium-sized feet. They have large chests, with full, wide ribs.

Staffordshire Bull Terrier

Breed Assessment
LIFE EXPECTANCY 11 years
EXERCISE Plenty
GROOMING Low maintenance
NOISE Very talkative
HEALTH PROBLEMS *Both* Parents and puppies should be eye-tested
SIZE *American Staffordshire Terrier* 17–19in (43–48cm);
Staffordshire Bull Terrier 14–16in (35.5–40.5cm)
BREEDS RECOGNIZED BY AKC, CKC, FCI *(American Staffordshire Terrier)*;
AKC, CKC, FCI, KC *(Staffordshire Bull Terrier)*

Breed Assessment
LIFE EXPECTANCY 13 years
EXERCISE Minimum
GROOMING Considerable
NOISE Fairly quiet
HEALTH PROBLEMS None known
SIZE 18–19in (46–48cm), bitches slightly smaller
CUSTOMARILY DOCKED Yes
BREED RECOGNIZED BY AKC, CKC, FCI, KC

Kerry Blue Terrier

A colorful character, this breed hails from County Kerry in Ireland, where it was originally a ratter. It was also a general farm dog and could be an impressive guard. The first reference to the breed was in the 19th century, but the Kerry was probably around a long time before then.

Characteristics
The Kerry is born black and the coat's blue tinge comes through gradually until the dog is two years old. A healthy and long-lived breed, it is an ideal pet for those with an aversion to dog hair, since its coat does not shed. It can be strong-willed and stubborn, but with confident handling and training it is a game, sporting, reliable and affectionate friend.

Appearance
The blue coloring distinguishes this breed from any other. Sometimes the color comes in unseen under the heavy black first coat, and is suddenly apparent on first trimming; it requires an experienced hand to keep the coat in shape. The dog's dark eyes are quite small, and its ears are also neat, understated, pointed and held fairly high. Its full tail is docked by some breeders, and it is carried high. It has small feet under its thick coat, high-sprung ribs and a firm, erect stance.

Soft-coated Wheaten Terrier

The Irish farmer's answer to vermin problems, the Soft-coated Wheaten is a good ratter and an excellent general farm dog. It is the oldest native terrier of Ireland.

Characteristics

This dog's distinctive, silky, gently curling coat is the warm color of ripening wheat. This is a breed that is becoming increasingly popular. It is trimmed differently for the show ring in the UK. It is a cheerful, active and playful dog that bonds closely with its family. Its strong personality and good sense of fun mean that it will occasionally misbehave, but with good early training it will prove a trustworthy companion to the right owner.

Appearance

Although beautiful to look at, this dog's coat, with its large, loose curls, needs considerable care to keep it in order. It is normally trimmed to a set style, with the hair on the face, feet, neck, chest and stomach longer than elsewhere. Its strong eyebrows hide mischievous dark eyes. The back edge of its ears stands out from its head, giving it an alert look. Its tail grows to about 4in (10cm), but is normally docked, and is carried high. Sturdy and compact, it is well proportioned, with a level back, straight front legs and strong, nimble feet.

Breed Assessment

LIFE EXPECTANCY 14 years
EXERCISE Moderate
GROOMING Considerable
NOISE Talkative
HEALTH PROBLEMS Hips and eyes need testing; kidney problems
SIZE Dogs 18–20in (46–49cm), bitches smaller
CUSTOMARILY DOCKED Yes
BREED RECOGNIZED BY AKC, CKC, FCI, KC

Breed Assessment

LIFE EXPECTANCY 13 years
EXERCISE Moderate
GROOMING Moderate
NOISE Talkative
HEALTH PROBLEMS None known
SIZE Approximately 11–12in (28–31cm)
BREED RECOGNIZED BY AKC, CKC, FCI, KC

Cairn Terrier

Originally from the Isle of Skye, this hard-working terrier was used in the Scottish Highlands to chase otters, foxes and badgers from their hiding places.

Characteristics

Sporty and vivacious, this terrier has a natural rugged charm, and will not resist a challenge when confronted. It has an independent streak, which means that it needs consistent early training, but it is normally eager to learn, and will try hard to please. It should be amiable to dogs, but may show a tendency to chase cats, although the family cat is usually accepted.

Appearance

The Cairn's coat is plentiful, with a good thick undercoat to keep it dry in Highland rain. Puppies are born dark, but become lighter when the hardier coat comes through. The color of the coat can be cream, wheaten, red, grey or nearly black, with dark points. The little face has widely separated dark eyes that are topped by shaggy eyebrows, and its pricked-up ears are small. Its front feet have thick, strong pads. The short, bushy tail is held proudly aloft. The dog stands fully forward on its front legs and is solidly rectangular in physique; it should be well proportioned.

Norfolk & Norwich Terriers

The main difference between these breeds is their ears, which are their truly defining features, and the prick-eared Norwich and the drop-eared Norfolk have had separate breed standards in the UK only since 1964.

Norfolk Terrier

Characteristics

Both breeds are persevering, almost stubborn, and energetic. Their characters are very similar, and although they are two of the smallest terriers, they are capable of a loud warning bark when the need arises. Generally easy-going, quiet dogs, they make cheerful, bouncy pets. Although playful and cunning, they learn quickly and will respond to modern motivational training methods.

Appearance

Either a fiery red, black and tan or, more rarely, grizzle, both the Norfolk and Norwich Terriers have a natural, lightly trimmed coat, which needs regular brushing and combing and the old hair plucked out. Their hair is wiry and straight with pretty, wispy whiskers and eyebrows. Oval shaped and deep set, their eyes are dark and sparkling. Tails are often docked and are carried upright. Their feet are small and round. Both breeds are stocky, short and broad, in spite of which they succeed in being nimble and sure-footed.

Norwich Terrier

Breed Assessment
LIFE EXPECTANCY 14 years
EXERCISE Moderate
GROOMING Considerable
NOISE Talkative
HEALTH PROBLEMS None known
SIZE Average 10in (25.5cm)
CUSTOMARILY DOCKED Yes
BREED RECOGNIZED BY AKC, CKC, FCI, KC

Breed Assessment
LIFE EXPECTANCY 14 years
EXERCISE Minimum
GROOMING Low maintenance
NOISE Fairly quiet
HEALTH PROBLEMS None known
SIZE Approximately 10in (25.5cm)
CUSTOMARILY DOCKED Yes
BREED RECOGNIZED BY AKC, CKC, FCI, KC

Australian Terrier

This dog was bred from several British terriers for the Australian homestead, and is capable of killing all small vermin, including rats and snakes. Its skills as a watchdog are also legendary, and it has become a popular working dog and family pet worldwide.

Characteristics

This terrier is not slow to voice its opinions, but it is not a noisy breed. It is lively, self-confident and normally easy to get along with. It should be able to adapt to life both in the city and the country. Forthright and friendly, this breed is also willing to please. It has a warm disposition and is a loyal and affectionate companion. Its coat will require regular plucking, but in good condition will lose little hair.

Appearance

It has an untrimmed, rough coat with a ruff about its neck. The breed has two distinct color groups: blue and tan or all red. It has a keen expression and kind, dark eyes. Its features include pointed, sensitive ears. It carries its tail high, but not bent over its back. Its feet are small and it moves with a springy step. It is longer in body than in height, and has a shapely body. The line of its back is level and it carries itself with grace.

Scottish Terrier

The development of the Scottish Terrier was not recorded until the late 19th century, but this breed is believed to date back several hundred years. All terriers with a Highland background descend from the Highland Terrier and share a courageous character. This dog is no exception, but it is now more likely to be seen in the showring than in a working environment.

Characteristics
A typical terrier, it is not a dog for the faint-hearted. It enjoys chasing, but it is not quick to be aggressive. Occasionally surly to strangers, it is a faithful and loyal companion that loves its home and will guard it conscientiously. It has a happy and playful nature.

Appearance
This dog's coat is either black, brindle or wheaten, with a soft, short undercoat and a dense and wiry outercoat. Its eyes are dark, deep set and fairly wide apart. Ears should not be too close together and should be carried erect at the top of the head. The tail should be held erect, either upright or with a slight bend. Feet are well padded, with the front feet slightly larger than the hind feet. The topline of the body is straight and the ribs well rounded and carried well back; the hind legs are strong.

Breed Assessment
LIFE EXPECTANCY 12 years
EXERCISE Moderate
GROOMING High maintenance
NOISE Fairly quiet
HEALTH PROBLEMS "Scottie cramp"
SIZE 10–11in (25.4–28cm)
BREED RECOGNIZED BY AKC, CKC, FCI, KC

Breed Assessment
LIFE EXPECTANCY 15 years
EXERCISE Minimum
GROOMING High maintenance
NOISE Moderate
HEALTH PROBLEMS Eye-testing strongly recommended
SIZE 12in (31cm)
CUSTOMARILY DOCKED Sometimes
BREED RECOGNIZED BY AKC, CKC, FCI, KC

Sealyham Terrier

The Sealyham Terrier's origins are in rural Wales, where it was bred specifically for its tenacious character. Bred in the village of Sealyham, it was intended as a hunting dog that was powerful yet small enough to follow a badger into its sett – requirements that this breed meets perfectly.

Characteristics
An adaptable little dog, happy in either the town or the country, the Sealyham loves human companionship. Normally active outdoors and calm indoors, it also makes an excellent watchdog. Charming and lovable, it can also be obstinate, so consistent early training is necessary. It is an intelligent dog and learns easily.

Appearance
The Sealyham's long and wiry topcoat, with its weather-resistant undercoat, needs regular attention to prevent matting, and should be hand-stripped at least twice a year. Its eyes are dark, well set and of medium size. Ears have rounded tips and are carried at the side of the cheek. Its tail is held erect, and the quarters should protrude beyond the set of the tail. Feet are round, with thick pads. The topline is level, and the ribs well sprung. Its broad chest should be set well down between its front legs.

West Highland White Terrier

Long favored by Scottish huntsmen, this dog is also a proficient ratter. The "Westie", as it is commonly called, is undoubtedly one of the most popular terriers, mainly because of its charm and intelligence. Although this breed is an extremely popular pet, it is still used as a working dog on some farms, and is the dog of choice for a famous British fox hunt.

Characteristics

The Westie is a sporting little dog but it appreciates comfort. It will adapt to life in the town but prefers the country. Its fun-loving nature makes it an ideal playmate for children, whose energy it is likely to match. A self-assured dog with a lust for life, it can be mischievous. This breed mixes well with other dogs and loves human companionship.

Appearance

Its outercoat is wiry, without curl, and its undercoat is soft and warm. Eyes are dark and set wide apart; ears should be erect and pointed. Its tail is 5–6in (12.5–15cm) long and is carried jauntily but not over the back. Feet are strong with thick pads, with the front feet larger than the hind. Its body is compact with a deep chest, and the upper ribs are arched.

Breed Assessment

LIFE EXPECTANCY 13 years
EXERCISE Moderate
GROOMING High maintenance
NOISE Very talkative
HEALTH PROBLEMS Dry eye and skin problems; Legge Perthes disease
SIZE 11in (28cm)
BREED RECOGNIZED BY AKC, CKC, FCI, KC

Breed Assessment

LIFE EXPECTANCY 12 years
EXERCISE Moderate
GROOMING High maintenance
NOISE Talkative
HEALTH PROBLEMS Eye-testing advised; some back problems
SIZE 10in (24cm)
BREED RECOGNIZED BY AKC, CKC, FCI, KC

Dandie Dinmont Terrier

The Dandie Dinmont's name derives from Sir Walter Scott's novel *Guy Mannering*, which features this jaunty little dog. Previous to this, it was known as the Mustard or Pepper. It is one of the oldest British terriers, and was originally bred in northern England for killing badgers.

Characteristics

Dignified and intelligent, the Dandie Dinmont was aptly described by Sir Walter Scott as "the big little dog". Its independent spirit means that it can be difficult to train, but it makes a good house dog. Its owner must earn its respect to get the best out of this courageous dog, but it will be loyal and devoted, usually to one person.

Appearance

It has a crisp outercoat with a soft undercoat. There are two colors: mustard, which is a pale fawn to rich tan with a creamy topknot, and pepper, which is a pale silver to bluish black with a silvery white topknot. Eyes are large, round, and dark hazel. Ears are set well back, wide apart and low on the cheek. Tail is 8–10in (20–25cm) long, with a slight curve. Front feet are smaller than the hind feet. Its body is long and strong, with round ribs and a back that is lower at the shoulders with a slight downward curve and a corresponding arch over the loins.

Skye Terrier

This terrier is named after the Scottish island of Skye. Its firm body and weather-resistant coat made it a versatile dog, and it soon proved its worth to hunters and gamekeepers. It was a favorite with nobility, and Queen Victoria bred a strain of Skye Terriers.

Characteristics
An intrepid dog that retains its sporting instincts, it has an elegant appearance and a dignified temperament. Its courageous, yet placid, demeanor makes it a good watchdog. Although distrustful of strangers, it is not normally vicious. The Skye Terrier does not forget a friend or foe, and tends to be a one-man dog.

Appearance
Its double coat has a long, hard outercoat free of curl, and a soft, woolly undercoat. Its eyes are brown and close set. Ears are pricked or dropped. When pricked, they should be high on the head and erect at the outer edges. When dropped, they should be larger and lie flat against the skull. Its tail is feathered and the lower half is curved when hanging. When upright, the tail should be an elongation of the body. Its front feet should be larger than its hind. It has a level back, and its straight-falling coat makes it appear flat from the side.

Breed Assessment
LIFE EXPECTANCY 13 years
EXERCISE Moderate
GROOMING Low maintenance
NOISE Very talkative
HEALTH PROBLEMS Back problems
SIZE 10–10.4in (25–26cm)
BREED RECOGNIZED BY AKC, CKC, FCI, KC

Breed Assessment
LIFE EXPECTANCY 13 years
EXERCISE Moderate
GROOMING Moderate
NOISE Fairly quiet
HEALTH PROBLEMS Puppies and parents should be eye-tested; hereditary liver problems
SIZE 16in (41cm)
BREED RECOGNIZED BY AKC, CKC, FCI, KC

Bedlington Terrier

Formerly known as the Northumberland Fox Terrier, this British breed was once used to hunt vermin and rabbits. Its hunting skills were such that it became a favorite with poachers and gained a reputation for being a gypsy's dog. From the beginning of the twentieth century this breed's elegance was more widely recognized, and today it is mainly a family dog.

Characteristics
Easier to relate to than many other terriers, the Bedlington is a quiet, enormously courageous dog. Although it retains much of its hunting instinct, it makes an excellent family pet and can be affectionate with children. This dog is full of fun and always ready for a game, but also is quick to protect those it loves.

Appearance
This terrier's distinctive coat should be thick, but not wiry; it has a tendency to twist, particularly on its head and face. The almost triangular eyes are expressive, small, dark and bright, and the ears are of medium size, set low and hanging flat on the cheek. The tapering, moderate-length tail is thick at the root. Feet are large, with thick, well-closed pads. Its back has a natural arch, creating a tucked-up underline, and its chest is broad and ribs flat.

Border Terrier

The Border Terrier developed in the border country between England and Scotland. It was bred to work alongside hunting hounds and takes its name from the Border Foxhounds with which it was associated.

Characteristics

This is an independent little dog, and its strong working instinct may lead it to undertake private hunting expeditions, so take care that yards are well fenced. The Border Terrier has admirable stamina and is said to be capable of running alongside a horse. Be sure to discourage any tendency to fight or it may become hard to control. Although affectionate, it is not overly demonstrative. It is very much a worker but makes a good family member.

Appearance

Its coat is harsh and lies close to the skin, with a soft undercoat. Eyes are dark with a keen expression, and its ears are small and V-shaped, dropping forward close to the cheek. Its tail is naturally short, fairly thick at the base and tapering. It should be set high and carried gaily, although it should not curl over its back. Its feet should be small with thick pads. The ribs are carried well back but are not over sprung.

Breed Assessment

LIFE EXPECTANCY 14 years
EXERCISE Moderate
GROOMING Considerable
NOISE Very talkative
HEALTH PROBLEMS Occasional back problems
SIZE 10in (25.5cm)
BREED RECOGNIZED BY AKC, CKC, FCI, KC

Breed Assessment

LIFE EXPECTANCY *Both* 12 years
EXERCISE *Standard* Plenty; *Miniature* Moderate
GROOMING Low maintenance
NOISE *Standard* Talkative; *Miniature* Fairly quiet
HEALTH PROBLEMS Parents of Miniatures should be eye-tested
SIZE *Standard* 17in (42cm); *Miniature* 14in (35.5cm)
BREED RECOGNIZED BY AKC, CKC, FCI, KC

Bull Terrier

Bred by crossing a Bulldog with a terrier, this dog was created to fight to the death in the bloody sport of bull baiting. It is now one of the most popular dogs in Britain and has proved itself to be an impeccable guard dog. The Miniature, which has existed for as long as the Standard, was recognized as a separate breed by the British Kennel Club in 1939.

Characteristics

Both Miniature and Standard Bull Terriers are friendly, placid dogs. Famous for their tenacity and courage, they match physical strength with obstinacy, and need to be kept active in both body and mind. Affectionate in the extreme, both types will place heavy demands on their owner's time. Neither breed is an an ideal dog for the first-time owner.

Appearance

The coat is short, flat and harsh to the touch; a soft undercoat may be present in the winter. Eyes are dark and narrow. Ears are small and close together, and the tail is short, set low and carried horizontally. Feet are compact, parallel and well rounded. The Bull Terrier's back is short and strong, and it has a broad chest. The line from brisket to belly should curve upward.

Utility Dogs

Types of utility dog ✦ Keeping utility dogs

The utility group comprises breeds that do not fit easily into other groups. It therefore encompasses a diverse mixture of dogs of varying shapes, sizes and origins – from the petite Tibetan Spaniel through to the giant Leonberger. Some experts have suggested that the group name should be changed to "special dogs", arguing that each dog in the group is out of the ordinary in one way or another. The utility group also boasts some of the oldest breeds of dog as its members.

Utility dogs are sometimes referred to as "companion" or "non-sporting" dogs, and some of the breeds in this group evolved for no other purpose than to offer warmth, company and entertainment. Others belong to this group because the task for which they were developed no longer exists, such as bull-baiting for the Bulldog.

Few countries are in total agreement as to which breeds belong in the utility group. The Japanese Akita, for example, is classed in the working group in the US, but is included in the utility group in Britain.

BREED DISTINCTIONS

While dogs in this group have little in common, they are some of the most beautiful, intelligent and popular breeds of dog. Many have an ancient pedigree and a fascinating history. The Lhasa Apso, for example, lived in Tibetan temples, and it was believed that lamas (holy men) were reincarnated as Lhasa Apsos if they failed to reach nirvana. Essentially a household companion dog, the Lhasa has a very different history to the energetic Dalmatian that ran alongside carriages to deter potential highwaymen.

The Chow dates back thousands of years, when he was used by Chinese noblemen for hunting. The Japanese Akita was a fighting dog, and hunted ferocious prey, including the black bear. The Japanese Akita has been honored as a national monument in its native country.

Below: The Tibetan Spaniel – in fact, not a spaniel at all – is thought to have served as a watchdog in monasteries many centuries ago.

Left: The Keeshond, once used as a companion on Dutch barges, still makes an effective watchdog.

Utility breeds are popular dogs the world over, as pets and in the show ring. The Poodle, which has been voted "Best in Show" at Crufts several times, was derived from German water retrievers and has an immaculate pedigree. The Bulldog is another imposing member of this group. No longer involved in the cruel "sport" of bull-baiting, it has become a British institution.

The Tibetan Terrier's name suggests that it should be classed with the terriers but, despite its name, it was originally used as a herding dog in Tibet. Because this breed was later developed for the purpose of companionship, it cannot be officially classed with the other larger, more energetic working or pastoral breeds.

Likewise, the Tibetan Spaniel is not included with other spaniels in the gundog group. A close relation of the Pekingese, Tibetan Spaniels were not bred to flush game in all weathers, as other spaniels were expected to do. Their working day involved being carried around under monks' robes to keep their masters warm.

Right: Today a popular pet, the Dalmatian has, over the centuries, had a variety of roles, including hunter, herder and carriage dog.

The utility group is the fastest-growing breed group, largely because of the number of crosses between the smaller breeds. For example, the Cockerpoo and the Pekepoo, in which poodles have been crossed with other breeds, have now become so popular that it is likely that they will soon be recognized as new breeds. Other examples of new breeds include the Labradoodle (Labrador crossed with Poodle) and the Markiesje (Toy Poodle crossed with continental spaniels), which is now officially recognized by the Dutch Kennel Club.

UTILITY DOGS AS PETS

Their histories may be varied, but there is one thing that links all utility breeds: they are all considered to be companion, or non-sporting, dogs. They usually form strong bonds with their owners, but it should be remembered that not all utility breeds make ideal pets for all households. The Japanese Akita, for example, is quite an independent breed and needs an experienced handler.

The diverse nature of the group does not allow for generalizations about maintenance or exercise requirements. It is important to seek expert advice if you are considering acquiring a utility dog.

Boston Terrier

The Boston Terrier is one of only a few of breeds that can claim to have originated in the USA. The breed came into being in the latter part of the 19th century, when stable workers tried their hand at crossbreeding the pedigree dogs of their owners. Although derived from fighting breeds, it has proven popular as a pet and show dog.

Characteristics
Despite its appearance, it is gentle, and its general obedience makes this breed an excellent house dog. It is self-confident and intelligent, and is not difficult to train. Its short coat needs minimal attention. A good-tempered dog, which can sometimes exhibit a strong will, this breed may become overly boisterous when playing.

Appearance
Short, smooth and lustrous, the coat should have a fine texture. Its eyes should be large, dark and round, set square in the skull and wide apart. Ears should be carried erect and as near to the corner of the skull as possible. Its tail should be short and tapering or screw; it should never be carried above horizontal. Feet should be round and compact with well-arched toes. Its chest should be of good width, and its back should be short. Its flank should be slightly cut up.

Breed Assessment
LIFE EXPECTANCY 13 years
EXERCISE Moderate
GROOMING Low maintenance
NOISE Fairly quiet
HEALTH PROBLEMS Eye problems
SIZE 14in (35.5cm)
BREED RECOGNIZED BY AKC, CKC, FCI, KC

Breed Assessment
LIFE EXPECTANCY 9 years
EXERCISE Moderate
GROOMING Moderate
NOISE Fairly quiet
HEALTH PROBLEMS Upper respiratory disease; skin problems; natural birth impossible for many
SIZE 19in (48cm)
BREED RECOGNIZED BY AKC, CKC, FCI, KC

Bulldog

Stubborn, determined and stoical, the qualities of this dog led it to be adopted by Britain as a national symbol. It was originally bred for bull baiting, and when the sport was outlawed in 1835 the breed suffered a decline. The breed later became popular in its own right, after it was bred to be more gentle.

Characteristics
Breeding for looks has had a detrimental effect on this breed's health, and there is concern about the number of bitches that have their puppies by Cesarean section, and also about the dogs' labored breathing. However, the breed has retained the stubborn and loyal traits for which it is renowned. Care and diligence are needed during training, since the dog can be strong willed. It is, however, overwhelmingly loyal.

Appearance
Its coat is short, straight and smooth. Eyes are dark and set well apart. Ears are set high, as far from the eyes as possible. Its tail can be straight or screw and should be set low. Forefeet should be straight and turned slightly out; hind feet should be round and compact. Its chest should be wide, round and deep, and its back should be strong, short and broad at the shoulder.

Chow Chow

The Chow Chow was originally bred in China more than 2000 years ago. It is commonly believed that its name stems from a Cantonese word for food, but there is little evidence to suggest that it was eaten. It is far more likely that it was used solely for hunting and guarding. This breed remained in China for hundreds of years and probably first arrived in Europe during the 18th century.

Characteristics
The Chow is friendly with its family but does tend to place its loyalty with one person and is aloof with strangers. It is generally genial but it can be aggressive if provoked. The Chow's independent streak makes it a difficult dog to train.

Appearance
The Rough's coat is dense and tight, with a coarse outercoat, a soft, woolly undercoat, and is thick around neck. The Smooth has a short, dense, straight coat, with a plush texture. Eyes are small, dark and oval. Ears are small, thick and erect and carried so as to give a scowling expression. Its tongue is blue-black. The tail is set high and is carried well over its back. Its feet are small and round. Ribs should be well sprung but not barrelled, and the back should be short, level and strong.

Breed Assessment
LIFE EXPECTANCY 14 years
EXERCISE Moderate
GROOMING Considerable
NOISE Fairly quiet
HEALTH PROBLEMS Eyelashes may need to be removed if inturned
SIZE 18–22in (46–56cm)
BREED RECOGNIZED BY AKC, CKC, FCI, KC

Breed Assessment
LIFE EXPECTANCY 11 years
EXERCISE A few miles daily
GROOMING Moderate
NOISE Fairly quiet
HEALTH PROBLEMS Hereditary deafness
SIZE 22–24in (55.9–61cm)
BREED RECOGNIZED BY AKC, CKC, FCI, KC

Dalmatian

In the 19th century, this elegant dog used to be seen running alongside carriages. Its job was to defend them against highwaymen and keep away animals that might frighten the horses. It was also used as a hunting dog, and therefore has high levels of endurance and energy. At one time it was incorrectly believed to have originated in Dalmatia, Yugoslavia, and the name has stuck.

Characteristics
This dog may have a reputation for being scatty, but it is a deceptively intelligent dog. Its boundless energy can make it difficult to manage, so if you are looking for a quiet companion, this is not the dog for you. Affectionate and gentle, this is a home-loving dog that enjoys human company.

Appearance
The Dalmatian's coat is short and dense, with a sleek appearance, and can be black- or liver-spotted. The medium-sized eyes are dark in black-spotted dogs and amber in liver-spotted ones. Ears are carried close to head, set rather high and of moderate size. The tail is carried with an upward curve, but is never curled. Feet are round and compact, with well-arched toes. Its body is muscular and slightly arched, with a deep but not too wide chest.

French Bulldog

The French Bulldog was probably developed from the British Toy Bulldog (a miniature version of the Bulldog), which was introduced into France by English lace-makers in the 19th century. It was then bred with short-faced bull-baiting dogs from other European countries, such as Spain's erect-eared bulldogs.

Characteristics
Courageous despite its diminutive size, it is an alert and intelligent dog. Although it is not a natural guard dog or generally noisy, it will bark to give warning of strangers. The "Frenchie", as it is affectionately known, is agile and vivacious. It fits in with most households, but needs owners who can give it their undivided attention, since this dog thrives on companionship.

Appearance
The short, smooth coat of the French Bulldog is brindle, pied or fawn. Its round, dark eyes are set wide apart and quite low down. The bat-like ears are set high and carried upright. The undocked tail is very short, and can be either straight or kinked, but does not curl over the back. Its short, muscular body has strong, wide shoulders and narrows toward the loins. Its strong hind legs are slightly longer than the front legs.

Breed Assessment
LIFE EXPECTANCY 12 years
EXERCISE Moderate
GROOMING Low maintenance
NOISE Fairly quiet
HEALTH PROBLEMS Back problems; eye disease
SIZE 12in (30.5cm) average
BREED RECOGNIZED BY AKC, CKC FCI, KC

Japanese Akita

Originally from Japan, this member of the Spitz family has existed for more than 300 years. When dog fighting was outlawed in Japan, this dog was employed to hunt deer, boar and black bear. At one time only royalty and the nobility could own these dogs, and since 1931 the Japanese government has declared champions of the breed to be national treasures.

Characteristics
The Japanese Akita is a very powerful, majestic dog that needs careful handling. It is intelligent and friendly, with a strong hunting instinct, and makes a good guard dog, without barking too much. It needs to be kept mentally and physically occupied, and can be independent, so requires confident handling.

Appearance
The outercoat is straight and coarse, with a soft, dense undercoat, and can be any color, including white, brindle and pinto. The dark brown eyes are almond-shaped and small, with dark rims. The ears are small and erect. The tail should be carried over the back with a full or double curl. The feet are thick, well knuckled and have hard pads. It has a wide, deep chest, a level back and muscular loins.

Breed Assessment
LIFE EXPECTANCY 12 years
EXERCISE Plenty
GROOMING Considerable
NOISE Talkative
HEALTH PROBLEMS Some eye problems under investigation
SIZE 24–28in (61–71cm)
BREED RECOGNIZED BY AKC, CKC, FCI, KC

Japanese Spitz

Developed in Japan in the 1930s, the Japanese Spitz is a small member of the Spitz family, believed to have been derived from the Russian White Spitz, the American Eskimo dog and the Pomeranian. It was exported to other parts of the world from Japan.

Characteristics
It is not difficult to see why this breed is fast growing in popularity: it is very glamorous in its snow-white coat, and is delicate looking and nimble. This dog can be noisy when warning of strangers and its coat needs regular attention, but it takes less time and effort than that of the Samoyed, of which it is something of a smaller version. Intelligent and alert, it loves human contact and makes an ideal companion and a rewarding pet.

Appearance
This Spitz's pure white outercoat is straight, and it has a dense, soft undercoat and a thick mane on its neck and shoulders. Its dark, oval-shaped eyes have black rims, and its small, angular ears are erect and set high. The distinctive bushy tail curls over its back. Its feet are small, round, cat-like and well cushioned, with black pads. It has a broad, deep chest and a fairly firm belly. Its short back is straight, and the loins broad and firm.

Breed Assessment
LIFE EXPECTANCY 14 years
EXERCISE Minimum
GROOMING Considerable
NOISE Fairly quiet
HEALTH PROBLEMS Knee problems
SIZE 12–14in (30–36cm), bitches slightly smaller
BREED RECOGNIZED BY FCI, KC

Keeshond

The Keeshond comes from Holland, where it lived on farms, in houses and on barges. It was probably named after a Dutch patriot called Kees, and during the 17th and 18th centuries became a symbol of national resistance; it is still remembered as a "peasant's dog". It is probably descended from earlier Spitz-type dogs, such as the Wolf Spitz, but its ancestry is not fully known.

Characteristics
It is a quick-witted watchdog, with a keen sense of hearing and a shrill warning bark. It learns quickly and responds well to training. In warm weather, care should be taken to ensure that it does not suffer from the heat. It is inquisitive, friendly and affectionate. A good house-dog, it makes a loving companion to all the family, although it usually bonds best with one family member.

Appearance
It has a harsh, straight coat in a mixture of grey and black, with an abundant ruff and a soft, light-colored undercoat. Its dark, almond-shaped eyes have unusual markings, and its erect ears are dark. The black-tipped tail curls tightly over the back. The feet are round and cat-like and have black nails. It is short, compact and square shaped, with strong, muscular hindquarters.

Breed Assessment
LIFE EXPECTANCY 13 years
EXERCISE Plenty
GROOMING Considerable
NOISE Very talkative
HEALTH PROBLEMS None known
SIZE 17–18in (43.2–45.7cm)
BREED RECOGNIZED BY AKC, CKC, FCI, KC

Lhasa Apso

This is an ancient Tibetan breed, used by monks and nobles as an indoor guard dog in palaces and temples. It was considered sacred and was usually given as a present, rather than being bought and sold.

Characteristics
An assertive little dog, the Lhasa Apso can be distrustful of strangers and will alert its owners to unannounced visitors. Its coat is an impressive sight, but attracts dirt as its skirts whisk along the ground. It is independent, and although it loves human company, will keep itself happily occupied around the house or backyard. It is not a troublemaker, but is quite capable of holding its own if challenged by other dogs.

Appearance
The long, hard topcoat can be of many colors, including golden, sandy, honey, dark grizzle, slate, smoke, black, white, brown or parti-color; it will reach the ground if left untrimmed. The thick undercoat is neither woolly nor silky. The eyes are dark and oval; the ears hang down. It has a proudly carried tail which kinks over to one side to drape over the body. Its hairy feet are cat-like in shape and well padded. Low to the ground, this is a balanced compact dog with a jaunty movement.

Breed Assessment
LIFE EXPECTANCY 13 years
EXERCISE Minimum
GROOMING High maintenance
NOISE Fairly quiet
HEALTH PROBLEMS Back problems; eye-testing recommended
SIZE 10in (25cm)
BREED RECOGNIZED BY AKC, CKC, FCI, KC

Breed Assessment
LIFE EXPECTANCY 14 years
EXERCISE Minimum
GROOMING Considerable
NOISE Fairly quiet
HEALTH PROBLEMS Back problems
SIZE Not more than 11in (26.7cm)
BREED RECOGNIZED BY AKC, CKC, FCI, KC

Shih Tzu

Not to be confused with the Lhasa Apso, this dog was developed in China. It is likely that it was found in the palaces of the Chinese Emperors. It is almost certainly a cross between Lhasa Apsos and ancestors of the Pekingese.

Characteristics
An extrovert dog with an infectious appetite for life, the Shih Tzu is a delightful companion that will be happy to be part of the family. It is friendly and independent and was bred solely as a pet. Its gentleness makes it an ideal dog for an older person, though the breed will in fact suit most people. It rarely barks.

Appearance
The Shih Tzu's long, dense coat is often wavy, and it is recommended that the hair on its head is tied up. It is found in most colors or parti-colors and quite often has a white blaze on the head and a white tip to the tail. The large, round, dark brown eyes are set well apart. Its long ears are very hairy, so they seem to merge with the coat on its body. The tail should be carried over its back. Feet are round, firm and well padded and give the impression of being large because of the amount of hair on them. Its body should be longer than it is high, with a level back. A broad, deep chest goes with its noble carriage.

Schipperke

Originating in Belgium and Holland, where it has been a distinct breed for centuries, the Schipperke was once used to guard canal boats, warn of strangers and catch rats and other vermin. It was from these duties that it derived its Flemish name, which translates as "Little Captain". This breed probably has distant links with the Belgian Shepherd Dog.

Characteristics

The Schipperke is a compact little dog that is lively and alert, making it an ideal house dog. It is also easy to keep clean. It enjoys all forms of exercise, like most dogs. Often mischievous, it remains ever-alert and watchful of strangers. It makes a loyal family pet. It can be noisy and high-spirited, but is eager to learn.

Appearance

Its gleaming thick coat feels harsh to the touch. It stands up around the neck and forms culottes on the back and thighs. Although the most common color is black, any solid color is acceptable. Its dark brown eyes add to its alert expression. The upright ears are strong enough not to fold over. Its tail can be docked short, but it is occasionally born without a tail. Its feet are small and cat-like. It has a broad, deep chest.

Breed Assessment

LIFE EXPECTANCY 14 years
EXERCISE Moderate
GROOMING Moderate
NOISE Talkative
HEALTH PROBLEMS None known
SIZE 13in (32cm)
CUSTOMARILY DOCKED Yes
BREED RECOGNIZED BY AKC, CKC, FCI, KC

Breed Assessment

LIFE EXPECTANCY 13 years
EXERCISE Plenty
GROOMING Moderate
NOISE Talkative
HEALTH PROBLEMS Eye-testing recommended
SIZE 13–14in (33–35.6cm)
CUSTOMARILY DOCKED Yes
BREED RECOGNIZED BY AKC, CKC, FCI, KC

Miniature Schnauzer

The smallest of three sizes of Schnauzer, the Miniature Schnauzer is also the most popular. It is an attractive dog which is probably related to the Affenpinscher as well as the larger Schnauzers. Originally from southern Germany, the Miniature Schnauzer's rugged appearance and versatility is in keeping with its humble beginnings as a general farm and drover's dog. It was prized as a good all-rounder: herding, protecting and rat-catching.

Characteristics

This dog enjoys human company and is always eager to please. It needs regular exercise and enjoys being in the country. Its wiry coat needs regular grooming and will require stripping to maintain its smart appearance. It looks like many terriers, but is quieter and less feisty.

Appearance

The harsh hair is normally trimmed into a distinctive shape that includes bushy eyebrows and a dense, hairy beard. Pepper and salt is the most common color, although black and black-and-silver are also found. The eyes are dark. It has neat, V-shaped ears that fall forward; in the USA and Europe, the ears are often cropped. The tail is set high. Its cat-like, compact round feet have firm black pads. This dog is strong and lithe.

Tibetan Spaniel

This old breed is thought to have originated from the Himalayan monasteries and villages of Tibet. They were much-loved companions to the monks, who would place them under their flowing robes in the winter for warmth.

Characteristics
The Tibetan Spaniel is a happy and assertive dog that will be content with any family. It is highly intelligent and enjoys both human and canine company. Often a sensitive dog, it can be responsive to its owner's moods and feelings. It loves to spend hours preening itself in the same manner as a cat. Consistent early training will discourage a wilful streak.

Appearance
It has a silky-textured double coat with a dense undercoat. Longer hair is present on the mane with feathering on the ears, feet, tail and buttocks. All solid colors are found, with mixtures permissible. Bright, expressive, dark brown eyes have dark rims. Its medium-sized ears are well feathered, high set and lift slightly away from the skull. Its feet are small, with neat feathering between the toes. A richly plumed tail is carried over the back to one side. Its body should have laid-back shoulders and tight elbows.

Breed Assessment
LIFE EXPECTANCY 14 years
EXERCISE Moderate
GROOMING Moderate
NOISE Talkative
HEALTH PROBLEMS Eye-testing recommended
SIZE 10in (25cm)
BREED RECOGNIZED BY AKC, CKC, FCI, KC

Breed Assessment
LIFE EXPECTANCY 11 years
EXERCISE Moderate
GROOMING Considerable
NOISE Fairly quiet
HEALTH PROBLEMS Hip- and eye-testing recommended
SIZE 14–16in (35.6–40.6cm)
BREED RECOGNIZED BY AKC, CKC, FCI, KC

Tibetan Terrier

This hardy little dog was developed to survive the harsh, variable weather of the Himalayan mountains. The biggest of the Tibetan breeds, it was used as a companion, guardian and herder by the monasteries and as a watchdog for the nomad encampments of traders who traveled to and from China.

Characteristics
The Tibetan is not terrier-like in either mind or body. It is enthusiastic and exuberant as a puppy, and an amiable and reserved adult. Although loyal and devoted to its owner, it can be stand-offish with strangers. It has a natural curiosity but is quick to get itself out of trouble. Its intelligence and spirit mean that it will enjoy frequent play, exercise and training.

Appearance
This dog's shaggy hair needs regular grooming to keep it tangle-free and looking good. The thick woolly undercoat sits under a wavy or straight topcoat in any color, or mixture, except chocolate or liver. Its eyes are large and round, and the ears hang down. The Tibetan terrier's hairy feet can be used in a cat-like manner, enabling it to hold and bat balls. Its tail is carried over its back and may have a kink.

Poodles (Toy, Miniature, Standard)

All three varieties of this breed are similar, apart from their size. The largest is the Standard, and it can claim the oldest history, with its image found on Roman coins. Although many believe it is a French breed, it is thought this breed originated in Russia and has German connections, since the name comes from the German *pudel*, meaning to splash. The Poodle was developed as a retrieving water dog, and it is thought that it was taken to France by 15th-century German soldiers. During the 17th and 18th centuries, the breed was popular at the French court. Demand grew for smaller types of Poodle, which would be more suited to the lifestyles and houses of the time, so the Toy (the smallest) and Miniature varieties were developed from the Standard.

Characteristics

Each variety has its own individual charm and all are natural entertainers. The most striking feature of the Poodle is its glamorous non-shedding coat. Although the exaggerated trim is often ridiculed, it has a historical pedigree: the coat was trimmed in order to keep the legs free when swimming, and left hairy around the joints and organs to protect them from the cold water. All three varieties are very intelligent and sensitive. The astute nature of these dogs allows them to do almost anything required, including obedience, tricks, hunting and retrieving. They can have a short concentration span, which gives them an endearing sense of fun, but they can, as a result, be mischievous if not kept occupied. Poodles are high-spirited dogs and are very independent. In a noisy environment, they will respond by being noisy dogs, but do not otherwise yap too much. They will live happily in an apartment and adapt to town living, but they do need plenty of exercise. Poodles normally get along with other dogs and pets, and they make excellent, sociable companions for people of all ages.

Appearance

This breed's very thick curly coat does not shed and has a harsh feel. The hair grows quickly and the dog needs regular trimming and bathing to keep it looking its best. The breed was once found corded, but this type of coat died out because it required so much maintenance: it needed to be oiled and tied up in rags to keep it in good condition. Traditionally, pet poodles are clipped in a style known as the "lion clip". The coat comes in all solid colors including white, cream, brown, apricot, silver and blue. The almond-shaped eyes should be full of fire and intelligence. The ears are long and low, and are set close to the head. The tail should be carried at a slight angle when the dog is active, in keeping with its free and easy movement. Its deep chest and short back give it a jaunty walk. Its back legs should be muscular, allowing it to swim well. Its front legs are straight and parallel with small, well-padded feet with arched toes.

Standard Poodle

Breed Assessment

LIFE EXPECTANCY 12 years

EXERCISE *Toy* Moderate; *Miniature* Moderate; *Standard* Plenty

GROOMING High maintenance

NOISE Talkative

HEALTH PROBLEMS Eye-testing recommended; some hip problems in the Standard and some slipping knee caps in Toy Poodles

SIZE *Standard* Over 15in (38cm); *Miniature* 11–15in (28–38cm); *Toy* Under 11in (28cm)

CUSTOMARILY DOCKED Yes

BREED RECOGNIZED BY AKC, CKC, FCI, KC

Standard Poodle

Working Dogs

Types of working dogs ✦ Working dogs as pets

The working dog group includes breeds that date back to times when dogs were used to guard settlements, carry loads and engage in battle. Mastiff-type working breeds feature in art from many thousands of years ago. Flockguards protected sheep from bears and wolves as far back as 10,000 years ago, and herders have been used by farmers for as long as they have kept animals.

GROUP DISTINCTIONS

In 1983, the American Kennel Club split the working dog group into two, to create the herding and working groups. In the UK, on January 1, 1999, a similar split was created in its working group. All types of herding dogs (see opposite) form the new pastoral group. Historically, dogs have had a wide range of uses outside the farm, and the breeds that remain in the working group reflect the diversity of jobs that dogs have performed for humans over the years.

Working dogs

Classic examples of working dogs include the Siberian Husky and Alaskan Malamute, sled dogs that were bred to pull heavy loads in treacherous conditions. The Portuguese Water Dog retrieved nets for fishermen, and the St Bernard searched for and rescued travelers lost in snow, reviving them with brandy from a barrel hung around its neck (see page 247). The Doberman Pinscher has always been an excellent guard dog and is still used as one today.

Herding or pastoral dogs

Some herding dogs developed from early Nordic or eastern sheepdogs that originally worked with reindeer. Several main types have been bred. Heelers would drive cattle forward by nipping at their heels. These dogs – which include the Lancashire Heeler, the Australian Cattle Dog, the Swedish Vallhund and the Welsh Corgi – were generally short legged to

Below: The Norwegian Buhund's strong herding instinct makes it an ideal farm guard dog; it is also a good companion.

Right: A shepherd's guardian throughout France for many years, the Briard today retains excellent guarding instincts.

prevent them from being kicked. They were capable of working independently of the farmer and searching out livestock that had strayed.

Flockguards are another type of working dog and should not be confused with herding dogs, although they form part of the new pastoral group. As their name suggests, they simply guarded their wards against theft or attack, and they had to be strong enough to defend against fierce predators. Flockguards often worked in bleak, mountainous areas and had to be sturdy, with a weather-resistant coat to survive extreme conditions all year round. Working independently from a shepherd, the dogs were required to be focused instinctively on their work. They also had to be utterly faithful to those they were protecting. When food was scarce, flockguards had to be trustworthy enough not to feast on animals left in their care, even when faced with starvation.

Sheep-herding dogs, or "strong-eyed" dogs, worked more closely with their masters, following commands. They continue to have strong bonds with their owners and have a great desire to please. Sheep-herders had to be gentler than the heelers, since sheep are not as sturdy and resilient as cattle, and could easily be harmed if they were nipped too hard.

Some farmers required sheepdogs that were sturdier, and could guard as well as herd. This was achieved by crossing sheepdogs with flockguards or mastiff types. These dogs are generally called shepherd dogs, rather than sheepdogs or sheep-herders. Many countries and regions developed their own sheep and shepherd dogs to suit their needs. France was the home of the Briard, Belgium of the Belgian Shepherd Dog and Germany of the German Shepherd dog. The British

Right: Today, teams of Newfoundlands, once used to pull nets and boats ashore in Canada, assist the emergency services in sea rescues.

Isles produced the Old English Sheepdog, the Shetland Sheepdog, and the Scottish-bred Collies.

WORKING DOGS AS PETS

Working and pastoral dogs are often energetic, large and strong. Coupled with their high intelligence, these characteristics can cause problems if the dogs are not kept active physically and mentally. If their energy is not channeled properly, you may end up with a dog that attempts to herd joggers or cyclists. However, with the right owner they usually make sound pets, forming strong bonds with their family. Many breeds in this group, particularly those bred as sheepdogs, excel at obedience and agility work.

The majority of working and pastoral breeds have long or thick coats, developed to cope with harsh weather conditions, and owners must be prepared to spend considerable amounts of time grooming them. If you object to hairs or pawprints on your belongings, you might want to consider breeds from another group.

Alaskan Malamute

This breed was originally used to pull sleds for the Mahlemuts, a tribe of Inuits in Alaska, who gave this dog its name. It was discovered by European settlers in the 1750s. When sled racing became popular, the breed almost became extinct as it was crossed with faster dogs.

Characteristics
Powerful and sporty, the Malamute makes an ideal jogging companion. It does not enjoy the heat, and thrives in colder climates. A playful companion, it needs to be kept fully occupied or it can become noisy and destructive. It is not a suitable dog for the inexperienced owner, but is affectionate, loyal and devoted to its family.

Appearance
The dog has a thick, coarse guard coat, and a dense oily undercoat. Its eyes are brown and almond shaped. The triangular ears, which are small in proportion to the head, fall forward when erect and are sometimes folded against the skull when it is working. The fairly high-set furry tail follows the line of the spine initially, then curls gently upward. The feet are large, with thick, rough pads and protective hair between the toes. This is a strong, powerfully built dog, with a deep chest and powerful loins. Its back slopes slightly from the shoulders.

Breed Assessment
LIFE EXPECTANCY 14 years
EXERCISE Plenty
GROOMING Moderate
NOISE Talkative
HEALTH PROBLEMS None known
SIZE 23–28in (58–71cm)
BREED RECOGNIZED BY AKC, CKC, FCI, KC

Breed Assessment
LIFE EXPECTANCY 14 years
EXERCISE A few miles daily
GROOMING Moderate
NOISE Very talkative
HEALTH PROBLEMS Eye problems
SIZE 20–24in (51–60cm)
BREED RECOGNIZED BY AKC, CKC, FCI, KC

Siberian Husky

The Siberian Husky has herded reindeer in Siberia for at least 3000 years. Introduced into Alaska at the beginning of the twentieth century, it soon became a champion at sled racing and is now also a popular pet.

Characteristics
This is not a breed for the inexperienced owner. It loves to wander and can leap most fences from a standing position, and dig under most obstacles. It needs lots of exercise, and careful lead-training to prevent pulling. The puppies of this breed were traditionally raised by the women of the Chukchi people of eastern Siberia, and legend has it that the breed's good temperament and ease in a family environment were established at this time.

Appearance
The undercoat, which sheds, is soft and dense. The guard hairs of the outercoat are straight and lie fairly smoothly. The almond-shaped eyes have a friendly, eager expression. The erect, triangular ears are quite close together, and are set high on the head. The tail is usually carried over the back in a sickle curve when the dog is alert and trails when the dog is working or at rest. The cushioned feet are slightly webbed. The body is straight and strong, and the loins well arched, muscled and lean.

Samoyed

Employed in northern Russia to guard and herd reindeer, the Samoyed acquired its name from the tribe it served. It was accustomed to working closely with its masters and to sleeping in their tents, and has always had a great love of life within a family.

Characteristics

Alert and intelligent, the Samoyed will warn of strangers, but will accept them if you invite them in. Its coat needs considerable daily attention and tends to shed. It can be vocal, but modern motivational training methods should eliminate any potential problems. It has a naturally "smiling" face and an equally happy temperament. It can be strong willed, so consistent early training is important.

Appearance

The thick, soft undercoat is protected by a weather-resistant, silver-tipped outercoat, which is white, cream, or white with biscuit. The slanting, almond-shaped eyes, rimmed with black, have an alert, intelligent expression. The ears are lightly rounded at the tips, set well apart and covered inside with hair; the adult's ears are erect. The long, hairy tail is carried over the back and to the side when the dog is alert. The feathered feet act as snowshoes. The moderate-length back is broad and muscular.

Breed Assessment

LIFE EXPECTANCY 14 years
EXERCISE Plenty
GROOMING High maintenance
NOISE Very talkative
HEALTH PROBLEMS None
SIZE 18–22in (46–56cm)
BREED RECOGNIZED BY AKC, CKC, FCI, KC

Breed Assessment

LIFE EXPECTANCY 13 years
EXERCISE Plenty
GROOMING Moderate
NOISE Very talkative
HEALTH PROBLEMS Eye problems
SIZE Ideal height for dogs 18in (45cm); bitches smaller
BREED RECOGNIZED BY FCI, KC

Norwegian Buhund

One of the earliest Nordic hunting dogs, possibly dating back 2000 years, the Buhund's name translates as "Farm Dog" or "Homestead Dog". It was first used as a farm watchdog and sheepdog and remains alert to strangers.

Characteristics

This dog's light build belies its capacity for arduous work. It enjoys training and physical and mental stimulation. This breed is lively and energetic, but needs comparatively little exercise to maintain its fitness, and is very clean and easy to groom. It does require consistent training as it can be headstrong. A natural guard dog, it is brave and vocal. This dog can be aloof, but loves its family and is known for its fondness for children.

Appearance

The outercoat is smooth and harsh, while the undercoat is soft and woolly. Colors include wheaten, black, red, and wolf-sable. Small symmetrical white markings are sometimes present. The dark brown eyes have a lively and fearless expression, and the sharply pointed ears are set high. The short, thick tail, with longer hair on the underside, is tightly curled and carried over the back. The feet are small and oval shaped. Short and strong, the Buhund has a light build.

Bearded Collie

The long-time friend of Scottish Highland farmers, the Bearded Collie is an intelligent dog that needed little supervision to drive sheep and cattle long distances to market. Now mainly a pet, it still needs regular stimulation.

Characteristics
This appealing shaggy dog's beautiful coat can become a full-time problem, since it collects mud and knots. It needs extra brushing for the first two years of its life, while the coat develops. Being bred for arduous work has resulted in an unexaggerated anatomy and it tends not to have many health problems. It can be noisy and mischievous if unstimulated, but is usually gentle.

Appearance
The harsh weatherproof topcoat, with a soft, fluffy undercoat, may be black, brown, fawn or blue with white collie-pattern markings, or tricolor. The Bearded Collie is born dark, but it coat nearly always lightens and it continues to change color throughout it life. Its big, gentle, enquiring eyes tone with the coat color. The ears rise slightly at the base when it is alert. Its tail is long enough to reach the hock. Feet are oval and well padded. Its ribcage is the shape of an inverted pear.

Breed Assessment
LIFE EXPECTANCY 14 years
EXERCISE A few miles daily
GROOMING High maintenance
NOISE Talkative
HEALTH PROBLEMS Hip- and eye-testing recommended
SIZE 20–22in (50–56 cm)
Breed recognized by AKC, CKC, FCI, KC

Breed Assessment
LIFE EXPECTANCY 10 years
EXERCISE A few miles daily
GROOMING High maintenance
NOISE Very talkative
HEALTH PROBLEMS Hip- and eye-testing strongly recommended
SIZE 22–24in (56–61cm)
CUSTOMARILY DOCKED Yes
BREED RECOGNIZED BY AKC, CKC, FCI, KC

Old English Sheepdog

This breed is native to Britain, and is sometimes called a "bobtail", due to its lack of tail. It was bred as a drover and herder, and its steady, trusting nature and protective instinct make it ideal for guarding flocks; occasionally it will go one step further and "adopt" children.

Characteristics
The the Old English Sheepdog's big, shaggy coat goes with a big personality, and boisterous puppies can grow into unruly adults if not suitably trained from a young age. For such a strongly built, sturdy breed it has amazing elasticity when moving, enabling it to turn quickly, although it can be clumsy. It has a very distinctive deep bark, which it uses to warn off strangers. This dog is generous with its affection to those it loves.

Appearance
Its huge coat, in all shades of grey or blue – a softer shade of grey – with white patches, has more body than length; the undercoat is waterproof. The wide-set eyes should be dark or blue. The ears are small enough to be lost in the head hair. The small round paws have thick hard pads. The tail is often docked very short. The dog's ambling movement when walking accentuates the rise in its back level from shoulder to rump.

Border Collie

The name of this breed stems from the fact that the dogs were used for herding sheep in the border counties of England and Scotland. A silent worker, the Border Collie will creep up to the flock in response to the shepherd's signals, then move them forward on command.

Characteristics

Dogs closer to the working lines have a strong predatory instinct, which has been diverted into superb herding ability. They need constant stimulation, otherwise they may become destructive or show other behavioral problems. This collie has tireless energy and its intelligence means that it learns quickly and is never happier than when playing a mentally stimulating game. It can be a faithful and loyal companion.

Appearance

Longer and shorter coats are found, both having a thick topcoat and soft, dense undercoat, with the hair forming a mane around the neck. Coats are of various colors but are never predominantly white. Wide-set, brown, oval-shaped eyes are the norm; sometimes merles have blue eyes. Medium-sized ears can tip over or stand upright. The tail is long enough to reach the hock. Oval, well-padded feet have arched toes. The dog is athletic in appearance.

Breed Assessment

LIFE EXPECTANCY 11 years
EXERCISE A few miles daily
GROOMING High maintenance
NOISE Talkative
HEALTH PROBLEMS Hip- and eye-testing recommended
SIZE 14–15in (35–37cm)
BREED RECOGNIZED BY AKC, CKC, FCI, KC

Rough Collie

Breed Assessment

LIFE EXPECTANCY 11 years
EXERCISE A few miles daily
GROOMING High maintenance
NOISE Talkative
HEALTH PROBLEMS Eye-testing strongly recommended
SIZE Sheltie 14–15in (35–37cm); Rough/Smooth 20–22in (51–6cm)
BREED RECOGNIZED BY AKC, CKC, FCI, KC

Rough & Smooth Collie & Shetland Sheepdog

Both Rough and Smooth Collie bitches have been known to produce litters with both coat types. The Shetland Sheepdog, known as the "Sheltie", is believed to have resulted from crossing Rough Collies with dogs from the Shetland Islands, lying to the north of Scotland. All were bred as working dogs, used for droving.

Characteristics

The Smooth is generally shyer and more retiring than the Rough. The Sheltie is affectionate, although it can be noisy. All these breeds enjoy mental and physical stimulation and make loyal family pets. The dogs all require thorough grooming to keep them looking attractive. They are nimble, intelligent, fast learners and enjoy all forms of motivational and active training.

Appearance

The Smooth has a short, dense coat; Rough and Sheltie coats are thicker; all have pronounced manes and feathering on the legs. Sable, tricolor and blue merle are the Collie colors, while the Sheltie is black and white or black and tan. Their long tails are carried low.

Belgian Shepherd Dogs

The four types of this breed from Belgium – Groenendael, Laekenois, Malinois and Tervueren – are identical except in coat and color. Their spirit and energy mark them as some of Europe's finest all-purpose working dogs.

Characteristics

A proud dog that is full of life, the Belgian Shepherd needs exercising in mind and muscle. Although its guarding instincts are still active and it can do well at agility, herding and obedience training, it can be noisy, and needs to be socialized from an early age and helped not to distrust strangers. It is a good family dog.

Appearance

The Groenendael and Tervueren share a long, straight coat with a thick undercoat; it forms a ruff around the neck and feathering on the legs. The Groenendael is black, while the Tervueren shares the red with black frosting and the face mask of the Malinois. The latter has a short, firm coat. The Laekenois has a reddish fawn wiry coat. Lively, enquiring dark brown eyes are of medium size. Distinct triangular ears are erect and stiff. A firmly set, medium-length tail lifts when moving. Feet are round with thick springy soles, and the breed has a well-muscled, elegant body. The chest curves up gracefully.

Breed Assessment

LIFE EXPECTANCY 13 years
EXERCISE A few miles daily
GROOMING Moderate
NOISE Very talkative
HEALTH PROBLEMS Eye-testing recommended
SIZE 22–26in (56–66cm)
BREED RECOGNIZED BY AKC *(ex. Lakenois)*, CKC, FCI, KC

Breed Assessment

LIFE EXPECTANCY 11 years
EXERCISE A few miles daily
GROOMING Considerable
NOISE Talkative
HEALTH PROBLEMS Hip-testing essential
SIZE 24–27in (59–68cm)
CUSTOMARILY DOCKED Yes
BREED RECOGNIZED BY AKC, CKC, FCI, KC

Bouvier des Flandres

This dog's name translates as "Flanders oxen-driver", and this is exactly its original task in the Flanders region of Belgium. It was one of the most skilful cattle dogs in Western Europe. The breed's guarding abilities nearly led to its extinction, when it suffered massive losses in its role as dog of war in the First World War. Clever breeding ensured its survival in the 1920s. Now a very popular police dog in several countries, the Bouvier is employed as a guard dog, guide dog and tracker.

Characteristics

The Bouvier des Flandres makes an excellent guard dog, and a good family dog that is gentle with children if brought up with them. It is remarkably nimble for its size. Intelligent and lively, it is also sensible and loyal.

Appearance

It has a thick, coarse and unkempt coat, with a crisp outercoat and a fine, fluffy undercoat. Dark alert eyes peer out from under bushy eyebrows. Ears are triangular and are cropped in America and parts of Europe. Its tail is customarily docked short. Its small, compact, round feet have thick, hard pads. Its square body is short and compact, as high as it is long, and its chest descends to the level of its elbows.

Briard

An extroverted rugged worker from the Brie region of France, the Briard had the dual role of guarding and herding sheep, and was used as a hunting and guard dog by the French aristocracy. It first took part in dog shows at the end of the 19th century. Today, it is usually a fearless dog with a heroic spirit and a zest for adventure.

Characteristics
A spirited breed, with strong guarding instincts, the Briard has kept many of its original characteristics and is very independent. It needs plenty of exercise and enjoys rough games; its powerful build means that this is not a dog for the weak-hearted. A charming dog, it is very loyal to its family. The shaggy coat has self-cleaning properties but must be groomed regularly.

Appearance
The long, slightly wavy, dry-textured coat has a fine but dense undercoat. The hair on its head has a distinctive middle parting and forms a moustache, beard and eyebrows, and its ears are hairy and high set. It can be black or fawn with dark frosting color. Dark brown eyes are intelligent. Strong, slightly rounded feet feature toes close together and dense, hard pads. A characteristic feature is double dew claws on the hind legs.

Breed Assessment
LIFE EXPECTANCY 11 years
EXERCISE A few miles daily
GROOMING High maintenance
NOISE Very talkative
HEALTH PROBLEMS Hip- and eye-testing essential
SIZE 22–27in (56–68cm)
BREED RECOGNIZED BY AKC, CKC, FCI, KC

Breed Assessment
LIFE EXPECTANCY 7 years
EXERCISE Plenty
GROOMING Considerable
NOISE Talkative
HEALTH PROBLEM Hip-testing and elbow screening recommended
SIZE 23–26in (58–66cm)
BREED RECOGNIZED BY AKC, CKC, FCI, KC

Bernese Mountain Dog

This multipurpose farm dog was also used by the weavers of Berne in Switzerland to pull carts. It is believed to be the result of interbreeding between native sheepdogs and mastiffs brought into Switzerland by the Romans during their invasion 2000 years ago.

Characteristics
This dog is naturally sweet-tempered. It is a devoted family pet that is intelligent and normally easily trained. It generally plays well with children and is vigilant and loyal to its family. It has a tendency to obesity, so care is needed with diet, and the thick coat means that it does not enjoy hot weather.

Appearance
Its long and wavy coat should be thick, with a bright natural sheen. The coat requires regular grooming where the hair is longer. The color is jet black, with reddish brown coloring around the cheeks, eyes, legs and chest, and a white blaze on the face, and white in the shape of a cross on the chest. Its dark brown, almond-shaped eyes reflect its kind nature. Triangular-shaped ears are high set and are raised when the dog is alert. It has relatively small, round, compact feet. Its long body and broad chest allow it to take long strides.

Boxer

The Boxer, which emerged between 1890 and 1900, originated in Germany, where it was developed from Mastiff-type bull-baiting breeds. Its main ancestor, the Bullenbeisser (whose name means "bull-biter" in German) was used for hunting boar and bear.

Characteristics
Its slightly wrinkled forehead and soulful eyes give the impression that it is worried, but it is a happy, playful dog. It is exuberant and lively and can be quite a handful – Boxers rarely grow up, even in their old age. This breed's natural guarding intincts sometimes make it distrustful of strangers, but it adores its family and is very loyal.

Appearence
Its coat is smooth, short and glossy, and a fawn coat can range from deep red to a light fawn. A brindle coat has a fawn base, with black stripes all over the body running parallel with the ribs. Eyes are dark brown with dark rims. The ears are set wide apart on the highest point of the head, and, in the US, are customarily cropped. The tail is set high, carried upward and customarily docked. The well-arched front feet are small and cat-like, with hard pads; hind feet are slightly longer. It has a deep chest that reaches the elbows.

Breed Assessment
LIFE EXPECTANCY 12 years
EXERCISE A few miles daily
GROOMING Minimum
NOISE Fairly quiet
HEALTH PROBLEMS Hip dysplasia; heart problems; prone to cancer
SIZE 21–25in (53–63cm)
CUSTOMARILY DOCKED Yes
BREED RECOGNIZED BY AKC, CKC, FCI, KC

Breed Assessment
LIFE EXPECTANCY 10 years
EXERCISE Plenty
GROOMING Moderate
NOISE Fairly quiet
HEALTH PROBLEMS Eye problems; OCD; dermoid sinus
SIZE 23–28in (58–69cm)
CUSTOMARILY DOCKED Yes
BREED RECOGNIZED BY AKC, CKC, FCI, KC

Rottweiler

The Rottweiler's career as a working dog has included hunting boar, guarding, droving cattle and working with the police. It is named after Rottweil, the town in south Germany where the breed started several centuries ago.

Characteristics
Good natured, loyal and obedient, the Rottweiler is devoted to its family. It has a surprisingly tranquil nature, despite its powerful and imposing physique. However, if challenged, it can be formidable. An energetic dog, it enjoys all types of vigorous exercise. It can be difficult to train and requires confident handling, so is not a suitable breed for the inexperienced owner. This breed has natural guarding instincts.

Appearence
The Rottweiler's topcoat is coarse and flat and always black in color, with tan to mahogany markings. The eyes are dark brown and almond shaped, and should not have baggy lids. Its ears lie flat and close to its cheeks. The Rottweiler's tail is carried horizontally but rises slightly when it is alert. Its feet have strong, well-arched toes and the hind feet are bigger than the front feet. Its compact, powerful body has a broad, deep chest. The back should be straight and slightly sloping.

German Shepherd Dog

Used originally to herd and guard sheep, this breed showed little uniformity until the 19th century. At the beginning of the 20th century, the German Shepherd Dog as we now know it started to emerge. The breed is now hugely popular around the world.

Characteristics

An intelligent dog that enjoys working, the German Shepherd needs a dedicated, consistent owner who will keep it occupied. Loyal and attentive, it builds good relationships with people it respects. Known for its steady, dependable temperament, it can be a successful guide dog. It also has common sense, versatility and a willingness to learn, making it useful for police work.

Appearance

The short, dense outercoat and thick undercoat can be black or black saddle with tan, or gold to light grey markings. All black or all grey with lighter or brown markings (sables) are also available. Eyes are almond-shaped. Ears have a broad base, are set high and are carried erect. The bushy tail rests in a slight saber-like curve. The feet have durable, well-cushioned pads and the toes should be rounded, well closed and arched. The chest is deep and the back slopes downward slightly.

Breed Assessment

LIFE EXPECTANCY 10 years
EXERCISE A few miles daily
GROOMING High maintenance
NOISE Talkative
HEALTH PROBLEMS Hip dysplasia; hemophilia testing for males recommended before breeding
SIZE 23–26in (57.5–64.5cm)
BREED RECOGNIZED BY AKC, CKC, FCI, KC

Breed Assessment

LIFE EXPECTANCY 8 years
EXERCISE Moderate
GROOMING Low maintenance
NOISE Talkative
HEALTH PROBLEMS Heart disease; hip and elbow problems; hip- and elbow-testing strongly recommended
SIZE Bitch: 28in (71cm) ; Dog: 30in (76cm)
BREED RECOGNIZED BY AKC, CKC, FCI, KC

Great Dane

The tall and elegantly built Great Dane is obviously "great" in stature, but since it was first bred in Germany, the use of the name "Dane" is confusing. It was originally used as a hunting and fighting dog, and is now the national dog of Germany.

Characteristics

Muscular but graceful, the Great Dane is a versatile, dignified and affectionate dog. It will be at home in the city, as long as it is exercised sufficiently, but great care should be taken in exercising and feeding puppies to avoid bone damage. It is a kind, friendly and outgoing dog, tolerant of children and other animals. It can be stubborn, but will respond to modern motivational training methods.

Appearence

The Great Dane's short, dense, sleek coat can be brindle, fawn, blue, black or harlequin. The eyes are quite deep set. The ears are customarily cropped in the US. The tail is carried in a straight line, level with the back. When the dog is moving, the tail curves slightly at the end. The feet should be cat-like and the toes should be well arched. The Great Dane's deep chest reaches to its elbows.

Mastiff & Bull Mastiff

An ancient breed, the Mastiff dates back to Egyptian times. It was used by farmers to drive and protect livestock. The Bull Mastiff was developed in the 19th century by crossing the Mastiff and the Bulldog. It was trained to capture poachers and hold them without mauling or killing. Both breeds have more recently been used as guard dogs and have become devoted family pets.

Bullmastiff

Characteristics
Both dogs are impressively built – the Mastiff remains one of the largest dogs – and give an overall impression of power and substance. They have "trademark" wrinked foreheads. Both the Mastiff and the Bull Mastiff are calm, intelligent and easily trained.

Appearance
The short coat is easily managed. The Mastiff is frequently found in apricot or silver-fawn shades, with or without brindling. The Bull Mastiff can be brindled in shades of fawn and red. Both breeds have black muzzles shading off towards the deep brown eyes, which are set off by dark markings and furrowed brows. The ears are V-shaped. The tail is high set and can be carried straight or curved. The feet are large and round with black nails. The chest is deep and muscular.

Breed Assessment
LIFE EXPECTANCY 10 years
EXERCISE Plenty
GROOMING Moderate
NOISE Fairly quiet
HEALTH PROBLEMS Hip-scoring recommended; heart disease and some eye problems in Bull Mastiffs
SIZE *Mastiff* 28–30in (70–76cm); *Bull Mastiff* 25–27in (63–68cm)
BREED RECOGNIZED BY AKC, CKC, FCI, KC

Breed Assessment
LIFE EXPECTANCY 8 years
EXERCISE Moderate
GROOMING High maintenance
NOISE Talkative
HEALTH PROBLEMS Hip- and heart-testing strongly recommended
SIZE 26–28in (65–70cm)
BREED RECOGNIZED BY AKC, CKC, FCI, KC

St Bernard

This large breed was first bred in the Swiss Alps at the Hospice of St Bernard, where the monks used it to help find travelers lost in violent snowstorms. Famed for its brandy barrel, it has been credited with saving countless lives. Thought to have descended from large Mastiff-type dogs, this is a popular pet but needs plenty of space.

Characteristics
One of the most massive dogs, the St Bernard is a gentle giant if you can cope with its size and tendency to salivate. It is good humored and equable provided it has sufficient space. A steady and intelligent dog, it is easily trained and a loyal friend. This breed has a caring nature and is generally devoted to children.

Appearance
Two types of coat are found in this breed, the more common being the rough coat, which is is dense with a ruff around the neck and hairy thighs. The smooth-coated dog has a close-fitting jacket, with slight feathering on the tail and white markings on a coat of either orange, mahogany-brindle or red-brindle. The dog's large head is set off by sparkling, gentle, diamond-shaped eyes. Its medium-sized ears should lie close to its cheeks. It has a wide muscular body with a deep chest.

Pyrenean Mountain Dog

The impressive Pyrenean Mountain dog has been used for centuries in the rugged mountains of the Pyrenees to protect flocks from wild animals and to pull sleds. Members of the breed were taken to the court of Louis XIV and were later also used in warfare. By the late 1800s, the breed had nearly disappeared, but was revived by enthusiasts; it was given its present name in 1908.

Characteristics

Hardy and healthy, this dog is slow to mature both physically and mentally. It is a good family dog, gentle with children and kind natured. It is remarkably nimble for its size. It will learn obedience readily in the hands of an experienced trainer. It is both affectionate and friendly, and is a good guard when necessary.

Appearance

The thick double coat is white or white with grey or tan patches like badger markings. It consists of fine hairs and a dense, coarse outercoat that forms a mane and trousers. The thick hair on the tail can sweep the floor or curve over the back. Almond-shaped, dark brown eyes give the dog an intelligent expression. Its small, triangular ears lie flat on the head. The feet are compact, slightly arched toes, and a broad chest with a muscular back.

Breed Assessment

LIFE EXPECTANCY 10 years
EXERCISE Moderate
GROOMING Considerable
NOISE Talkative
HEALTH PROBLEMS None known
SIZE Minimum 26–28in (65–70cm)
BREED RECOGNIZED BY AKC, CKC, FCI, KC

Breed Assessment

LIFE EXPECTANCY 10 years
EXERCISE Plenty
GROOMING Low maintenance
NOISE Fairly quiet
HEALTH PROBLEMS Blood clotting disorder and hip problems
SIZE 26–28in (65–69cm)
CUSTOMARILY DOCKED Yes
BREED RECOGNIZED BY AKC, CKC, FCI, KC

Doberman

This breed was created by a German tax-collector, Louis Dobermann, in the late 1860s to protect him in his work. The Doberman was developed from a variety of breeds, probably including the Rottweiler, Pinscher and Manchester Terrier, among others. Recognized by the German Kennel Club in 1900, the Doberman served as a guard and patrol dog in the First World War.

Characteristics

The Doberman is an elegant dog, capable of great speed. Its agility and energy mean it needs plenty of exercise. Intelligent, loyal and obedient, it also needs considerable mental stimulation and human contact. It is a strong and athletic dog better suited to experienced dog owners. Brought up properly, it makes a good family dog with natural guarding ability.

Appearance

Its short, thick, smooth coat can be black, brown, blue or fawn, all with tan markings. Eyes are almond shaped. Ears droop naturally, but in some countries, including in the US, it is customary to have them surgically trimmed so that they stand erect. The tail is a continuation of the spine. Feet are compact and cat-like. It has a square muscular body with a slightly sloping back.

Komondor & Puli

The Komondor is twice the size of the Puli, but both of these Hungarian dogs were used for herding sheep, and their natural instincts may need to be controlled. Their strange coats are their most distinguishing feature and the dogs are sometimes called "moving carpets".

Characteristics
The coat is both a highlight and a curse and can take up to three years to form. The hair matts into cords and can become unmanageable if left unattended. Both breeds can be determined and somewhat territorial; they require a great deal of exercise. The smaller Puli is more nimble than the Komondor, whose strength can be imposing, so early training and socializing are important.

Appearance
The coarse outercoat and soft undercoat cling together to produce distinctive cords, which feel like felt and are heavy and often floor-length. The medium-sized, dark eyes are hidden behind the dogs' coats, and their ears are barely noticeable. The Komondor's tail rises slightly at the tip and can be distinguished from its general rump area; the Puli's tail is curled up tightly when it is alert. The Komondor has larger feet than the Puli. In both dogs, the level back leads to a broad, slightly sloping rump.

Komondor

Breed Assessment
LIFE EXPECTANCY *Komondor* 10 years; *Puli* 11 years
EXERCISE *Both* Plenty
GROOMING High maintenance
NOISE Talkative
HEALTH PROBLEMS *Komondor* Hips should be tested; *Puli* Hips and eyes should be tested
SIZE *Komondor* On average 28–32in (70–80cm);
Puli 15–18in (37–44cm)
BREEDS RECOGNIZED BY AKC, CKC, FCI, KC

Standard Schnauzer

Breed Assessment
LIFE EXPECTANCY *Giant* 10 years; *Standard* 11 years
EXERCISE *Both* Plenty
GROOMING *Giant* Considerable; *Standard* High maintenance
NOISE *Giant* Fairly quiet; *Standard* Talkative
HEALTH PROBLEMS None known
SIZE *Giant* 24–28in (60–70cm);
Standard On average 18–19in (45.7–48.3cm)
CUSTOMARILY DOCKED Yes
BREED RECOGNIZED BY AKC, CKC, FCI, KC

Giant & Standard Schnauzer

The Schnauzer originated in southern Germany. The Standard is the oldest member of the family; the larger and more robust Giant is used for droving and guarding. Because of its strength and ability, the Giant is now classed separately as a working breed. There is also a third size of Schnauzer, the Miniature (see page 213).

Characteristics
The word Schnauzer means "snout", and this dog has a very conspicuous wiry beard that emphasizes its muzzle. For the showring, this is accentuated by trimming and it has become its hallmark. It is slow to mature and is very powerful. Its no-nonsense approach to life makes it suitable for police and army work. It is patient and trustworthy and can easily make a 10-mile (16-km) hike.

Appearance
The Schnauzer's coat is harsh and wiry, with a thick undercoat, and will need plenty of care. It has dark eyes in a dark face. Its ears are set high and drop forward. It carries its normally docked tail high. The feet should not turn in or out, and they are short and tightly arched. The Giant is simply a larger version of the Standard. It has a larger rib cage and its body length should equal its height.

Pembroke & Cardigan Corgi

The two types of Welsh Corgi were developed relatively independently from each other for hundreds of years, although their breeding lines connect. The Cardigan is, possibly, an older breed than the Pembroke. A good farm dog, the Corgi's connection with royalty in the UK has increased its popularity there.

Characteristics

The "Cardie" is long-bodied, long-tailed and calmer than its cousin. It is also known as the "Yard Dog" because from tip to tail it measures one Welsh yard (about 40in or 1m). The Pembroke is smaller. Both types are sociable: the Pembroke is perhaps more outgoing, but neither is shy. They have a reputation for nipping, but with early training and socialization they can make good pets and are often patient with children.

Appearance

The Cardigan has more colors, but the coat of both should be straight with good weatherproofing. The ears are quite large and are normally pricked. The Cardigan has a long, ground-sweeping brush-like tail, that of the Pembroke is very short. Both breeds have large, well-padded feet. Both have very low slung and sturdy bodies, but the Cardigan's body is longer.

Pembroke Corgi

Breed Assessment

LIFE EXPECTANCY 13 years
EXERCISE Moderate
GROOMING Low maintenance
NOISE Talkative
HEALTH PROBLEMS *Pembroke* None known;
Cardigan Eyes should be tested
SIZE *Pembroke* On average 10–12in (25.5–30.5cm);
Cardigan Ideally 12in (30cm)
CUSTOMARILY DOCKED The Pembroke may be docked
BREED RECOGNIZED BY AKC, CKC, FCI, KC

Breed Assessment

LIFE EXPECTANCY 13 years
EXERCISE Moderate
GROOMING Low maintenance
NOISE Very talkative
HEALTH PROBLEMS None known
SIZE 12–14in (31–35cm)
CUSTOMARILY DOCKED Yes
BREED RECOGNIZED BY FCI, KC

Swedish Vallhund

The Swedish Vallhund was used by the Vikings as a watchdog and cattle dog. In looks and temperament it resembles the Welsh Corgi. The breed became so rare that it nearly died out, until it was rescued in the 1940s by Count Björn von Rosen, a Swedish breeder.

Characteristics

Two types of the breed exist today, one slightly weightier than the other and with a thicker, fuller-bodied coat. Although it looks like the Welsh Corgi in many ways and shows many of its attributes, the Swedish Vallhund is an entirely different dog with a distinct personality. It is tough and tenacious and makes a good guard dog with a quick, warning bark. Friendly and eager to please, it is a good companion dog.

Appearance

The Vallhund generally has a full, dense coat with a soft, woolly undercoat that gives it a tousled look, and a slight ruffle at the neck. It has dark, oval eyes and an eager expression. Its ears are alert and fairly pointed. The length of a full tail should not exceed 4in (10cm). It has strong, thick-set legs and medium-sized feet that are oval in shape. Its back should be level and well muscled. It is a sturdy, well-balanced dog.

Toy Dogs

History ✦ Types of toy dog ✦ Keeping toy dogs

The dogs included in the toy group come from a diversity of backgrounds. Terriers (such as the Yorkshire Terrier), gundogs (the King Charles Spaniel), sighthounds (the Italian Greyhound) and Spitz dogs (the Pomeranian) are all represented in this group, although always in miniaturized form.

TOY HISTORY

Dog dwarfism is not uncommon, but many breeders – in particular Asian breeders – were fascinated by the phenomenon and bred from small specimens to create tiny versions of existing breeds. The hairless dogs, such as the Chinese Crested, were developed when breeders further adapted the tiny breeds in order to make them more useful. A genetic mutation creates such baldness, but the Chinese nurtured any dogs affected, and eventually created bald breeds. These dogs provided amusement, but also had a more practical purpose, becoming sources of warmth that were small enough to fit into a coat sleeve, and devoted enough to lie quietly under the bedclothes, at the feet of their owners. The Löwchen was trimmed in such a way as to ensure that heat could easily be transmitted to the owner through the shaved or "hairless" areas on the dog's body. Even today, some toy breeds are happy to remain perfectly still under a duvet, warming their owner's toes.

Until quite recently, toy breeds belonged exclusively to nobility and royalty. For example, the Japanese Chin reigned supreme in Japanese royal circles, the Pekingese held court in China and the King Charles Spaniel had English royal connections. European royalty favored the Bichon, Maltese and Bolognese, among others.

The Chinese Crested was originally employed to guard treasure before it was miniaturized further to become a companion dog. Until recently, its flesh was considered a great delicacy in China, and this, coupled with the anti-pet policy of Communist China, has led to its demise in its native land. Fortunately, because it is also valued

Below: The Papillon, so named because its ears resemble a pair of butterfly's wings, originates from Continental Europe.

as a pet in other parts of the world, there is now little risk of the breed becoming extinct.

GROUP DISTINCTIONS

As well as being uniformly small, toy breeds share a history of service as companions. Unlike other breeds, the toys were not bred to work for their owners. Their only job was to provide companionship, usually for wealthy women who spent much of their lives at home. Over the years, toy breeds were also known as "lap dogs", "pillow dogs" or "sleeve dogs".

Some dogs come in both toy and standard sizes for the purposes of the show ring. For example, the Manchester Terrier is bred in both sizes, but both sizes are categorized within the terrier group. Equally, the Toy Poodle is very much a miniaturized breed, but all poodles are considered to be utility or "non-sporting" dogs by the kennel clubs.

Because of their size, toy dogs are popular pets, particularly in cities, where their size and gentle temperament make them ideally suited to living in an apartment. They tend to be plucky and courageous dogs, and usually make good alarm dogs. However, many toy dogs have coats that require a great deal of maintenance. Historically, toy dogs were companion dogs to mainly wealthy owners, so trimming and grooming were never a problem. Even hairless breeds need considerable attention, since they can be prone to sunburn or heat rash.

TOY DOGS AS PETS

Bred specifically as companion dogs, the toys make excellent pets. They require a great deal of attention from their owners and are often unhappy when left alone for any length of time. They do not usually require vast amounts of exercise, but are surprisingly energetic. Despite their size, toy breeds are often resilient, but care must be taken with any young children in the house. For example, the tiny Chihuahua may look like an appealing plaything, but if dropped it can be seriously injured. Excited children may step on a toy breed, or

Above: Today's pampered Yorkshire Terriers are a far cry from the tenacious fighters orginally bred to catch rats in mines.

Below: The Pekingese, according to Chinese legend, is the product of a union between the noble lion and the graceful monkey.

their fingers may prod and poke too roughly, causing pain and damage. For this reason, children should be taught to handle the dogs correctly, and to take special care.

Many of the toy breeds are very loyal, and may become attached to their owners to the point of jealousy. However, proper socialization, with plenty of exposure to other people and pets, will help overcome this problem in most instances.

Right: The Löwchen, native to southern Europe, is also called the "Little Lion Dog". Adults are usually trimmed like Poodles.

Affenpinscher

This German breed, which looks similar to the Brussels Griffon, is shown in paintings from the 14th century and so may be one of the oldest toy breeds in Europe. It was formerly used on farms to catch rats.

Characteristics

This lively, self-confident, scruffy-looking dog can be an entertaining companion. Its exercise needs are not very high, but, being dependent and sharp-witted, it may have a tendency to get into mischief. Despite the small stature, this breed is quite fearless of intruders and fiercely loyal to its family. Affenpinschers normally get along well with children and other dogs.

Appearance

The rough, shaggy coat should form a "lion's mane" on the head and shoulders, which emphasizes the monkey-like expression. Black, which may grey with age, is the only color found in Britain. The round, dark, sparkling eyes should never protrude and the ears should be set high on the head. The tail may drop down when the dog is standing but should be carried proudly over the back when it moves, and must not curl around tightly. The feet are small, compact and cat-like. The sturdy body is square and compact, with a well-rounded ribcage.

Breed Assessment

LIFE EXPECTANCY 11 years
EXERCISE Moderate
GROOMING Low maintenance
NOISE Talkative
HEALTH PROBLEMS None known
SIZE 9.6–11in (24–28cm)
CUSTOMARILY DOCKED Tail docked in some countries, but left natural in Britain
BREED RECOGNIZED BY AKC, CKC, FCI, KC

Cavalier King Charles Spaniel

Breed Assessment

LIFE EXPECTANCY 11 years
EXERCISE Moderate
GROOMING Moderate
NOISE Talkative
HEALTH PROBLEMS *King Charles* None known; *Cavalier* Heart disease very common and eye-testing recommended
SIZE 12in (30cm)
BREED RECOGNIZED BY AKC, CKC, FCI, KC

Cavalier & King Charles Spaniels

King Charles II of England loved these dogs, hence the name. The two breeds share a common ancestry, the prefix "Cavalier" indicating the longer-nosed type first recognized as a breed in the 1940s. Originally used as little gundogs, they are now mainly companion dogs.

Characteristics

Both breeds have sweet natures and will enjoy trekking through fields, wandering around the shops or sitting by the fire with a human friend. Both King Charles Spaniels and Cavalier King Charles Spaniels are born companions, with happy affectionate dispositions. The King Charles may be a little more relaxed than the Cavalier, but both are gentle with calm children.

Appearance

The coat should be long and silky, with a slight wave. It requires no trimming and is easy to groom. Both breeds are found in four colors: black and tan, ruby (red), Blenheim (red and white) and tricolor (black and white with red spots). The large dark eyes should be round. The ears are long and silky. The tail should not rise above the back. The feet are compact and well feathered. The chest should be wide and deep, and the back level. The King Charles is smaller than the Cavalier.

Chihuahua
(Long- & Smooth-coated)

Brought to the USA in the late 19th century, this breed takes its name from Chihuahua in Mexico. Its precise origins are obscure, but most believe this feisty individual was reared by the Aztecs or Incas. The Chihuahua is the smallest breed in the world, sometimes weighing less than 2¼lb (1kg).

Characteristics

An agile, courageous and fiery dog, the Chihuahua is oblivious of its size and has the same determination as many larger breeds. It makes a noisy watchdog and is fearless enough to take on the biggest of intruders. Its small size means it needs to be protected from the cold.

Appearance

The Long-coated type, with a large ruff around the neck and longer hair on the ears, feet and legs, is soft to touch. The Smooth-coated has hair close to the skin, which gives it a sleek, glossy look. Both varieties can be any color or mixture of colors. Eyes should be large, round and set well apart and the color should match the coat. Ears are large and flared. The tail is held over the back. The body should be slightly longer than it is tall, with a deep chest.

Breed Assessment

LIFE EXPECTANCY 13 years
EXERCISE Minimum
GROOMING Moderate
NOISE Talkative
HEALTH PROBLEMS Slipping kneecap and occasional heart murmurs
SIZE 5in (13cm)
BREED RECOGNIZED BY AKC, CKC, FCI, KC

Breed Assessment

LIFE EXPECTANCY 14 years
EXERCISE Minimum
GROOMING High maintenance
NOISE Very talkative
HEALTH PROBLEMS None known
SIZE 9–11in (23–28cm)
BREED RECOGNIZED BY AKC, CKC, FCI, KC

Bichon Frisé

Once known as the Tenerife Dog, owing to the theory that it was brought to the Mediterranean from the Canary Islands in the 14th century, this breed is now regarded as French. After much controversy, the breed was given its current French name, which simply means "fluffy little dog", in the early part of the twentieth century.

Characteristics

This little dog is noted for its cheerful and confident outlook on life, which allows it to adapt to the most varied circumstances. It can be gentle mannered with children, but is also be playful and affectionate. The breed has a unique trim that gives the head a chrysanthemum shape. Keeping this lively dog in fine condition requires dedicated grooming and regular trimming.

Appearance

The distinctive puffball shape of this dog is created by the corkscrew-curly outercoat, which covers a soft, thick undercoat. The coat is white, and dedication is needed to retain the color. The eyes are dark and round with black rims. The ears, covered with flowing hair, lie close to the head and are raised when it is alert. The tail is carried curved over the body. The tight, round feet have black nails. The sturdy body is square, with a well-developed chest.

Chinese Crested

Established in China as early as the 13th century, the Chinese Crested was used to guard treasure and to hunt. There are now two types, one with hair on only the head, feet and tail and a second, known as the Powder Puff, which has long silky hair all over its body.

Characteristics
Within the Hairless and Powder Puff varieties, there are also two distinct types of Chinese Cresteds. The "Deer" is a racy, fine-boned type, while the "Cobby" is heavier. Care must be taken to ensure the skin of the Hairless does not dry out or burn in the sun. Years of domestication have made this breed a devoted companion that loves human company and home comforts. It is intelligent and makes a good watchdog. Very active, it rarely sits still for long.

Appearance
The skin of the Hairless is smooth and warm, and hair is usually found on its head, feet and tail. The Powder Puff has an undercoat and a soft veil of long hair. The wide-set eyes are dark, and the ears large and erect, although the Powder Puff may have drop ears. The tail is carried up or out when moving and hangs down at rest. The lower two-thirds of the tail has a long plume. The body is supple, the forelegs slender and the hindquarters muscular.

Breed Assessment
LIFE EXPECTANCY 13 years
EXERCISE Moderate
GROOMING High maintenance
NOISE Talkative
HEALTH PROBLEMS Skin problems in the Hairless
SIZE 9–13in (23–33cm)
BREED RECOGNIZED BY AKC, CKC, FCI, KC

Breed Assessment
LIFE EXPECTANCY 12 years
EXERCISE Moderate
GROOMING Considerable
NOISE Talkative
HEALTH PROBLEMS Knee and heart problems
SIZE 9in (23cm) average
BREED RECOGNIZED BY AKC, CKC, FCI, KC

Japanese Chin

Originally from China, this breed arrived in Japan as a present from a Chinese empress to the Japanese royal family. Chinese Buddhist missionaries to Japan may also have been responsible for introducing the breed to the country, where it developed into the dog we know today.

Characteristics
The word *chin* means cat-like, which describes the breed well. This dog is graceful, washes its face like a cat, loves sitting on furniture and being petted on a warm lap. Like most toy breeds, the Chin needs lots of attention and physical contact. It is intelligent, always bright and happy. Although it is lively and often playful, it has a regal air. Its sweet nature makes it a good companion.

Appearance
The Japanese Chin has a long, profuse coat that is soft, straight and silky. Colors include black and white or red and white. Large, dark eyes are set wide apart and white may show at the inner corners making the dog look as if it were surprised. The feathered ears sit high on the head and are carried slightly forward. The well-feathered tail is curved closely over the back. The hare-feet are slender and feathered. Square and cobby, the dog has a wide chest and straight forelegs and hindquarters.

Papillon

This breed may date back 700 years, and was widespread in Europe by the 16th century, when it was popular with many royal families. It developed from the same toy spaniel stock as the King Charles Spaniel.

Characteristics
The name Papillon is French for "butterfly", and was given to this breed because its erect fringed ears resemble butterfly wings. The Phalene, a type taking its name from the French word for "moth", is identical apart from its drop ears. Dainty but resilient, the Papillon loves exercise. It is intelligent, friendly and alert, but can be jealous of strangers. It can become very attached to its owners and needs plenty of human companionship.

Appearance
The abundant long, silky coat is flat and does not have an undercoat. The breed should be white, with patches of any color except liver. The dark, round eyes have dark rims and are set low on the head. The very large ears are heavily fringed and rounded. They are mobile and when erect should form a 45-degree angle to the head. The long fringed tail arches over the back. The feet are long and hare-like, with long tufts between the toes. The body is quite long, with a level top and a slightly arched belly.

Breed Assessment
LIFE EXPECTANCY 16 years
EXERCISE Plenty
GROOMING Considerable
NOISE Talkative
HEALTH PROBLEMS Knee problems
SIZE 8–11in (20–28cm)
BREED RECOGNIZED BY AKC, CKC, FCI, KC

Breed Assessment
LIFE EXPECTANCY 12 years
EXERCISE Plenty
GROOMING Low maintenance
NOISE Fairly quiet
HEALTH PROBLEMS None known
SIZE 10–12in (25–30cm)
BREED RECOGNIZED BY FCI, KC

English Toy Terrier

Although small terriers existed in the 15th century, today's breed appeared in the 1880s as a rat-catcher, and it was also used to flush out foxes that had gone to ground.

Characteristics
The name suits this breed well, for although it is a tiny toy breed, it has many terrier traits. It is robust and the ratting instinct is still very keen. The breed can suffer from the heat and may be susceptible to heat rashes; but may also be uncomfortable in the cold owing to the thin coat. The English Toy Terrier is a loyal dog, devoted to its owners, but it can be wary of strangers. Always alert, it is also perceptive and seems to have an instinctive awareness of its owner's moods. It is intelligent and lively and makes a good family pet.

Appearance
The English Toy Terrier's thick, glossy coat is black with well-defined tan markings. The small, sparkling eyes are very dark. The erect ears are shaped like a candle flame and, if bent forward, should not reach the eyes. The tail is set low. The feet are dainty and compact, and the two middle toes on the front feet are longer than the others. The body is compact, the chest should be narrow and the buttocks well rounded.

Brussels Griffon

First bred in 1880 and once known as the "Belgian street urchin", this little dog began as a stable dog used for killing rats. However, it soon became popular with the nobility and was the pet dog of choice for the elite. The Brussels Griffon is now growing in popularity as more and more people become aware of its charms.

Characteristics

Much of this dog's charm comes from its monkey-like face. Although a member of the toy group, it has something of a terrier's disposition and is hardy and full of fun. This highly intelligent dog makes a wonderful companion and enjoys comfort.

Appearance

The Brussels Griffon is available in Rough and Smooth varieties. Roughs have a harsh, wiry coat with a soft undercoat, while Smooths have a short, straight coat. Coloring in both varieties should be red, black, or black and tan. The eyes should be large and round with black rims. The ears should be semi-erect, wide apart and high set. The tail is usually docked and should be carried high. The feet are small and cat-like. The back should be short, and level from withers to tail. The ribs should be deep and well sprung.

Breed Assessment

LIFE EXPECTANCY 12 years
EXERCISE Plenty
GROOMING Considerable
NOISE Very talkative
HEALTH PROBLEMS None known
SIZE 10in (25.5cm)
CUSTOMARILY DOCKED Yes
BREED RECOGNIZED BY AKC, CKC, FCI, KC

Löwchen

This breed originated in France and is also known as the "Little Lion Dog" because of the unusual manner in which it is clipped. There is some debate as to how this distinctive haircut came about, but it is believed that this small dog was used as a living hot water bottle in the Middle Ages. The shaved area of the body gave instant access to a natural source of warmth for people to thaw out cold fingers and toes. To this day, a Löwchen will be eager to climb under the bed covers and lie there without making a move.

Characteristics

The Löwchen makes a great pet and loves being in a home environment. It will mix well with other dogs. Naturally outgoing and happy, it is intelligent, affectionate and, despite its diminutive size, always lively.

Appearance

The coat should be long and silky, with a slight wave, and may be any color or combination of colors. The eyes should be round, dark and large. The ears should be pendent and well fringed so that the hair merges with that of the mane. The tail should be clipped to leave a tuft of hair at the tip. The feet should be small and round. The body is short, strong and square, with a level topline.

Breed Assessment

LIFE EXPECTANCY 14 years
EXERCISE Moderate
GROOMING High maintenance
NOISE Very talkative
HEALTH PROBLEMS Slipping patella
SIZE 10–13in (25–33cm)
BREED RECOGNIZED BY FCI, KC

Maltese

This breed is believed to have existed in Roman times, or even earlier. If this is true, it would make the Maltese the oldest European breed of toy dog. Maltese merchants used the dog as a trade commodity, ensuring a wide distribution for the breed. It was bred as a lap dog and, according to tradition, was used as a sleeve dog, being carried up the sleeve by European nobility centuries ago.

Characteristics

A merry and friendly dog with a sweet temper, this breed makes an excellent family dog but its glorious coat needs regular attention. It is both affectionate and lively, and will be a loyal house-dog, although it can be suspicious of strangers. It will get along well with children, and enjoys being with its family.

Appearance

The coat should be straight, silky and long, but should not impede movement. The eyes should be oval and dark brown and should not bulge. The ears should be long, with good feathering, and hang close to the head so that the hair mingles with the coat at the shoulders. The tail should be carried arched over the back. The feet are round with black pads. The ribs should be well sprung and the back level from withers to tail.

Breed Assessment

LIFE EXPECTANCY 15 years
EXERCISE Minimum
GROOMING High maintenance
NOISE Fairly quiet
HEALTH PROBLEMS Prone to slipping patellas
SIZE 10in (25.5cm)
BREED RECOGNIZED BY AKC, CKC, FCI, KC

Breed Assessment

LIFE EXPECTANCY 14 years
EXERCISE Moderate
GROOMING Low maintenance
NOISE Very talkative
HEALTH PROBLEMS Slipping patella
SIZE 10–12in (25.5–30cm)
CUSTOMARILY DOCKED Yes
BREED RECOGNIZED BY AKC, CKC, FCI KC

Miniature Pinscher

Developed from the larger, smooth-coated variety of Pinscher, this breed originated in Germany. It was recognized in Germany in 1895 and spread to other countries in the 1920s. In Germany, it is known as the Reh (roe) Pinscher because of its striking resemblance to the roe deer. This tiny dog has been developed with the show ring in mind, and is popular internationally.

Characteristics

Although not closely related to the Doberman Pinscher, this small dog bears many resemblances to the larger breed. Its alert mind and excellent hearing make it a wonderful watchdog, and it enjoys barking. This is a proud little dog, and a great hunter, with a passion for chasing. It learns very quickly and can be obedient if well trained.

Appearance

The smooth, short and glossy coat should be black, blue or chocolate, with tan markings on the cheeks. The eyes are black and slightly slanted. The ears are small, set high and either erect or dropped. The tail is often docked and should be carried high. The feet are short, with dark nails. The ribs should be deep, and the hindquarters well developed. The straight back slopes towards the rear.

Pekingese

Pekingese were so prized by Imperial Chinese dynasties, that commoners were forbidden to own them. When Western armies stormed the palace at Peking in 1860, five dogs were brought to Europe as spoils of war. The modern breed is descended from these.

Characteristics
The Pekingese is just the right size to tuck under an arm and carry. However, this is not a sedentary dog; it enjoys exercise and is lively and mischievous. Legend claims that this ancient breed is the offspring of a lion and a marmoset. With its mane and fearless nature the dog bears some similarity to the lion and will hold its own if aggrieved. It can be stubborn and needs a patient owner.

Appearance
The long, straight coat, which needs extensive grooming to keep it in good condition, forms a thick mane. Several colors are found, from red and fawn brindles to blacks and parti-colors. The eyes are large, round, dark and lustrous, and the profusely feathered heart-shaped ears are held level with the skull. The feathered tail is set high and is slightly curved over the back. The feet are large and flat and the front feet turn out slightly. The body is pear shaped with a short, broad chest and clearly defined waist.

Breed Assessment
LIFE EXPECTANCY 15 years
EXERCISE Minimum
GROOMING Considerable
NOISE Fairly quiet
HEALTH PROBLEMS Occasional back, eye, and upper respiratory tract problems
SIZE 7in (18cm)
BREED RECOGNIZED BY AKC, CKC, FCI, KC

Breed Assessment
LIFE EXPECTANCY 13 years
EXERCISE Moderate
GROOMING High maintenance
NOISE Very talkative
HEALTH PROBLEMS Occasional patella problems
SIZE 8in (20cm) average
BREED RECOGNIZED BY AKC, CKC, FCI, KC

Pomeranian

Descended from Arctic sled-pulling breeds, this Spitz-type dog came originally from Pomerania in Germany. It was developed in Britain in the late 19th century and quickly became popular. It is a rewarding companion dog.

Characteristics
This foxy-faced dog has a large personality in a small body. Small and sturdy, it is very vocal, but can easily be encouraged, through consistent training, to be quieter. The coat needs considerable attention. It is an active and lively extrovert. Affectionate and loyal, it makes a good pet, but is perhaps not ideal for families with very young children. It is happy with short walks and playtimes, but can walk long distances.

Appearance
The Pomeranian has a soft, fluffy undercoat and a long, straight outercoat, which is particularly abundant around the neck, shoulders and chest. Whole colors include white, black, brown, pale blue, bright orange, beaver and cream, while sable and parti-colors are also available. The eyes are slightly oval, bright and dark. The ears are small and erect. The high-set tail is turned over the back. The feet are small and cat-like. The short, compact body is well proportioned and has a deep chest.

Pug

The Pug appears to have originated in the Far East, but its later development took place in and around the Netherlands and Britain. Popular with royalty and the aristocracy, it was and is a prized companion dog.

Characteristics
The flat face, with its prominent wrinkles, make the Pug look worried, but it is a happy dog with a carefree disposition. It is affectionate and intelligent, and makes a great companion – although its snoring may be a problem. It needs little grooming and the minimum of exercise; it is also easily trained, which makes this a good breed for a busy family. Pugs get on well with other dogs and pets and are normally good with children.

Appearance
The Pug has a short, glossy coat, which is soft and smooth and comes in silver, apricot, fawn or black. The dark eyes are large and expressive. Being prominent, the eyes are prone to damage, so extra care must be taken. The ears are like black velvet. There are two types: "rose ear" where the ear folds over and back to reveal the burr, and "button ear" where the flap folds forward and covers the ear's opening. The tail is set high and is curled tightly over the hip. Short and square, the Pug has a wide chest.

Breed Assessment
LIFE EXPECTANCY 13 years
EXERCISE Minimum
GROOMING Low maintenance
NOISE Fairly quiet
HEALTH PROBLEMS Rare cases of hip dysplasia; eye and upper respiratory problems
SIZE 18–22in (46–54cm)
BREED RECOGNIZED BY AKC, CKC, FCI, KC

Breed Assessment
LIFE EXPECTANCY 15 years
EXERCISE Moderate
GROOMING High maintenance
NOISE Talkative
HEALTH PROBLEMS Slipping patella; Legge Perthe's disease
SIZE 7in (18cm)
CUSTOMARILY DOCKED Yes
BREED RECOGNIZED BY AKC, CKC, FCI, KC

Yorkshire Terrier

The first Yorkshire Terriers, affectionately known as "Yorkies", were bred in Yorkshire, England, in about the 1850s. They were larger than today's dogs and were used for ratting.

Characteristics
Despite its tiny size and fancy coat, the Yorkie has not forgotten its terrier roots. It is hardy and spirited, has a natural hunting instinct and enjoys a good walk. It is a robust soul, who loves the outdoors. The Yorkie's versatile "happy-go-lucky" spirit has seen many dogs compete in mini-agility tests. It enjoys being kept occupied, is even-tempered, and makes an ideal companion dog, if you can cope with the grooming commitments.

Appearance
The long, silky coat should be a dark steel blue with tan head, chest and legs. The tan hair is dark at the root and lighter towards the tip. The hair on the head is usually tied up to keep it away from the eyes, which are dark and sparkling, with dark edges to the eyelids. The V-shaped ears are erect and covered with short hair. The tail is darker than the rest of the body, particularly at the tip. The feet are round and the nails are black. The compact body has moderately sprung ribs and a level back.

Show Dogs

Preparing for a dog show ✦ Show procedure ✦ Judging

Humans are competitive by nature, and there is little doubt that from an early time dogs were used to satisfy their need to compete. Early contests probably concentrated on finding the best hunting dog or fighter, rather than on obedience or agility skills. Judging dogs on looks alone has been a fairly recent addition to such competition, yet it is proving to be one of the most popular dog "sports" in the world.

TYPES OF DOG SHOW

Dog shows are classified in different ways, which may vary from country to country. On the whole, they are divided into fun shows, which can be entered on the day, and more serious competitions, where exhibitors are required to enter in advance.

Fun dog shows are often held in conjunction with a fête or summer fair. They include categories like pedigree puppies or sporting dogs, as well as less formal classes such as best crossbreed, dog with the waggiest tail,

and even "Dog the judge would most like to take home!" Judges at these shows are looking for a dog that is well-behaved, in good condition and well handled, rather than an excellent specimen of its breed.

In the other types of show, dogs compete for the title of "Best of Breed". Here, judges are looking for the minute details which make one dog more representative of the breed standard than another. Judges spend considerable time examining the dogs for their construction, movement and condition.

PREPARING FOR THE RING

Presentation is extremely important if you are going to show your dog. No judge will look twice at an exhibit that has a grimy coat, dirty ears or unclipped nails. Most Kennel Clubs issue quite strict rules about the preparation of dogs for shows, stating that no dyes or unnatural substances can be used to enhance a dog's appearance. This means that good diet and exercise are essential to ensure that your dog's coat and musculature are in top condition.

Some breeds require special bathing, trimming or clipping if they are to be shown. Poodles, for example, require a high level of grooming and only certain "clips" are acceptable in the show ring. Many terriers also need hand stripping, when dead hair is removed by plucking. Ask a breed expert for help to ensure that you display your dog's best points to the full.

Your dog must be fit before being entered in a show. A sick dog should not be subjected to the rigors of a show, nor should other dogs be exposed to the risk of infection. Aggressive, nervous or unsociable dogs should never be shown.

Left: It is important that your dog is of sound temperament. In the ring it will be required to stand close to others, to trot or walk on a loose lead, and to be handled by the judge.

"triangle", where the dog is trotted in a straight line away from it, then across the top of the ring, then straight back. This allows the judge to assess the dog's rear movement, see it moving in profile, and then observe the front movement.

Once the judge has inspected all the entrants individually, the dogs are required to stand again. The judge then makes his decision as to which dog most closely resembles the breed standard, and picks the winners.

No matter who wins or loses, good sportsmanship must always be shown by the handlers. It is worth remembering that whatever the outcome, you will take home the best dog of all at the end of the day!

THE JUDGE'S DECISION

◆

Judges are usually experts in their breed or breeds, who are often successful and experienced exhibitors themselves. Their decision is always based on how closely a dog matches the criteria set down in the "breed standard". This standard is provided by the Kennel Club and describes the attributes of that particular breed. It also indicates what colors are permissible, how large the breed should be and gives an outline of the breed's specific characteristics. Breed standards are available from the Kennel Clubs of all countries involved in the showing of dogs. Obtaining and studying the breed standard is an important first step for anyone who intends to show their dog, as it allows the dog to be compared to an objective standard, without looking through the rose colored glasses of the owner or breeder.

Most dogs need schooling before entering the ring. They should be taught to stand still and allow the judge to handle them. They will need to move around the ring to demonstrate their movement, but without stopping or breaking into a gallop. "Ringcraft" classes exist to teach these skills to dogs and their handlers. They are also an ideal place to discuss dog showing with other enthusiasts, and to gain information about your breed.

While fun dog shows are informal, the more serious shows have a full set of rules and an emphasis on show "etiquette". Regardless of the type of show, the judges usually require each exhibitor to complete the same actions in the ring, so that they can assess the dog's potential.

WHAT TO EXPECT AT A SHOW

Dogs in the same class enter the ring together and each exhibitor must wear the ring number given. Each owner stands their dog in "show stance", so that the judge can take a first look at all the dogs. The dog's stance, whether it is standing square or with its legs positioned specifically, will depend on the breed.

Each dog is then brought out individually for the judge's examination. The judge looks at the dog's teeth to assess its "bite" and will run his or her hands all over the dog, to confirm the dog's skeletal and muscular construction. Having examined the dog, the judge asks the handler to move the dog around the ring. By tradition, the judge asks the handler to perform a

Dogs in History

Although a 50,000-year-old cave painting in Europe seems to show a dog-like animal hunting with men, most experts believe that the dog was domesticated within the last 15,000 years. The earliest dog skeleton was excavated in 1979, when 12,000-year-old bones were discovered at a site called ein Mallaha in Israel. Authorities agree that the dog was the first of man's domesticated animals. Fossil remains from the early Bronze Age (about 6500 years ago) make it possible to identify five major groups of early dogs. Selective breeding and natural genetic mutation in these five groups produced the hundreds of breeds in existence today.

Egyptian deities

The Ancient Egyptians entrusted the dog deity Anubis, the god of death, with the responsibility of accompanying their souls to be judged. Anubis was portrayed with the head of a jackal or a dog. The Egyptians were great lovers of dogs and were responsible for developing many breeds by crossing dogs with jackals, wolves and foxes. Herodotus wrote that the Egyptians mourned when dogs or cats died, and indeed many mummified dogs have been found within the tombs of the pharaohs.

BEWARE THE DOG

◆

When Pompeii – the Roman city destroyed by the volcano Vesuvius in AD 79 – was finally excavated, searchers found the remains of a dog lying across a child, apparently trying to protect him. The Ancient Romans relied heavily on watchdogs, a belief thought to have derived from the legend that a dog guarded the gate to hell. So many dogs were kept in the larger Roman cities that any house with a watchdog was required to have a sign warning *Cave Canem* (Beware the Dog). The Romans also used dogs for military purposes, some as attack dogs and some as messengers. They equipped their Mastiffs with light armor and sent them into battle against the enemy, carrying spikes and cauldrons of flaming sulphur.

Above: A mosaic meaning "Beware the Dog", which would have appeared on the doorsteps in many ancient Roman cities.
Right: *Hunters with their Catch*, a mosaic from the Roman villa of Casale Piazza Armerina, showing a hunting dog.

Right: Hunting scene from illuminated manuscript (15th C., *Livre de Gaston-Phebus*).

Changing roles

Over the centuries, dogs have been eaten and deified, hunted and trained. The following landmarks chart the history of the dog in society.

✦ In some cultures, dogs were (and still are) used as food: the ancient Romans are said to have prized dog stew. The Aztecs of ancient Mexico raised tiny dogs to feed large carnivores in the private zoos. Today, dog meat is still eaten in some parts of China.

✦ Canute (c.995–1035), King of England, Denmark and Norway, introduced a restriction on the ownership of dogs. He allowed only freemen to own Greyhounds, which were the favorite hunting dogs.

✦ In past centuries, drastic measures were taken to prevent dogs from interfering with the royal hunt. William the Conquerer (1028–87) decreed that all dog owners should remove three toes from each foot of their animals to reduce their speed.

✦ In medieval times, the Greyhound became a favorite with royal and noble hunters, appearing widely on heraldry.

✦ Many of the European hound breeds were developed in the Middle Ages, when hunting was popular with the nobility.

✦ Breed histories and pedigrees were not methodically compiled until the 19th century, with the establishment of the first kennel clubs. The world's first dog show took place in Britain in 1859.

✦ The use of guide dogs by the blind can be traced to the First World War, when a German doctor was struck by the caring attitude of an Alsatian towards a blind man.

✦ The first "Hearing Dog" center in the world was set up in San Francisco in 1977. Since then, a growing number of deaf people have used dogs as "ears", enhancing their independence.

Chinese miniatures

During the 400 years of the Han Dynasty of China, which began during the 3rd century BC, dogs were portrayed in many pieces of pottery. These were effigy pieces depicting the burial of favored dogs with their masters.

Much of the early domestication of the dog took place in China, and many experts believe that dwarfing and miniaturization first occurred in that country. Toy dogs were particularly popular among the people of ancient China: the little animals were used to provide warmth when carried in the wide sleeves of their gowns. Black dogs held the same supernatural significance as black cats did in Europe. The "Fu Dog" or "Lion Dog", which was a recurring theme in Chinese folklore, religion and mythology, was believed to bring good fortune and happiness to the owner.

Left: Bronze Chinese "Fu Dog", or "Lion Dog" (17th C.).

A DOG BOOK OF RECORDS

✦ The heaviest domestic breeds are the Old English Mastiff and the St Bernard; both can weigh 170–200lb (77–91kg) at maturity. The heaviest dog ever recorded was Aicama Zorba of La-Susa, who tipped the scale at 319lb (144.55kg).

✦ The smallest mature dog on record was a Yorkshire terrier. This tiny dog, which died in 1945, aged nearly 2, stood only 2½in (6.3cm) at the shoulder.

✦ The oldest dog – Bluey of Victoria, Australia – reached the age of 29.

✦ The tallest dogs are the Great Dane and the Irish Wolfhound, both of which can exceed 39in (90cm) at the shoulder. The tallest Great Dane stood 41in (105.4cm) before he died in 1984.

Famous Dogs & Dogs of the Famous

Since the first dogs came to live near to human settlements, they have played an important role in our lives. Originally used as watchdogs, they were soon bred to accompany hunters, and to protect and guard sheep. Working dogs became highly specialized, pulling carts and sleds, taking on roles in the military, with the police and in the community, assisting the disabled and undertaking rescue work. Not surprisingly, many dogs have become well-known for feats of daring or loyalty, or activities that have set them apart from their canine cousins. Many dogs have also shared the limelight with their celebrated owners, becoming recognizable and well-known features of some of the great moments of Western culture.

The bond with a true dog is as lasting as the ties of this earth will ever be.

KONRAD LORENZ, MAN MEETS DOG, 1963

Greyfriars Bobby

This famous Scottish Skye Terrier lived in the mid-1800s, and earned his name in history by refusing to leave his master's grave until he himself died some 10 years later.

DOGS IN SPACE

The female dog Laika was the first living creature to be sent into outer space. She was launched by the former USSR on November 3 1957 in the 1120-lb (508-kg) Sputnik 2 satellite, which stood at a height of only 4ft (1.2 meters). Laika traveled in a sealed, cylindrical cabin that contained equipment for recording data including her pulse rate, heartbeat, respiration and blood pressure.

The craft was not designed to return Laika to Earth, and she died after a few days. Soviet statements assured the public that she would have been given a poisoned meal before the Sputnik re-entered the atmosphere. Three years later, the Soviets were to send a total of 10 dogs into space, on six different missions, as part of their Vostok space program.

DOGS OF THE FAMOUS

NAME	OWNER	BREED
Argus	Odysseus	–
Azure	Baron von Steuben	–
Beagle	Lyndon B. Johnson	Beagle
Blemmie	Eugene O'Neil	Dalmatian
Boatswain	Lord Byron	Newfoundland
Buddy	President Clinton	Labrador
Butterfly	John F. Kennedy	Welsh Terrier
Cavall	King Arthur	–
Charley	John Steinbeck	Poodle
Chuleh	Beatrix Potter	Pekingese
Diamond	Isaac Newton	–
Flossey	Anne Brontë	Cocker Spaniel
Flush	Elizabeth Barrett Browning	Cocker Spaniel
Igloo	Admiral Richard Byrd	Fox Terrier
Inez	Madame Pompador	Papillon
Jo-Fi	Sigmund Freud	Chow Chow
Kasbec	Pablo Picasso	Afghan Hound
Lucy	Jodie Foster	Brown and White Boxer
Maggie	Truman Capote	Bulldog
Maida	Sir Walter Scott	Scottish Deerhound
Martha	Paul McCartney	Sheepdog
Muggsie	Marilyn Morroe	Collie
Peritas	Alexander the Great	–
Poor Pooh	Prince Charles	Jack Russell
Urian	Anne Boleyn	Wolfhound

Odysseus and
Argus

Marilyn Monroe
and Muggsie

Against the elements

In June 1910 the Norwegian Roald Amundsen (1872–1928) sailed from Norway, intending to be the first to reach the South Pole. He knew of a similar expedition being launched by the British under the direction of Robert Falcon Scott. Their race captured the imagination of Europe. Amundsen, with a shorter overland route and a disciplined plan involving the use of dogs to pull the sleds and provide food for the return journey, arrived at the

John F. Kennedy
and Butterfly

pole with four men in December 1911, one month ahead of the British. Amundsen was renowned for his humane treatment of his dogs, and part of his team included specialist dog carers and trainers. Some of his canine team members are pictured above with Amundsen's assistant Hanssen.

Burdened with a name

A show catalog is the ideal place to uncover the newest and most unusual dog names, and it is evident that dogs must bear the weight of their owner's sense of humor. The military action in the Persian Gulf, for example, led to a number of Stormin' Normans, Desert Storms, and Desert Sands. Other newsworthy names are Open Door Policy, Wall Street Wizard, Senator, Morning Newsmaker and Foreign Cliche.

Dogs & the Imagination

Art has always reflected the unique relationship between humans and dogs, and there are works of art from every period in history in which a dog is an adjunct to the main subject. Even prehistoric paintings from 10,000 years ago show dog-like animals accompanying humans while they perform their daily activities. Dogs are also shown in the sculpture and the pottery of ancient Assyria, Egypt and Greece. Myths, legends and, more recently, books and films, have featured dogs, illustrating how integral the dog is to our human culture.

Right: Gustav Courbet's *Femme nue au chien*, or *Nude Woman with a Dog* (1861).

Fine arts

✦ Portraits of dogs were popular in early European culture, although by Roman times portraiture had nearly disappeared, to be replaced by miniatures of dogs in illuminated manuscripts, including *Les Tres Riches Heures du Duc de Berry*, and in later tapestries, including the Bayeux Tapestry.

✦ During the Renaissance, detailed portraits of dogs were the subject of many paintings. Painters who included dogs in their works include: Leonardo da Vinci, Antonio Moro (1517–75), Jan Van Eyck (1390–1411), Albrecht Durer (1471–1528), Aleandre-François Desportes (1661–1743).

✦ Portraiture of the dog became popular around the beginning of the 18th century. Notable artists include: George Stubbs (1724–1806), Thomas Gainsborough (1727–88) and Sir Edwin Landseer (1802–73).

✦ Many of the Impressionists included dogs in their works, among them Auguste Renoir (1840–1919) and Henri Toulouse-Lautrec (1864–1901). Later, Pablo Picasso (1881–1973), Joan Miró (1893–1993) and Alberto Giacometti (1901–66) brought them alive in modern art.

Left: Self-portrait by English painter William Hogarth (1697–1764): *Painter and His Pug*.

Over the centuries, cultures around the world have included dogs in the fabric of their mythology and folklore. While dogs played little part in the religions of many European countries, they were a confirmed part of their allegorical heritage and feature in stories, myths and fables from cultures as diverse as Ancient Greece and Islam.

◆ One of the most famous dogs in Greek mythology is Argos, the loyal pet of Odysseus. When Odysseus returned home after the Trojan War, presumed dead for 20 years, his faithful dog, ran forward to greet him. Odysseus, not ready to reveal his identity, was forced to ignore his dog, who immediately died of a broken heart.

◆ In Egyptian mythology, Anubis was the dog-headed god who took the souls of the dead to be assessed on their worthiness to pass to the afterlife.

◆ The King Arthur cycle of tales in British mythology includes references to his dog, Cavall, which left its footprints in stone in Wales.

◆ Cuchulainn, in ancient Celtic mythology, whose name means "hound of Culann", earned his name by slaying a giant watchdog.

◆ The ancient Chinese "Fu Dog", or "Lion Dog" was considered to bring fortune and happiness to its owner, and featured in many legends and works of art.

◆ According to northern English (Yorkshire) legend, Barghest, a monstrous dog with huge teeth and claws, appeared only at night. It was

Above: The best known of all Irish heroes was Cuchulainn, who slayed a smith's watchdog and agreed to take its place as penance.

believed that anyone who saw such a dog would die soon afterwards. In Wales, the dog was the red-eyed Gwyllgi, the Dog of Darkness. On the Isle of Man it was called Mauthe Doog, a demonic spaniel that haunted Peel Castle. This fearsome apparition may well have provided the inspiration for the Sherlock Holmes detective story *The Hound of the Baskervilles*, written by Sir Arthur Conan Doyle.

Right: This Greek vase (c.530–525 BC) features Hercules leading Cerberus to Eurystheus in the last of his 12 deeds. Cerberus, a monstrous dog with three heads – of a dog, a wolf and a lion – on a Mastiff's body, was the guardian of Hades, or hell.

Sir Edwin Landseer

One of the most prolific painters of dogs was the Victorian artist Sir Edwin Landseer (1802–73). His painting *Alpine Mastiffs Reanimating a Traveler* (1820), was the first to show a St Bernard carrying a tiny barrel of brandy around its neck, a notion based not on fact, but on Landseer's imagination. This image proved so compelling that St Bernards used in mountain rescue were, subsequently, often provided with barrels of brandy to ease the suffering of wayward travelers.

Dignity and Impudence (1837), shown here, features Landseer's own dogs: Myrtle, a Retriever, and Brutus, a white terrier mongrel.

Now thou art dead, no eye
shall ever see
For shape and service spaniel
like to thee.
This shall my love do, give thy
sad death one
Tear, that deserves of me
a million.

ROBERT HERRICK,
"UPON MY SPANIEL, TRACIE", 1648

Dogs & the imagination

A devoted owner

Sir Walter Scott's (1731–1832) dog was called Maida, and was described by the Scottish novelist as being a cross between a Deerhound and a Mastiff. Maida was painted with the writer several times, in particular by the artist Sir Edwin Landseer (see page 247). Scott recorded that he in fact had to sit with another dog on one occasion, because Maida was so tired of sitting for artists that the mere sight of a palette and brush was enough to make him get up and leave the room.

Scott wrote: "The misery of keeping a dog is his dying so soon. But, to be sure, if he lived for 50 years and then died, what would become of me?" When Maida died, Scott built a marble mausoleum for Maida at his home in Abbotsford, which bore the following inscription:

Sit tibi terra levis, or
May the earth lie lightly upon you.

The dog has seldom been successful in pulling man up to its level of sagacity, but man has frequently dragged the dog down to his.

JAMES THURBER,
MEN, WOMEN AND DOGS, 1940

DOGS IN PRINT

In the last 500 years, the special relationship between man and dog has developed beyond that of working companion. As dogs took on a new role as loyal confidant, and were welcomed into our homes, stories and tales of their generosity and spirit formed a new genre in Western literature. Shakespeare mentions dogs in many of his works, often anachronistically, but he is most eloquent in *The Two Gentleman of Verona*, when Launce describes his devoted dog, Crab. Jack London and Zane Grey wrote fascinating accounts of canine courage, and Canadian Farley Mowat, who spent time living among the wolves in Northern Canada, helped us to understand the intelligence and almost human qualities of dogs in the wild. Literary dog owners include:
◆ John Steinbeck, who was accompanied by his dog Charley on his travels across

Above: *Aesop's Fables*, "The Two Dogs". Aesop, a Greek folk hero who lived in the 6th century BC, acquired a great reputation as a teller of animal fables. Because his fables are short, simply expressed, and entertaining, they have been used since classical times in schools. The most popular English version is probably that by Samuel Croxall, originally published in 1722.

DOGS ON THE SCREEN

Dogs have been used for entertainment, both in sport and in the circus ring, for hundreds of years, eventually making their way to the silver screen, where they have, in many cases, become as popular as their human counterparts. The

special relationship between man and dog has also been celebrated on the screen, featured as the subject of dozens of landmark films, including *A Dog's Best Friend*, *Lassie* and *The Littlest Hobo*. Most memorable characters include:
◆ Rin Tin Tin, who starred in 22 black-and-white films.
◆ Lassie, for which 300 dogs auditioned; Pal got the part in the first film.
◆ Hooch, from the film *Turner and Hooch*.
◆ Tramp, a love-smitten mongrel from Disney's *Lady and the Tramp*.
◆ Snoopy, Charles Schultz's famous *Peanuts* character.
◆ Apollo, "Magnum PI"; one of Higgins' famous Dobermans.
◆ 101 charming Dalmatians, both animated and live, in a 1997 box-office hit starring Glenn Close.

Left: Tom Hanks and his canine co-star in *Turner and Hooch*.

the USA, and eloquently describes their relationship in *Travels with Charley*.

✦ Elizabeth Barrett Browning's spaniel Flush, a gift from a friend, became the object of her undying devotion. He was the subject of many letters and poems, including "Flush or Faunus". In this poem, she was startled while resting, and thinking she had been wakened by a faun, was delighted to find Flush at her side. She thanked the god Pan: "Who, by low creatures, leads to heights of love".

Above: Elizabeth Barrett Browning and her beloved spaniel Flush.

✦ Americans E.B. White and James Thurber took dog literature to new heights in the 20th century, presenting warmly humorous portrayals of dogs that revealed their affectionate understanding of their housemates. E.B. White wrote, in *The Fox of Peapack and Other Stories*:

The Dachshund's affectionate
He wants to wed with you:
Lie down to sleep,
And he's in bed with you.
Sit in a chair,
He's there.
Depart,
You break his heart.

In 1938, Eric Knight published a short story in the *Saturday Evening Post* about a Collie who makes an epic journey to find her original owner. So popular was the story that two years later the author published it as a book, which appeared in 25 languages. The touching story inspired the 1943 film *Lassie Come Home* and its sequels, as well as a radio and TV series.

✦ Beethoven, from the film of the same name: a St Bernard with home-wrecking and heart-winning ways.
✦ A sensible Labrador and a streetwise Bull Terrier in Walt Disney's successful film *The Incredible Journey*.
✦ Benji, from the films of the same name; a bright, terrier-mix mongrel.
✦ Boomer, Jasmine and Dylan's Yellow Labrador in *Independence Day*.
✦ Scud, the spring-wired Dachshund in *Toy Story*.

Above: Benji, film and television action hero.
Right: John Belushi and his German Shepherd partner in the 1988 police comedy film *K9*.

Useful Addresses

General Organizations

American Animal Hospital
Association
12575 West Bayaud Avenue
Lakewood, CO 80228
Phone: (303) 986-2800
Website: www.healthypet.com

American Boarding Kennels
Association
4575 Galley Road, Suite 400A
Colorado Springs, CO 80915
Phone: (719) 591-1113
Fax: (719) 597-0006
Website: www.abka.com

American Dog Breeders Association
PO Box 1771
Salt Lake City, UT 84110
Phone: (801) 298-7513
Website: members.aol.com/bstofshw/
best.html

American Kennel Club
5580 Centerview Drive, Suite 200
Raleigh, NC 27606-3390
Phone: (919) 233-9767
 Fax: (919) 233-3627
Website: www.akc.org

American Society for the Prevention
of Cruelty to Animals
424 E. 92nd Street
New York, NY 10128
Phone: (212) 876-7700
Website: www.aspca.org

American Veterinary Medical
Association
1931 North Meacham Road –
Suite 100, Schaumberg, IL 60173
Phone: (847) 925-8070
Fax: (847) 925-1329
Website: www.avma.org

Canine Resource and Referral
Helpline: (212) 727-7257
Website: www.inch.com/~dogs

Canine Companions for Independence
PO Box 446
Santa Rosa, CA 95402-0446
Phone: (800) 572-2275
Website: www.caninecompanions.org

Dog Infomat
Website: www.doginfomat.com

The Humane Society of the
United States
2100 L. Street, NW
Washington, DC 20037
Phone: (202) 452-1100
Website: www.hsus.org

Orthepedic Foundation For Animals
2300 Nifong Boulevard
Columbia, MO 65201
Phone: (573) 442-0418
Website: www.prodogs.com//chn/ofa/
index.html

People for the Ethical Treatment
of Animals
501 Front Street
Norfolk, VA 23510
Phone: (757) 622-7382
Fax: (757) 628-0782
Website: www.peta-online.org

Prodogs
PO Box 729
Princeton Junction, NJ 08550
Phone: (609) 936-1883
Fax: (609) 936-1443
Website: www.prodogs.com

Therapy Dogs Incorporated
PO Box 5868
Cheyenne, WY 82003-5868
Phone: (877) 843-7364
Website: www.tdi-dog.org

US Kennel Club
PO Box 754
Plainview, NY 11803
Phone: (516) 942-4395
Website: www.dogpapers.com

World Society for the Protection
of Animals
PO Box 190
Jamaica Plain, MA 02130
Phone: (617) 522-7000
Website: www.wspa.org.uk

Dog – The
Complete
Guide
*Useful
Addresses*

250

Further Reading

Books

The Adoption Option: Choosing and Raising the Shelter Dog for You
by Eliza Rubenstein and
Shari Kalina
Howell Book House

Caring For Your Older Dog
by Chris Pinney
Barron's Educational Series

Choosing a Shelter Dog
by Bob Christiansen
Canine Learning Center

Choosing the Perfect Dog for You and Your Family
by Mordecai Siegal
Contemporary Books

The Common Sense Book of Puppy and Dog Care
by Harry Miller
Bantam Books

The Complete Dog Book (18th ed.)
John J. Madeville and
Ab Sidewater, eds.
Howell Book House

Coping with Sorrow on the Loss of Your Pet
by Moira Anderson
Alpine Publications

Dog Training: The Gentle Modern Method
by David Weston
Howell Book House

Dog Owner's Veterinary Handbook
by Delbert G. Carlson, DVM and
Dr. James M. Griffin
Howell Book House

Dr. Pitcairn's Complete Guide to Natural Health for Dogs and Cats
by Richard H. Pitcairn, DVM
Rodale Press

The Holistic Guide for a Healthy Dog
by Wendy Volhard and
Kerry Brown
Howell Book House

How to be Your Dog's Best Friend
by The Monks of New Skete
Little, Brown & Company

How to Teach a New Dog Old Tricks
by Dr. Ian Dunbar
James & Kenneth Publishers

Making Friends: Training Your Dog Positively
by Linda Colflesh
Howell Books

The Nature of Animal Healing: The Path to Your Pet's Health, Happiness, and Longevity
by Martin Goldstein, DVM
Alfred A. Knopf, Inc.

The Owner's Guide to Better Behavior in Dogs (2nd ed.)
by William E. Campbell
Alpine Publications

Saved: A Guide to Success With Your Shelter Dog
by Myrna Papurt
Barron's Educational Series

Save That Dog! Everything You Need to Know About Adopting a Purebred Rescue Dog
by Liz Palika
Howell Book House

UC Davis School of Veterinary Medicine Book of Dogs
by Mordecai Siegal
Harper Collins

Understanding and Training Your Dog or Puppy
by H. Ellen Whiteley, DVM
Crown Trade Paperbacks

The Well Dog Book
by Terri McGinnis, DVM
Random House

Periodicals

AKC Gazette
5580 Centerview Drive, Suite 200
Raleigh, NC 27606-3390
Phone: (919) 233-9767
Fax: (919) 233-3627
Website: www.akc.org

Dog World Magazine
500 North Dearborn, Suite 1100
Chicago, IL 60610
Phone: (312) 396-0600
Website: www.dogworldmag.com

Dog Fancy Magazine
PO Box 53264
Boulder, CO 80322-3264
Phone: (303) 604-1464
Website: www.
animalnetwork.com

DOG – THE
COMPLETE
GUIDE
*Further
Reading*

251

Index

A

adolescence in dogs 42–3, 48
Affenpinscher 232
Afghan Hound 19, 34, 37, 60, 172
    grooming 113
ageing in dogs 43, 145, 243
aggression in dogs 39, 92–3, 102, 103
    towards humans 103
Aicama Zorba (record heavy dog)
    243
Airedale Terrier 20, 196
Alaskan Malamute 216, 218
allergic dermatitis 139
Alsatian 243
American Cocker Spaniel 186
American Foxhound 177
American Staffordshire Bull Terrier
    195, 199
American Water Spaniel 189
anemia 137
anal area 107, 109
    cleaning 117
    emptying glands 115
anal sacculitis 139
Anubis 242, 247
arnica 147
arthritis 141
ataxia 136
Australian Terrier 195, 201
Auvergne Pointer 180

B

backyards 77, 99
Barghest 247
barking 39, 93, 99, 102
Basenji 154, 178
Basset Hound 29, 31, 37, 38–9, 113,
    171, 176
baths 107, 114
Beagle 37, 113, 176
Bearded Collie 113, 220
Bedlington Terrier 204
beds for dogs 68, 80, 81, 96–7, 119
Beecher, Henry Ward 10
behavior 44–5, 52, 74–5
    discipline 55, 92–3
    influences on 72–3
    patterns 122
    problems 102–5
    training 86, 88–9, 90, 105
Belgian Shepherd Dog 39, 222
Benji (dog in film) 249
Bernese Mountain Dog 34, 223
Bichon Frisé 112, 233

birth 152, 158
biscuits 111
bitches 65
    breeding from 152–3
    fostering 160
    giving birth 158–9
    mating 154–5
    as mothers 66, 160–1
    pregnancy 156–7
        false pregnancy 144
    reproductive cycle 154–5
    reproductive disorders 144–5
    in season 38, 42, 65, 154–5
    spaying 132–3
bite, types of 19
biting 84–5, 103
bladder disease 145
bleeding 150
blood conditions 137
blood tests 131
Bloodhound 21, 29, 37, 38–9, 177
bloodsuckers 143
"Bluey" (oldest dog) 243
boarding kennels 101
body language 51, 53, 54, 70–1
body shapes 20–1
bones, dogs' 18–19
    disorders and injuries 140–1,
        151
bones for dogs 111
    burying 97
    chewing 98
Border Collie 33, 62, 113, 153, 221
Border Terrier 194, 205
Borzoi 19, 27, 172
Boston Terrier 113, 195, 208
Bouvier des Flandres 222
Boxer 19, 35, 43, 113, 153, 224
breath 109, 135
breathing 25
    first aid 150
breeders 66, 67
breeding 20–1, 152–3
    earliest 17
    for hunting 21, 36
    selecting a mate 154
Briard 217, 223
Brittany 192
Brussels Griffon 236
Buffon, Count of 54
Bull Mastiff 113, 226
Bull Terrier 27, 29, 113, 195, 205
Bulldog 19, 21, 27, 29, 143, 207, 208
    grooming 113
burns 150
Butler, Samuel 10

C

Cairn Terrier 195, 200

cancer 131, 141, 142, 149
    mammary 145
    skin tumors 139, 149
Canidae 16
Canis lupus pallipes 16
car travel 69, 77, 100
Cardigan Corgi 229
cardiomyopathy 137
cartilage, damaged 141
cataracts 130, 131, 134
cats 63, 78, 79
Cavalier King Charles Spaniel 112,
    153, 232
chain collars 68, 119
Chesapeake Bay Retriever 37,
    185
chewing 91, 98
cheyletiella mites 138
Chihuahua 21, 62, 112, 120, 231,
    233
    pregnancy 144
    skulls 19
children and dogs 48, 49, 58, 79,
    82, 85, 231
Chinese Crested Dog 22, 112,
    230–1, 234
chocolate, effect on dogs 77, 106
choking 150
Chow Chow 27, 62, 206, 209
Choweiler 154
Clare, John 166
classes, training 61, 88, 89
    ringcraft 241
    socialization 85
nails 23, 109, 113, 115,
    116
clipping
    coat 112–13, 114
    nails 115, 116
clubs, breed 6, 63
Clumber Spaniel 187
coat 22–3
    care of 60, 112–13
    colors 23
    healthy 109
    smooth 113
Cocker Spaniel 68, 135, 153, 186
Cockerpoo 207
colitis 143
collars 68, 77, 82, 119, 129
    copper 141
    Elizabethan 132, 133
Collie 17, 26, 74
colors, coat 23
combs 118
communication 50–5, 61
    body language 51, 53, 54, 70–1
    vocal 53, 72
conditioning 52, 86
conformation 32

conjunctivitis 134
Coonhound 37, 177
corneal scarring 134
corticosteroids 141
Cowper, William 166
cross-breed dogs 65, 154, 207
Curly-coated retriever 37, 184
Cushing's disease 139
cuts, treating 150
Cynodictis 16
Czesky Fousek 181

D

Dachshund 21, 31, 136, 174, 249
Dalmatian 113, 206, 207, 209
Dandie Dinmont Terrier 203
Deerhound 34, 37, 113, 175
defense strategies of dogs 102
demodectic mange mites 138
dental disease 129, 135
dependency 75
dew claw 109
diarrhea 143
diet, dog's 16, 77, 106, 110–11
digestion 24, 52, 77, 106
    problems 143
digging 99
Diogenes 164
discipline 55, 92–3, 103
diseases
    dental 129, 135
    hereditary 63, 130–1, 153
    joint 140–1
    prevented by vaccination 129
    reproductive 144–5
    urinary 145
distemper 129
DNA tests 131
Doberman Pinscher 62, 113, 137,
    216, 227
docking 6
dog days 59
dog flaps 119
dog shows 240–1, 243
domestication 17, 242, 243
drowning 150–1
drug-sniffing 39
dwarfism 21, 230, 243

E

ear drops 148–9
ears 28–9
    cleaning 117
    examining 107, 108
    long 68, 97
    problems 134, 135
Eliot, George 13
Elizabethan collar 132, 133

Elkhound 29, **179**
elongated soft palate 143
emergencies 150–1
Emerson, Ralph Waldo 49
endocardiosis 137
English Foxhound **177**
English Pointer 112
English Setter **182**
English Springer Spaniel **188**
English Toy Terrier 195, **235**
epilepsy 131
equipment 118–19
euthanasia 151
Evans, George Bird 167
evolution 14–17, 50
excretion 24–5
exercise 34, 59, 63, 106, 122–3, 169
eye ointment 148
eyes, dogs' 26–7
  checking 129
  cleaning 117
  defects and diseases 130, 131,
    153
  healthy 107, 108
  problems 134

F

feces
  disposal 95, 125
  scent signals 38, 124–5
feeding 68, 77, 97, 106
  sick dogs 148
  see also food, dog
Field Spaniel **187**
fighting 34–5, 44, 75, 102
Finnish Spitz **170**
first aid 150–1
fits 136, 151
Flat-coated Retriever 37, 98, **185**
fleas 97, 109, 129, 138, 139
"Flush" (Elizabeth Barrett
  Browning's dog) 245, 249
food, dog 68, 77
  guarding 104
  labels 111
  nutrition 110–11
  types 111
  weaning 161
  see also digestion; feeding
food, dogs eaten as 230, 243
fostering puppies 160
Foxhound 37
fractures 151
French Bulldog **210**

G

games 124–5
gastro-enteritis 143
genitals 109
German Hunting Terrier 20
German Longhaired Pointer **193**
German Shepherd 21, 27, 29, 31,
  153, **225**
German Short-haired Pointer 37,
  112
German Wirehaired Pointer **190**

giant breeds 21, 62, 68. 228
Golden Retriever 32, 37, 52, 98, 112,
  153, 181, **184**
Gordon Setter 181, **182**
Great Dane 113, **225**, 243
grey wolf 17
"Greyfriars Bobby" 244
Greyhound 17, 20 27, 29, 34, 36, 37,
  79, **173**, 243
  grooming 113
groomers, professional 115
grooming 69, 112–17, 169
grooming glove 112
growling 102
guard dogs 21, 39
guide dogs for the blind 243
gundogs 112, 180–1

H

hair 22–3
  cutting 114, 115
  growth 23
  see also coat
Hamiltonstövare **171**
handling dogs 82–3
hand-rearing 16–17, 160, 161
"hand shy" dogs 92
Harrier **177**
health 108–9
healthcare 128–9
hearing 28–9, 36
  problems 135
"hearing dogs" for the deaf 243
heart 136
  problems 137, 153
heartworms 137
herding dogs 17, 36, 113, 216
hereditary diseases 63, 153
  joint 140–1
Hesperocyon 16
Hill, Gene 13, 152
hip dysplasia 131, 140, 153
Hoagland, Edward 11
homeopathy 133, 147
hookworms 143
hormonal imbalances 139
hormones 25
hounds 170–9
  grooming 113
  group distinctions 171
  history 170–1
  hunting 36–7
  as pets 171
house-training 81
howling 53
humans
  communication with dogs
    54–5, 57, 61, 70, 72–3
  dogs' aggression towards 103
  relationships with dogs 8–13,
    16–17, 247, 248–9
Hungarian Vizsla 112, **191**
hunting 34, 36–7
  breeding for 20, 21
  early 16–17, 242, 243
  hounds 171
hygiene 94–5, 97, 107

I

Ibizan Hound **174**
identification of dogs 68, 77, 82,
  119, 129
incontinence 145
infectious hepatitis 129
injuries 141, 150–1
insecticides 139
intelligence 45, 54, 75
Irish Red and White Setter **183**
Irish Setter 106, **183**
Irish Terrier **197**
Irish Water Spaniel **189**
Irish Wolfhound 21, 37, 113, **175**,
  243
Italian Spinone **192**

J

Jack Russell 21, 29
jackals 16
Japanese Akita 152, 206, 207, **210**
Japanese Chin **234**
Japanese Spitz **211**
joint diseases 140–1
judging dogs 241
jumping 35
jumping up 104

K

Keeshond 207, **211**
Kennel Clubs 66, 152–3, 241, 243,
  250, 251
kennel cough 129, 142
kennels
  boarding 101
  indoor 68–9, 80, 96
  outdoor 99
Kerry Blue Terrier 194, **199**
kidney disease 145
King Charles Spaniel 112, 153, 181,
  232
Koelher, W. R. 103
Komondor 22, 113, **228**

L

Labradoodle 154, 207
Labrador Retriever 37, 112, 120–1,
  139, 153, 181, **185**
  weight 143
"Laika" (pioneer space traveler) 244
Lakeland Terrier **197**
lameness 140
laryngeal paralysis 142–3
leashes 68–9
  pulling 104–5
  walking on 87, 88, 89, 91
leptospirosis 129
Lhasa Apso 60, 206, **212**
lice 138–9
lifting dogs 82, 83
line breeding 154
"Lion Dog" 243, 247
litters 153, 156
"Little Lion Dog" *see* Löwchen
London, Jack 164, 165

"Low Pressure" (stud Greyhound)
  155
Löwchen 230, 231, **236**
lung cancer 143
Lurcher 36, 79
lymphosarcoma 149

M

Malinois 39
Maltese 112, **237**
mammary neoplasia 145
Manchester Terrier 113, **198**, 231
Mann, Thomas 75
Markiesje **207**
Mastiff 17, 21, 195, **226**, 242
mating 154–5, 156
McCaig, Donald 45
medication, administering to dogs
  148–9
Mexican Hairless Dog 22
Miacis 16
miniature dogs 21, 181, 243
  Poodle **215**
  Schnauzer **213**
mixed-breed dogs 65, 154, 207
mouth 107, 108–91
  problems 135
mouthing 84–5
Munsterlander 181
muscles 18, 33
  disorders 140–1
muzzling 150

N

nail clippers 118
nail clipping 115, 116
nasal problems 142
nervous problems 136
neutering 132–3
Newfoundland 34, 106, **217**
Norfolk Terrier **201**
Norwegian Buhund 216, **219**
Norwich Terrier **201**
nose 30–1, 108
  problems 142
Nova Scotia Duck Tolling Retriever
  37
nutrition *see* diet

O

old age 43, 145, 243
Old English Mastiff **243**
Old English Sheepdog 113, **220**
operations, surgical 132–3,
  133, 148, 149
osteomyelitis 141
Otitis media 135
Otterhound **178**

P

pack behavior 44–5, 50, 75, 90
pads, paw 109
Papillon 29, 181, 230, **235**
parasite control 129

parasites, internal 143
parasitic skin problems 138-9
parvovirus 129
pastoral dogs 216-17
patella luxation 140-1
Pavlov, Ivan 52
paws 23, 107, 109
    grooming 115, 116
pedigree dogs 64-5
    breeding 17, 20-1, 36, 154
    diseases 130-1, 153
Pekepoo 207
Pekingese 231, 238
Pembroke Corgi 229
pen, safety 80, 98
Perthe's disease 141
Petit Basset Griffon Vendéen 176
Pharaoh Hound 171, 174
physiotherapy 141
Pinscher, Miniature 237
plants, poisonous to dogs 77, 99
play biting 84-5, 103
play fighting 51, 102
playing, dogs 69, 74, 124-5
    with owner 61, 120-1
    see also toys
pleurisy 143
pneumonia 143
Pointer 180-1, 190
poisoning 151
poisons 77, 99
Pomeranian 238
Poodle 62, 163, 181, 215, 240
    grooming 113
    miniature and toy 215, 231
    origins 207, 215
poop scoop 95, 125
Portuguese Water Dog 34, 181, 216
pregnancy 144, 156-7
    accidental 155
    false 144, 157
Pudel Pointer 181
Pug 21, 143, 239
pulling
    on leash 68-9, 88-9, 104-5
    loads 34, 35, 216, 245
pulmonary edema 143
puppies 30, 40-2
    birth 152, 157, 158-9
    breeding 152-3
    choosing 66-7
    embryonic 156-7
    fostering 160
    health checks 130
    litters 153, 156
    in new home 70-1, 78, 80, 81
    newborn 40, 46, 157, 158-9, 160
    owning 62-3, 64
    personality 73
    socialization 41, 46-9, 85, 128, 160
    training 84-5
    two together 66-7
    vaccinations 128-9
    weaning 161
pyoderma 138
pyometra 144-5
Pyrenean Mountain Dog 109, 227

R
rabies 129
races, sled dogs 34, 35
recall training 124, 181
record-breaking dogs 155, 243
registration 152-3
reproduction 25
    disorders 144-5
    see also breeding
rescue centers 59, 67
respiration 24, 25
respiratory diseases 142-3
retrievers 36, 37, 87, 98-9, 181, 184-5
retrieving 34, 74, 98-9, 121, 122
rewards 54-5, 84, 86-7, 88, 89, 124
Rhodesian Ridgeback 179
rhus toxidendron 147
ringworm 139
"Rocky" (drug-sniffer) 39
Rogerson, John 75
Rottweiler 21, 224
Rough Collie 113, 221
roundworms 129, 143
running 34, 35, 36, 123

S
safety 76-7, 80, 98-9
Saluki 27, 173
Samoyed 219
sarcoptic mange mites 138
scavenging 17, 104
scent 38-9
    signals 38-9, 42, 51, 95, 124-5
scenthounds 171
Schipperke 213
Schnauzer 113, 195, 228
    Giant 228
    Miniature 213
Scotch Terrier 202
Scott, Sir Walter 12, 248
Scottish Deerhound 20
scratching 138
Sealyham Terrier 202
season, bitches in 38, 42, 54-5
setters 181, 182-3
sexual maturity 42, 43
shampoo for dogs 114, 118
Shar Pei 21, 35, 113, 134, 153
sheepdogs 39, 113, 217, 220, 221
Shetland Sheepdog 221
Shih Tzu 212
Shorthaired Pointer 190
Siberian Husky 16, 216, 218
sight 26-7
sight-hounds 20, 34, 36, 37, 171
sixth sense 29
size of dogs 21, 61
    record 243
    see also giant breeds; miniature
        dogs; toy dogs
skeleton, dog's 18
skin 22-3, 109
    disorders 138-9, 149
Skinner, B. F. 52
skull, dog's 19
Skye Terrier 113, 204, 244

sled dogs 34, 35
sleeping 77, 80-1, 96-7
smell 30-1, 38-9, 70
    see also scent
Smooth Collie 221
Smooth Hair Fox Terrier 13, 113, 195, 198
snapping 103
snarling 102-3
sniffing 70
socialization 41, 46-9, 128, 160
    classes 85
    problems 86
Soft-Coated Wheaten Terrier 113, 194-5, 200
spaniels 29, 37, 98, 112, 181, 186-9
spaying 132-3
spinal cord 136-7
sprains 151
St Bernard 21, 134, 216, 243
St Hubert Hound 170
Staffordshire Bull Terrier 113, 195, 199
stomach 109
stud dogs 66, 153, 154, 155, 155, 156
submission 53, 75
Sussex Spaniel 187
Swedish Vallhund 229
swimming 34, 121

T
tail 53
tapeworms 143
taste, sense of 30-1
teeth 19, 84-5
    brushing 117, 129, 135
    examining 128
    problems 135
temperature, taking dog's 128
terriers 194-205
    body shape 20
    grooming 113
    history 194-5
    hunting 34, 36
    as pets 195
    showing 240
testicles
    undescended 130, 145
thermometer 128
Thurber, James 248, 249
Tibetan Spaniel 206, 207, 214
Tibetan Terrier 195, 207, 214
ticks 138
toilet training 81, 94-5
Tomarctus 16
toothbrushes, for dogs 118
toothpaste, for dogs 118
toy dogs 112, 230-39, 243
    group distinctions 231
    history 230-1
    as pets 231
    poodles 215
toys, dogs' 69, 74, 91, 98, 19, 120-1, 124-5
tracking 125
training 54-5

puppies 62, 84-6
    continuing 86-7
    adult dog 88-9
    commands 86, 87, 89
    discipline 55, 92-3
    at home 88
    pets 61
    professional 105
        classes 61, 88, 89
    recall 124, 181
    socialization 85
travel 48, 69, 77, 100-1
traveling kit 119
trimming 112-13, 114, 115
tumors 131, 141, 149
    mammary 145
    skin 139, 149

U
urination
    problems 95
    scent signals 38-9, 42, 51, 95, 124-5
    toilet training 62, 81, 94-5
utility dogs 113, 206-15
    breed distinctions 206-7
    as pets 207

V
vaccinations 128-9
vets 126-7, 128-9, 133
vision 26-7
visitors 39, 105
vocal communication 53, 72
vomeronasal organ 30-1

W
walking 106, 124-5
    off-lead 122-3
    on a lead 87, 88, 89, 91, 122
watchdogs 39, 242
water, drinking 77, 106, 110
water dogs 181
weaning 161
weight 110, 143, 243
Weimaraner 112, 181, 191
Welsh Springer Spaniel 188
Welsh Terrier 196
West Highland White Terrier 139, 203
whelping box 158, 159
Whippet 27, 29, 37, 64, 173
whipworms 143
Wirehaired Fox Terrier 29, 198
Wirehaired Pointing Griffon 193
wolves 16-17, 44-5, 53, 155, 165
working dogs 113, 216-29
    group distinctions 216-17
    as pets 217
worms 129, 137, 143
wounds 150, 151

Y
Yorkshire Terrier 112, 195, 231, 239

Credits

Photograph sources

Abbreviations

b   bottom
c   center
l   left
r   right
t   top

Page 1 Warren Photographic/J Burton; 2–3 Animal Photography/R Willbie; 4–5 FLPA/Foto Natura; 6–7 Tony Stone Images/R Lynn; 8–9 Warren Photographic/J Burton; 10 tl FLPA/Foto Natura/J & P Wegener, bl Ardea/M Watson, br Oxford Scientific Films/Survival Anglia/J Blossom; 10–11 t Ardea/S Gooders; 11 bl FLPA/Foto Natura/J & P Wegener, br Tony Stone Images/R Lynn; 12 t FLPA/R Tidman, bl & br FLPA/Foto Natura; 13 t FLPA/M Newman, bl FLPA/Sunset/P Moulu, br Oxford Scientific Films/N Rosing; 14 bl FLPA/G Lacz; 14–15 FLPA/ Foto Natura/J Van Arkel; 16 tr FLPA/G Lacz, l e.t. Archive/Pella Museum, Greece; 17 b Ardea/L Bomford; 19 bc Animal Photography/S A Thompson, br Warren Photographic/J Burton; 20 t FLPA/D Grewcock: b FLPA/G Lacz; 21 tl FLPA/ G Lacz, tr Ardea/J Daniels, bl Ardea/J-P Ferrero; 22 tl Animal Photography/S A Thompson, tr Ardea/J Daniels, 26 t FLPA/ Panda/N Biet; 27 bl Animal Photography/S A Thompson, bc Solitaire Photographic/A Rixon; 28 FLPA/G Lacz; 30 Solitaire Photographic/A Rixon; 31 tl FLPA/D Dalton, tr Animal Photography/S A Thompson, b FLPA/ Foto Natura/J & P Wegener; 32 FLPA/ Foto Natura; 33 Ardea; 34 Ardea/J Daniels; 35 t FLPA/Foto Natura,c Ardea/J Daniels; 36 Ardea/ J Daniels; 37 t Ardea, c FLPA/D Dalton, b FLPA/Foto Natura; 38 t Ardea/J Daniels, b FLPA/ G Lacz; 39 tl Ardea/J Daniels, tr Animal Photography/R Willbie, b Solitaire Photographic/A Rixon; 40–42 Warren Photographic/J Burton; 43 t FLPA/G Lacz, b Warren Photographic/J Burton; 44 Warren Photographic/J Burton; 45 t Animal Photography /D Philpott, b Warren Photographic/J Burton; 46 Warren Photographic/J Burton; 47 t FLPA/Foto Natura, b FLPA/ Foto Natura/Bios/ Gunther; 48 FLPA/ D Grewcock; 49 FLPA/ Foto Natura/J & P Wegener; 50 t Warren Photographic/J Burton, b Ardea/J Daniels; 51 tr FLPA/W Rohdich, b Warren Photographic/J Burton; 52–53 Warren Photographic/J Burton; 54 t FLPA/D Hosking, b Oxford Scientific Films/W Johnson; 55 Oxford Scientific Films/ G I Bernard; 56–57 Ardea/ J Daniels; 56 Ardea/J Daniels; 58 tr Ardea, bc FLPA/G Lacz; 59 l FLPA/ Foto Natura/J & P Wegener, tr FLPA/G Lacz, br FLPA/McCarthy; 60 Warren Photographic/J Burton; 61 tl & tr Warren Photographic/J Burton, bl FLPA/ Sunset/G Lacz, br FLPA/Foto Natura/K Hubert; 62 tr Warren Photographic/J Burton, b FLPA/ R Tidman; 63 t Warren Photographic/ J Burton,b Solitaire Photographic/A Rixon; 64 tc

FLPA/D Dalton, tr Warren Photographic/ J Burton, b FLPA/G Lacz; 65 Tony Stone Images/ R Lynn; 66 tr Ardea/J Daniels,c Warren Photographic/J Burton; 67 tr FLPA/ J Zimmermann, cr Solitaire Photographic/ A Rixon; 68 tl & bl Ardea/J Daniels, tr Warren Photographic/J Burton, br FLPA/D Hosking; 69 tc & cr Ardea/J Daniels FLPA/Sunset/G Lacz, br FLPA/ Foto Natura/W Meinders; 70 tr Ardea/ J Daniels, br Warren Photographic/J Burton; 71 tr Warren Photographic/J Burton, br FLPA/Sunset/P Moulu; 72 tc Ardea/J Daniels, brFLPA/ Sunset/G Lacz; 73 tl FLPA/Foto Natura, bl FLPA/Panda/G Memmi; 74 tl & b Warren Photographic/J Burton, tr FLPA/ Foto Natura/J & P Wegener; 75 tl FLPA/H Clark, bl FLPA/G Lacz; 76 c FLPA/Foto Natura; 77 br Ardea/J Daniels; 78 b FLPA/G Lacz, t Warren Photographic/J Burton; 79 tr FLPA/D Hosking, br FLPA/Foto Natura; 80 tr FLPA/Panda/S Nardulli, b Animal Photography/ S A Thompson; 81 tr FLPA/D Dalton, br FLPA/ Foto Natura; 82 tr Warren Photographic/ J Burton, bl FLPA/J Hosking, br FLPA/D Hosking; 83 tr FLPA/G Lacz, bl & bc FLPA/D Hosking; 84 tc Ardea/J Daniels, b Warren Photographic/ J Burton; 85 tl & trFLPA/Sunset/G Lacz, bl FLPA/ Foto Natura; 86 bl Warren Photographic/ J Burton; 86–87 b Ardea/J Daniels; 87 tl & tr FLPA/D Hosking, br Solitaire Photographic/ A Rixon; 88 t Ardea, b FLPA/Sunset/G Lacz; 89 tr FLPA/R Wilmhurst, cr FLPA/R Tidman; 90 tr FLPA/Sunset/G Lacz, br FLPA/Foto Natura; 91 bl Ardea/J Daniels tc, FLPA/ Foto Natura, br Warren Photographic/J Burton; 92 c Warren Photographic/J Burton, bl FLPA/Foto Natura; 93 tl Ardea/J Daniels, tr FLPA/G Lacz; 94 Ardea/ J Daniels; 95 tl Warren Photographic/J Burton, tr Ardea/J Daniels, cl Ardea/Y Arthus-Bertrand; 96 t Ardea/J Daniels, b Animal Photography/ R Willbie; 97 t Solitaire Photographic/A Rixon, b B Viner/Novaris Animal Health; 98 c & br FLPA/D Hosking, bl Animal Photography/S A Thompson; 99 tl FLPA/P Dean, tr FLPA/ D Hosking, b Warren Photographic/K Taylor; 100 t Animal Photography/S A Thompson, b FLPA/R Tidman; 101 t FLPA/D Hosking, bl Shannon/K & D Dannen, br Animal Photography/S A Thompson; 102 t Warren Photographic/J Burton, bl Animal Photography/S A Thompson, br Dogs Today; 103 t EMAP Pet Magazines, bl & br Dogs Today; 104 t FLPA/Sunset/G Lacz, bl FLPA/Foto Natura, br Emap Pet Magazines; 105 Emap Pet Magazines; 106 bl Animal Photography/ R Willbie; 106–107 b Animal Photography/S A Thompson; 107 t Animal Photography/S A Thompson, tr Animal Photography/R Willbie; 108 b FLPA/Sunset/P Moulu; 108–9 Ardea/ J Daniels; 109 b Animal Photography/R Willbie; 110 t Warren Photographic/J Burton, b Animals Unlimited/P Cutts; 111 t Animal Photography/ S A Thompson, bl Animal Photography/ R Willbie, br FLPA/D Hosking; 112 t Animal Photography/S A Thompson, b FLPA/Foto

Natura; 113 t FLPA/G Lacz, b Animal Photography/S A Thompson; 114 t Animal Photography/S A Thompson/R Willbie, b Animal Photography/S A Thompson; 115 t FLPA/ R Bender, b FLPA/R Tidman; 116 t Animal Photography/S A Thompson, bl & br EMAP Pet Magazines; 117 t Animal Photography/S A Thompson, bl & br EMAP Pet Magazines; 118 M Newton; 119 tl Dogs Today, tr & cr M Newton, cl & br EMAP Pet Magazines; 120 Animal Photography/R Willbie; 121 tc, cl & bl M Newton, cr Warren Photographic/K Taylor, br Animal Photography/S A Thompson; 122–3 t Ardea/J Daniels; 122 b Animal Photography/ R Willbie; 123 tr FLPA/Foto Natura/J &P Wegener, b FLPA/Foto Natura; 124 t FLPA/Foto Natura, bl & br M Newton; 125 t FLPA/Foto Natura, cl, bl & br M Newton; 126 l ARDEA/ J Daniels; 126–127 ARDEA/J Daniels; 128 B Viner; 129 B Viner; 130 t Warren Photographic/ J Burton, b FLPA/D Hosking; 131 t Animal Photography/S A Thompson, bl FLPA/M Withers, br B Viner; 132 Animal Photography/S A Thompson; 133 tl EMAP Pet Magazines, tc FLPA/H D Brandl, br M Newton; 134 B Viner; 135 t FLPA/R Tidman, b Animal Photography/ S A Thompson; 136 Animal Photography/S A Thompson/R Willbie; 137 tl B Viner, tr Warren Photographic/J Burton, b Solitaire Photographic/A Rixon; 138 t B Viner, b FLPA/Silvestris; 139 t FLPA/M Withers; 140 t FLPA/R Tidman, c & b Warren Photographic/ J Burton; 141 t & c B Viner, b Ardea/R Gibbons; 142 Warren Photographic/J Burton; 143 t B Viner, b FLPA/M Withers; 144 b FLPA/Foto Natura; 145 FLPA/D Hosking; 146 Warren Photographic/J Burton; 148 t Warren Photographic/J Burton, b B Viner; 149 FLPA/ Sunset/G Lacz; 150 t Animal Photography/S A Thompson, b FLPA/R Tidman; 151 tl & b Warren Photographic/J Burton, tr B Viner; 152 t Ardea/ J Daniels, b Animal Photography/S A Thompson; 153 Animal Photography/R Willbie; 154 t Ardea/J-P Ferrero, b EMAP Pet Magazines; 155 t Ardea/J Daniels; 156 Warren Photographic/ J Burton; 158 t Animal Photography/R Willbie, bl & bc Warren Photographic/J Burton, br FLPA/Sunset/G Lacz; 159 tl FLPA/Sunset/A Christof, tr Animal Photography/S A Thompson, b Warren Photographic/J Burton; 160 c & tr Animal Photography/R Willbie; 161 b Animal Photography/S A Thompson; 162–3 Ardea/J Daniels; 164 tl Ardea, bl FLPA/Silvestris, r FLPA/M Newman; 165 t Ardea/J-P Ferrero, bl FLPA/Foto Natura, br Ardea/E Dragesco; 166 t Ardea/J Daniels, c & b FLPA/G Lacz; 167 l Tony Stone Images/T Davis, tr Ardea/E Dragesco, br Tony Stone Images/D Tipling; 168 bl Animals Unlimited/P Cutts; 168–169 Ardea/J M Labat; 170 Animals Unlimited/P Cutts; 171 tl Animal Photography/S A Thompson, tr Animals Unlimited/P Cutts; 172 t Animal Photography/S A Thompson, b Animal Photography/R Willbie; 173 t Animal Photography/S A Thompson, b